"If you love to read a gripping story, if you are awed by the talent of an artist, then look no further: Chester Brown's LOUIS RIEL is comix history in the making, and with it, history never looked so good."— THE GLOBE AND MAIL

"Complete with exhaustive footnotes and an index, it has the thoroughness of a history book yet reads with the personalized vision of a novel. LOUIS RIEL coalesces many of the themes Brown had explored in his earlier works: the relative 'truth' of nonfiction, the relationship between madness and religious experience, the dubious intentions of authority." —TIME

"[LOUIS RIEL] is extraordinary. Brown makes no bones about whose side he's on (the dispossessed Métis'), but he leaves the eternal questions about Riel himself–madman or visionary, traitor or patriot–to readers' judgment....the words work flawlessly with the muted atmospherics and minimalist settings."
—MACLEAN'S

"Brown has invented a biographical form unique to his medium. LOUIS RIEL has too vivid a personal spin to pass as documentary, but it's not quite historical fiction, either–Brown's not interested in making things up."
—THE VILLAGE VOICE

"Chester Brown's graphic novel LOUIS RIEL: A COMIC-STRIP BIOGRAPHY is an overwhelming, eye-boggling achievement, my favourite book of the year. What you have here is Brown at the height of his abilities as an artist, his handling of line and composition is absolutely beautiful, and he'- made a fascinating and intelligent portrait of one of Cana⌐-' ⸻ ⸍ersial historical figures. To me, this isn't ins⸺ ⸺ ⸺ ⸺ear, it's one of the most impo YA Riel -B
— Lee Henderson, N
Brown, C.
Louis Riel.

"For history buffs, art lovers or anyone with an interest in the life Louis Riel, Chester Brown's book is a must-have addition to the collection."
—THE BRANDON SUN

"This is a story with plenty of dash and a mysterious, charismatic figure at its centre...With his words and pictures, Brown puts a lie to the idea that Canadian history is boring."—UPTOWN MAGAZINE (Winnipeg)

"LOUIS RIEL stands among the most detached of 'serious' comic books. Despite its exacting construction, it confounds a superficial reading of history. It has been rigorously scrubbed of staged drama and crowd-pleasing effects, emptied of sure-fire appeals and cheap thrills....Like the 'classics' of education's yesteryear, once read it is difficult to forget. It continues to invite appraisal, sustain consideration, and reward contemplation of itself and the larger world." —THE COMICS JOURNAL

"...maintains a thoughtful, mature sensibility and a respect for historicity..."
—THE BEAVER: CANADA'S HISTORY MAGAZINE

"Brown's writing and artwork have never been better, and LOUIS RIEL is a must-have for comics lovers."—NEW CITY (Chicago)

"Brown tells the story with evenhanded naturalism whether he's depicting a historical battle or Riel's divine visions, and the lengthy book is drawn with a grace and solidity new to his work. Don't skip the endnotes, where Brown humorously critiques his own work." —PHILADELPHIA CITY PAPER

"Brown's exploration of the life of...19th century Canadian revolutionary Riel is a strong contender for the best graphic novel ever...This is an ingenious comic and a major achievement." —PUBLISHERS WEEKLY (starred review)

"Comics artists have tackled history before but seldom as artfully and intelligently as Brown does here."—BOOKLIST

"LOUIS RIEL is an educational, moving, challenging graphic novel that shows a talented cartoonist at the peak of his storytelling."
—THE OKLAHOMAN

LOUIS RIEL

Also by Chester Brown:

ED THE HAPPY CLOWN (1989)
THE PLAYBOY (1992)
I NEVER LIKED YOU (1994)
THE LITTLE MAN (1998)

LOUIS RIEL
A COMIC-STRIP BIOGRAPHY

CHESTER BROWN

DRAWN AND QUARTERLY PUBLICATIONS
MONTREAL

Drawn & Quarterly
Post Office Box 48056
Montreal, Quebec
Canada H2V 4S8
www.drawnandquarterly.com

First hardcover edition: September 2003.
Second hardcover printing: January 2004.
Third hardcover printing: September 2004.

First paperback edition: June 2006.
Second paperback printing: March 2007.
Third paperback printing: October 2008.
ISBN 978-1-894937-89-4
Printed in Canada.

10 9 8 7 6 5 4 3

Library and Archives Canada Cataloguing in Publication
Brown, Chester, 1960—
    Louis Riel; A comic-strip biography / Chester Brown.
ISBN 1-894937-89-9 (hardcover edition)
    I. Title.
PN6733.B76A13 2006   741.5'971   C2006-901119-2

Drawn & Quarterly acknowledges the financial contribution of the Government of Canada
through the Book Publishing Industry Development Program (BPIDP) and the Canada
Council for the Arts for our publishing activities and for support of this edition.

Distributed in the USA by:
Farrar, Straus and Giroux
18 West 18th Street
New York, NY 10011
Orders: 888.330.8477

Distributed in Canada by:
Raincoast Books
9050 Shaughnessy Street
Vancouver, BC V6P 6E5
Orders: 800.663.5714

For Gord

FOREWORD

Because it's unusual for a comic-book to have one, I want to point out that this book does have an index, even if it is a bit limited in scope. (It only lists 19th century individuals.)

This "comic-strip biography" is not a full biographical treatment of Riel's story. Long periods of time are skipped over, and many aspects of his life are completely ignored. I've mostly concentrated on Riel's antagonistic relationship with the Canadian government, and even that has been simplified and distorted in order to make it fit into a 241-page comic-strip narrative. In the endnotes, I point out many of my distortions, as well as other stuff that I think may be of interest.

In case this book triggers a desire in you to read further, here are a few recommendations:
In my opinion, the best, most comprehensive biography is RIEL: A LIFE OF REVOLUTION by Maggie Siggins. She presents the Métis rebel as a heroic figure.
For a less sympathetic judgement of the man, try Thomas Flanagan's RIEL AND THE REBELLION: 1885 RECONSIDERED. Also worth reading by Flanagan is LOUIS 'DAVID' RIEL: 'PROPHET OF THE NEW WORLD' -- a fascinating study of the development of Riel's religious thinking. (I'm familiar with the two Flanagan books in their revised editions.)

PRAIRIE FIRE: THE 1885 NORTH-WEST REBELLION, by Bob Beal and Rod Macleod, is a good book that doesn't just focus on Riel.
I don't want this list to get too long, so I'm going to cut it off there, even though several other books that helped me in the creation of this strip were as enjoyable to read as the above ones. See the bibliography for a more complete list.

Several people have asked me if Hergé influenced the artwork in LOUIS RIEL. I love Hergé -- his Tintin books have probably affected my drawing-style to some degree -- but my main visual inspiration here was Harold Gray's work on Little Orphan Annie. I hesitate to acknowledge this because I'm well aware that my scratchings fall far short of the beauty of Gray's imagery.

My thanks to the following people for various forms of assistance and/or encouragement while I worked on this project: Peter Birkemoe, Jacques Boivin, Gordon Brown, Jeet Heer, Sook-Yin Lee, Marina Lesenko, Joe Matt, Akemi Nakamura, Chris Oliveros, Seth, Dave Sim, Colin Upton, and Elizabeth Walker.
Thanks also to THE CANADA COUNCIL FOR THE ARTS for providing me with financial assistance.

Chester
Brown
June 2003

FIRST
MAP SECTION

In 1670 the king of England granted Rupert's Land to a fur-trading enterprise called the Hudson's Bay Company.

In 1812 the company started the first agricultural settlement in Rupert's Land when it brought 170 people over from Scotland and placed them by the Red River.

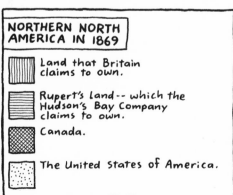

NORTHERN NORTH AMERICA IN 1869

Land that Britain claims to own.

Rupert's land -- which the Hudson's Bay Company claims to own.

Canada.

The United States of America.

The Red River Settlement grew, and by 1869 almost 12,000 people lived there. More than 80 percent of this population were Métis -- people who have both Indians and whites in their family background. A large number of the whites who had come into the area had been French fur-traders, so a majority of the Red River Métis spoke French.

Canada in 1869 consisted of four provinces: Ontario, Quebec, New Brunswick, and Nova Scotia. Both Canada and the United States were eager to expand their borders.

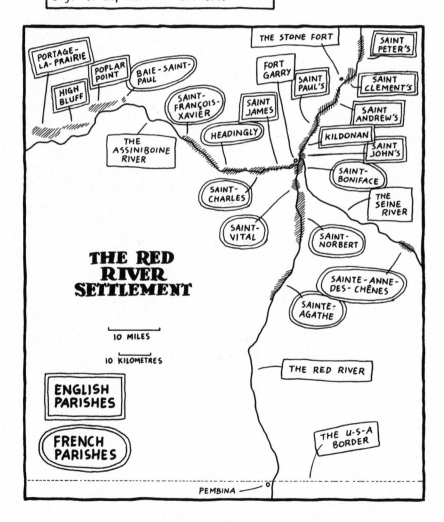

THE STONE FORT

SAINT PETER'S

PORTAGE-LA-PRAIRIE

POPLAR POINT

BAIE-SAINT-PAUL

HIGH BLUFF

SAINT-FRANÇOIS-XAVIER

THE ASSINIBOINE RIVER

HEADINGLY

SAINT-CHARLES

SAINT-VITAL

FORT GARRY

SAINT PAUL'S

SAINT JAMES

SAINT CLEMENT'S

SAINT ANDREW'S

KILDONAN

SAINT JOHN'S

SAINT-BONIFACE

THE SEINE RIVER

SAINT-NORBERT

SAINTE-ANNE-DES-CHÊNES

SAINTE-AGATHE

THE RED RIVER SETTLEMENT

10 MILES

10 KILOMETRES

THE RED RIVER

ENGLISH PARISHES

FRENCH PARISHES

THE U-S-A BORDER

PEMBINA

PART ONE

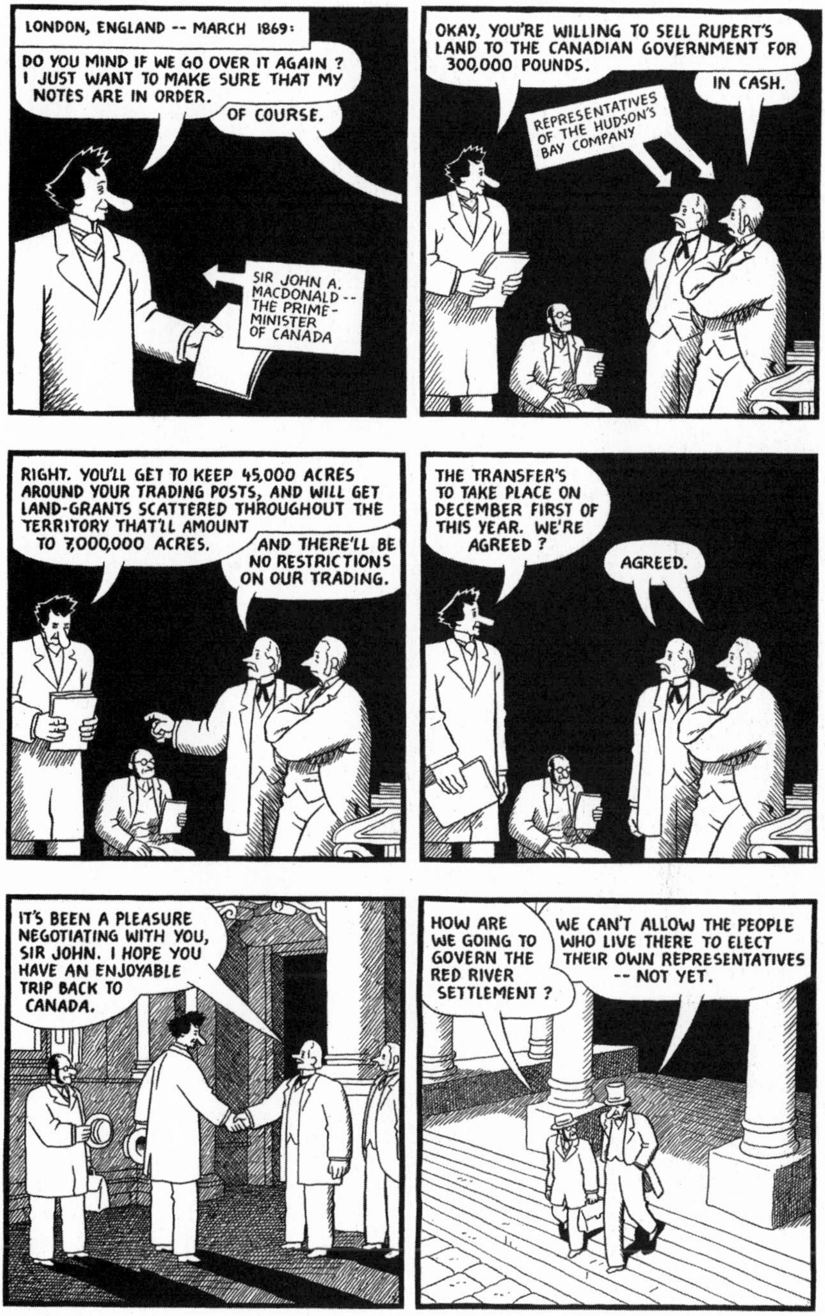

LONDON, ENGLAND -- MARCH 1869:
DO YOU MIND IF WE GO OVER IT AGAIN ? I JUST WANT TO MAKE SURE THAT MY NOTES ARE IN ORDER.
OF COURSE.
SIR JOHN A. MACDONALD -- THE PRIME-MINISTER OF CANADA
OKAY, YOU'RE WILLING TO SELL RUPERT'S LAND TO THE CANADIAN GOVERNMENT FOR 300,000 POUNDS.
REPRESENTATIVES OF THE HUDSON'S BAY COMPANY
IN CASH.
RIGHT. YOU'LL GET TO KEEP 45,000 ACRES AROUND YOUR TRADING POSTS, AND WILL GET LAND-GRANTS SCATTERED THROUGHOUT THE TERRITORY THAT'LL AMOUNT TO 7,000,000 ACRES.
AND THERE'LL BE NO RESTRICTIONS ON OUR TRADING.
THE TRANSFER'S TO TAKE PLACE ON DECEMBER FIRST OF THIS YEAR. WE'RE AGREED ?
AGREED.
IT'S BEEN A PLEASURE NEGOTIATING WITH YOU, SIR JOHN. I HOPE YOU HAVE AN ENJOYABLE TRIP BACK TO CANADA.
HOW ARE WE GOING TO GOVERN THE RED RIVER SETTLEMENT ?
WE CAN'T ALLOW THE PEOPLE WHO LIVE THERE TO ELECT THEIR OWN REPRESENTATIVES -- NOT YET.

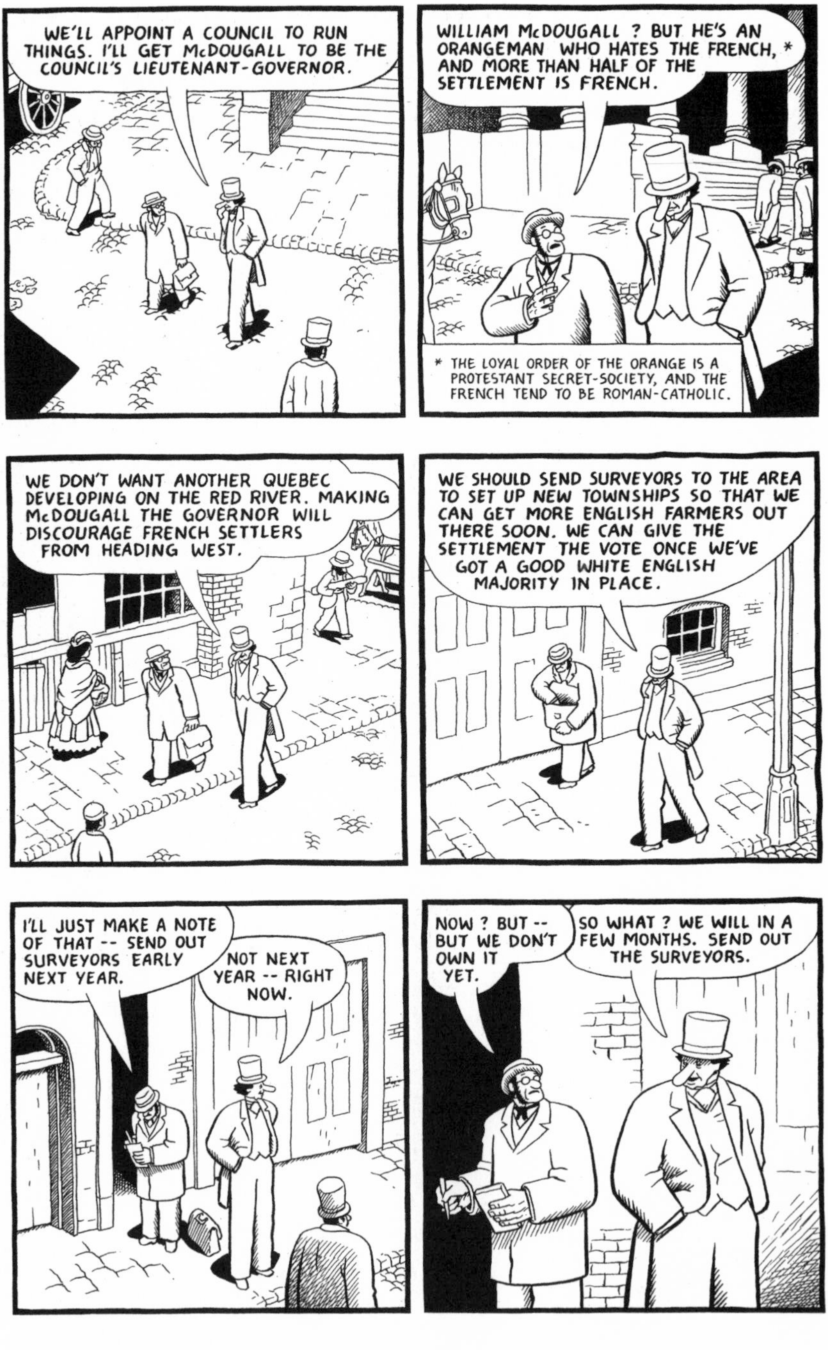

WE'LL APPOINT A COUNCIL TO RUN THINGS. I'LL GET McDOUGALL TO BE THE COUNCIL'S LIEUTENANT-GOVERNOR.
WILLIAM McDOUGALL ? BUT HE'S AN ORANGEMAN WHO HATES THE FRENCH, * AND MORE THAN HALF OF THE SETTLEMENT IS FRENCH.
* THE LOYAL ORDER OF THE ORANGE IS A PROTESTANT SECRET-SOCIETY, AND THE FRENCH TEND TO BE ROMAN-CATHOLIC.
WE DON'T WANT ANOTHER QUEBEC DEVELOPING ON THE RED RIVER. MAKING McDOUGALL THE GOVERNOR WILL DISCOURAGE FRENCH SETTLERS FROM HEADING WEST.
WE SHOULD SEND SURVEYORS TO THE AREA TO SET UP NEW TOWNSHIPS SO THAT WE CAN GET MORE ENGLISH FARMERS OUT THERE SOON. WE CAN GIVE THE SETTLEMENT THE VOTE ONCE WE'VE GOT A GOOD WHITE ENGLISH MAJORITY IN PLACE.
I'LL JUST MAKE A NOTE OF THAT -- SEND OUT SURVEYORS EARLY NEXT YEAR.
NOT NEXT YEAR -- RIGHT NOW.
NOW ? BUT -- BUT WE DON'T OWN IT YET.
SO WHAT ? WE WILL IN A FEW MONTHS. SEND OUT THE SURVEYORS.

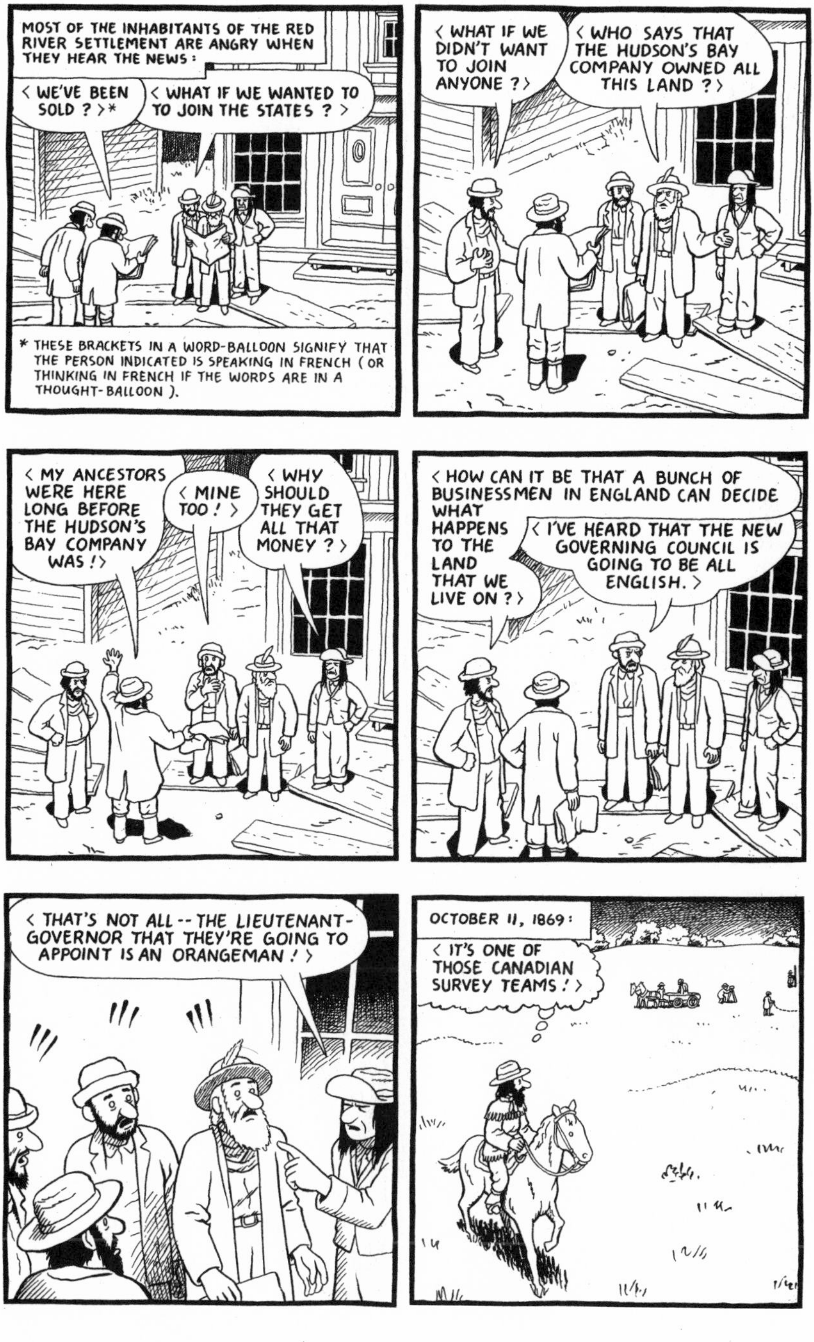
MOST OF THE INHABITANTS OF THE RED RIVER SETTLEMENT ARE ANGRY WHEN THEY HEAR THE NEWS:
< WE'VE BEEN SOLD ? >*
< WHAT IF WE WANTED TO TO JOIN THE STATES ? >
* THESE BRACKETS IN A WORD-BALLOON SIGNIFY THAT THE PERSON INDICATED IS SPEAKING IN FRENCH (OR THINKING IN FRENCH IF THE WORDS ARE IN A THOUGHT-BALLOON).
< WHAT IF WE DIDN'T WANT TO JOIN ANYONE ? >
< WHO SAYS THAT THE HUDSON'S BAY COMPANY OWNED ALL THIS LAND ? >
< MY ANCESTORS WERE HERE LONG BEFORE THE HUDSON'S BAY COMPANY WAS ! >
< MINE TOO ! >
< WHY SHOULD THEY GET ALL THAT MONEY ? >
< HOW CAN IT BE THAT A BUNCH OF BUSINESSMEN IN ENGLAND CAN DECIDE WHAT HAPPENS TO THE LAND THAT WE LIVE ON ? >
< I'VE HEARD THAT THE NEW GOVERNING COUNCIL IS GOING TO BE ALL ENGLISH. >
< THAT'S NOT ALL -- THE LIEUTENANT-GOVERNOR THAT THEY'RE GOING TO APPOINT IS AN ORANGEMAN ! >
!!!
!!!
!!!
OCTOBER 11, 1869:
< IT'S ONE OF THOSE CANADIAN SURVEY TEAMS ! >

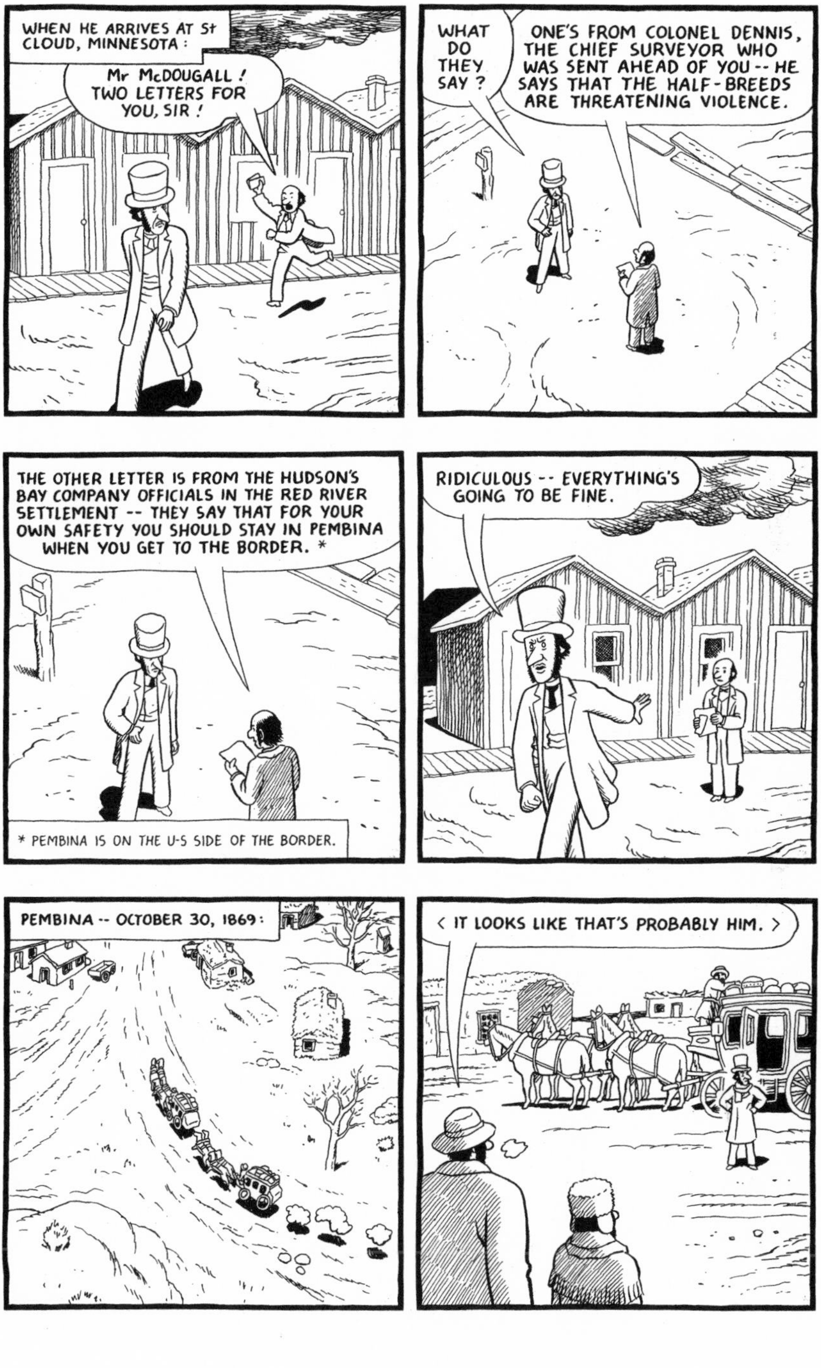
WHEN HE ARRIVES AT St CLOUD, MINNESOTA:
Mr McDOUGALL! TWO LETTERS FOR YOU, SIR!
WHAT DO THEY SAY?
ONE'S FROM COLONEL DENNIS, THE CHIEF SURVEYOR WHO WAS SENT AHEAD OF YOU -- HE SAYS THAT THE HALF-BREEDS ARE THREATENING VIOLENCE.
THE OTHER LETTER IS FROM THE HUDSON'S BAY COMPANY OFFICIALS IN THE RED RIVER SETTLEMENT -- THEY SAY THAT FOR YOUR OWN SAFETY YOU SHOULD STAY IN PEMBINA WHEN YOU GET TO THE BORDER. *
* PEMBINA IS ON THE U-S SIDE OF THE BORDER.
RIDICULOUS -- EVERYTHING'S GOING TO BE FINE.
PEMBINA -- OCTOBER 30, 1869:
< IT LOOKS LIKE THAT'S PROBABLY HIM. >

15

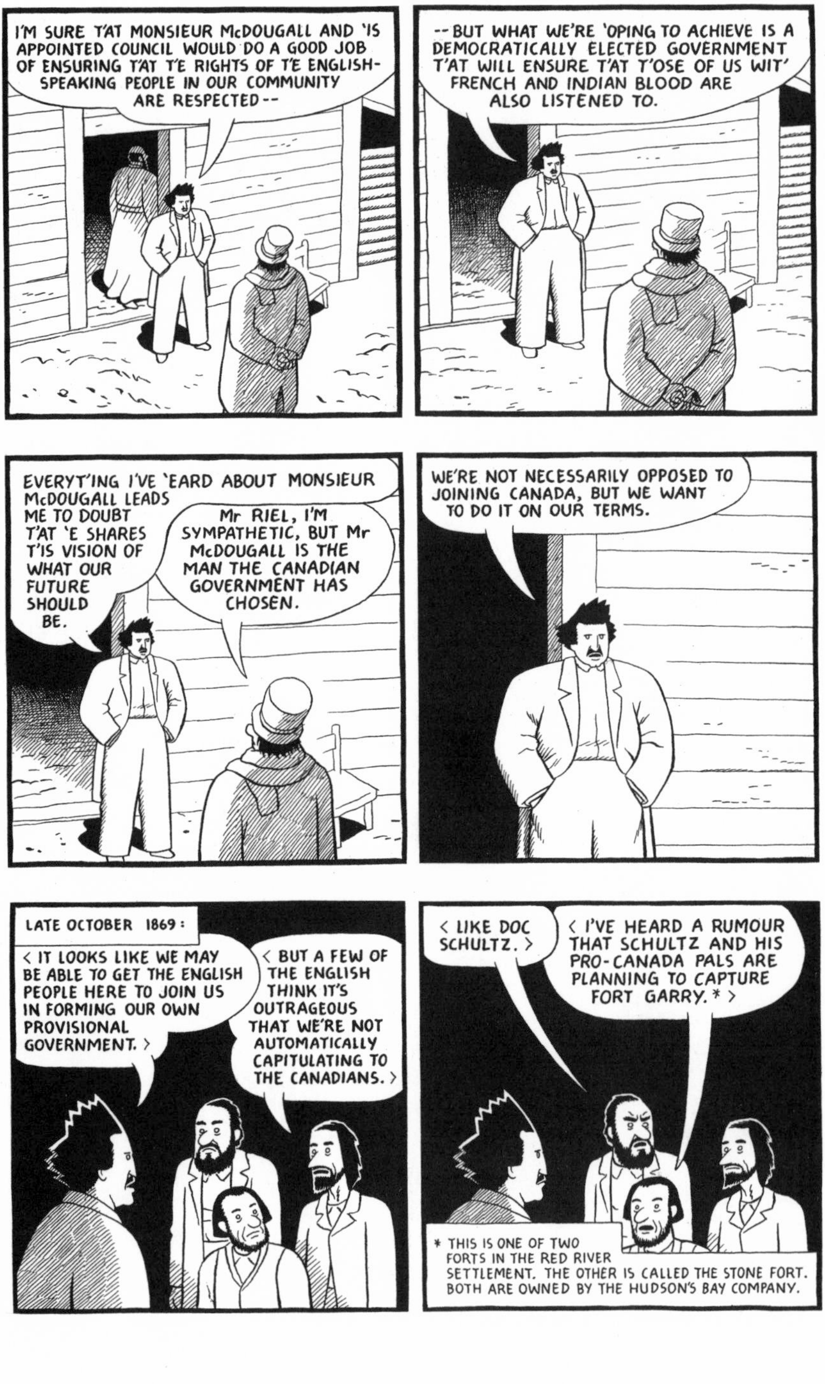

I'M SURE T'AT MONSIEUR McDOUGALL AND 'IS APPOINTED COUNCIL WOULD DO A GOOD JOB OF ENSURING T'AT T'E RIGHTS OF T'E ENGLISH-SPEAKING PEOPLE IN OUR COMMUNITY ARE RESPECTED--
--BUT WHAT WE'RE 'OPING TO ACHIEVE IS A DEMOCRATICALLY ELECTED GOVERNMENT T'AT WILL ENSURE T'AT T'OSE OF US WIT' FRENCH AND INDIAN BLOOD ARE ALSO LISTENED TO.
EVERYT'ING I'VE 'EARD ABOUT MONSIEUR McDOUGALL LEADS ME TO DOUBT T'AT 'E SHARES T'IS VISION OF WHAT OUR FUTURE SHOULD BE.
Mr RIEL, I'M SYMPATHETIC, BUT Mr McDOUGALL IS THE MAN THE CANADIAN GOVERNMENT HAS CHOSEN.
WE'RE NOT NECESSARILY OPPOSED TO JOINING CANADA, BUT WE WANT TO DO IT ON OUR TERMS.
LATE OCTOBER 1869:
< IT LOOKS LIKE WE MAY BE ABLE TO GET THE ENGLISH PEOPLE HERE TO JOIN US IN FORMING OUR OWN PROVISIONAL GOVERNMENT. >
< BUT A FEW OF THE ENGLISH THINK IT'S OUTRAGEOUS THAT WE'RE NOT AUTOMATICALLY CAPITULATING TO THE CANADIANS. >
< LIKE DOC SCHULTZ. >
< I'VE HEARD A RUMOUR THAT SCHULTZ AND HIS PRO-CANADA PALS ARE PLANNING TO CAPTURE FORT GARRY.* >
* THIS IS ONE OF TWO FORTS IN THE RED RIVER SETTLEMENT. THE OTHER IS CALLED THE STONE FORT. BOTH ARE OWNED BY THE HUDSON'S BAY COMPANY.

< THERE'S A LOT OF FOOD STORED THERE, AS WELL AS 300 MUSKETS. >

< WE'VE MANAGED TO GATHER AN ARMY OF ABOUT 400. WE'RE GOING TO NEED THAT FOOD. >

< THE GUNS WOULD COME IN HANDY TOO. >

< AND WE WOULDN'T WANT THOSE GUNS TO FALL INTO THE HANDS OF DOC SCHULTZ. >

< I GUESS WE HAVE TO CAPTURE THE FORT. >

OUTSIDE FORT GARRY -- NOVEMBER 2, 1869:

< I'LL GO IN AND, IF IT SEEMS CLEAR, I'LL WAVE. >

17

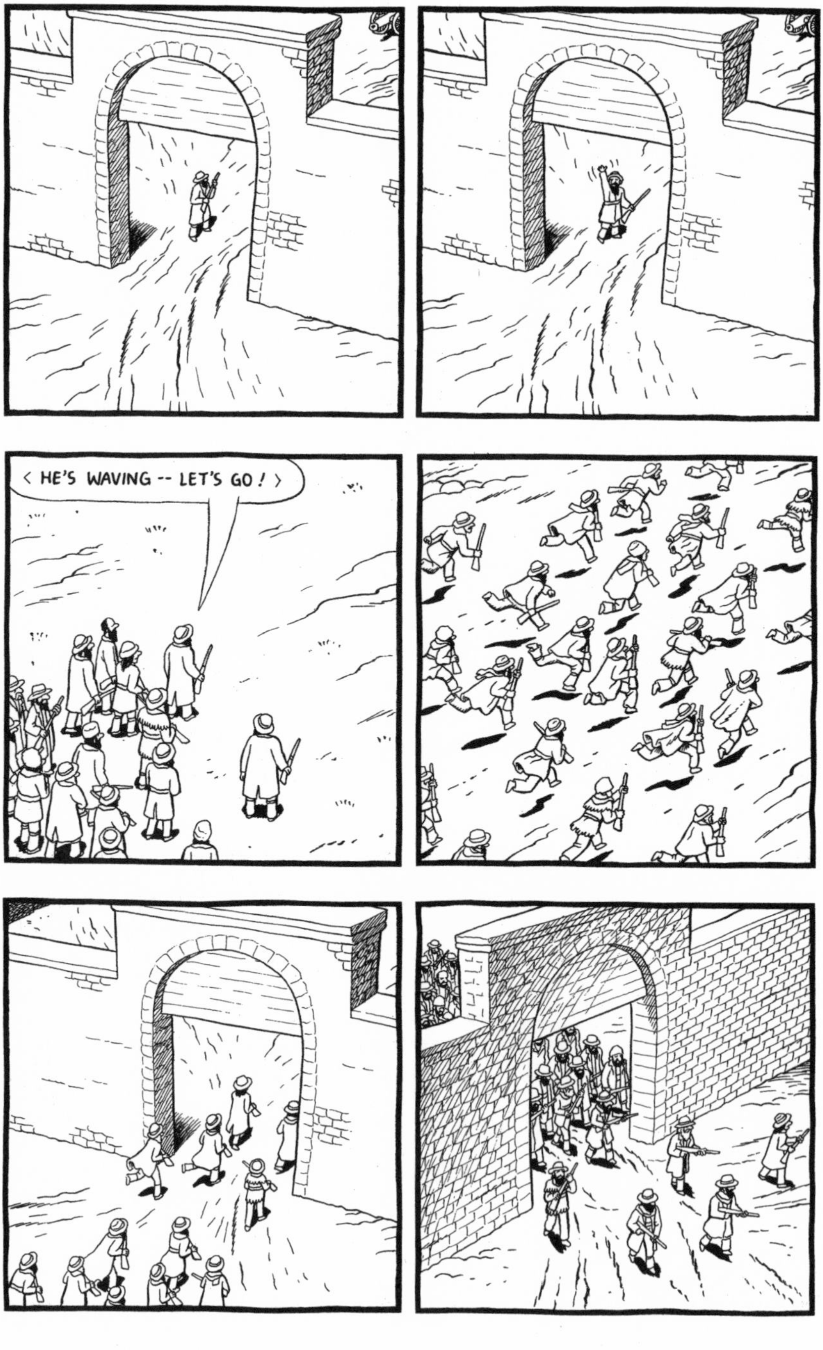
< HE'S WAVING -- LET'S GO! >

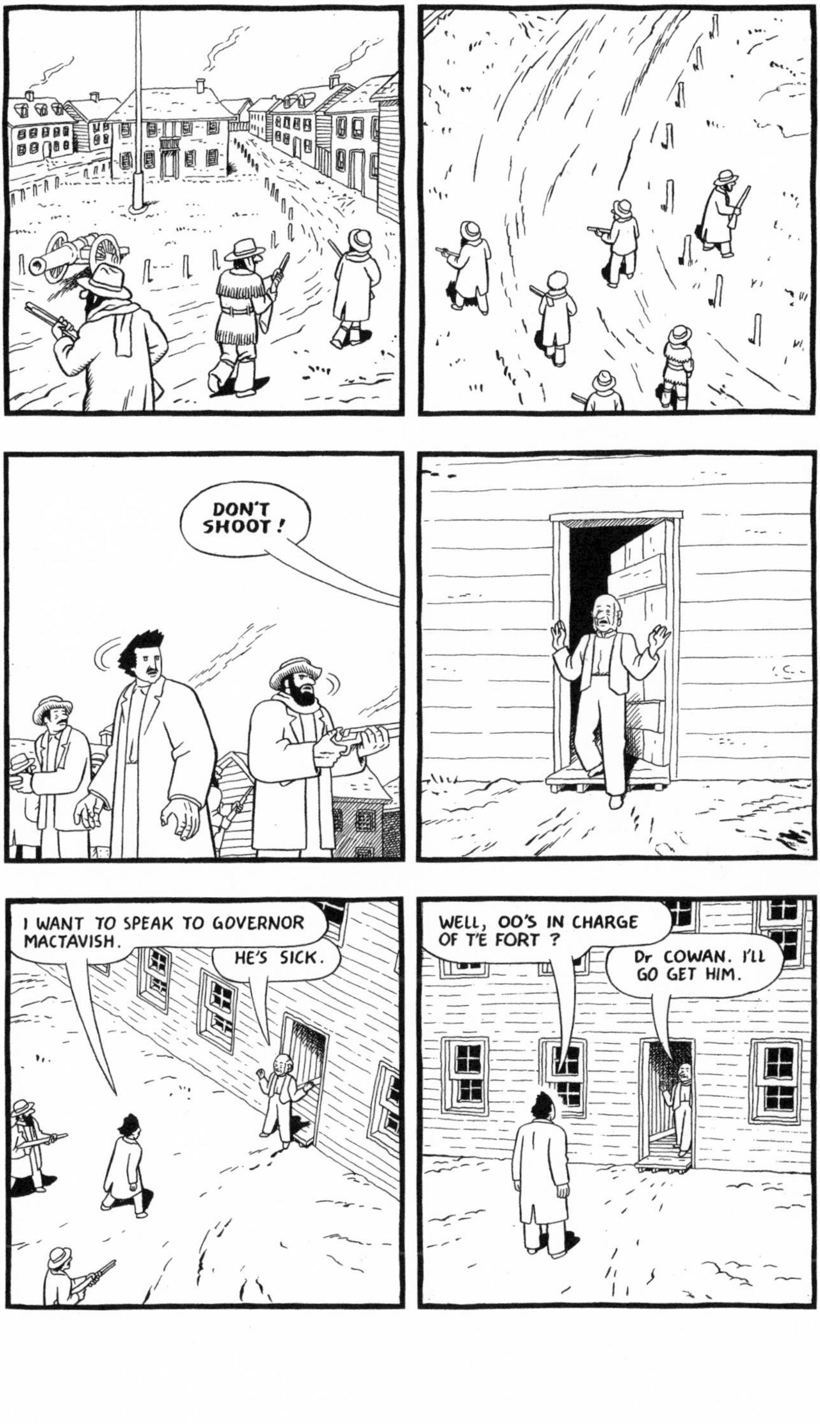
DON'T SHOOT !
I WANT TO SPEAK TO GOVERNOR MACTAVISH.
HE'S SICK.
WELL, OO'S IN CHARGE OF T'E FORT ?
Dr COWAN. I'LL GO GET HIM.

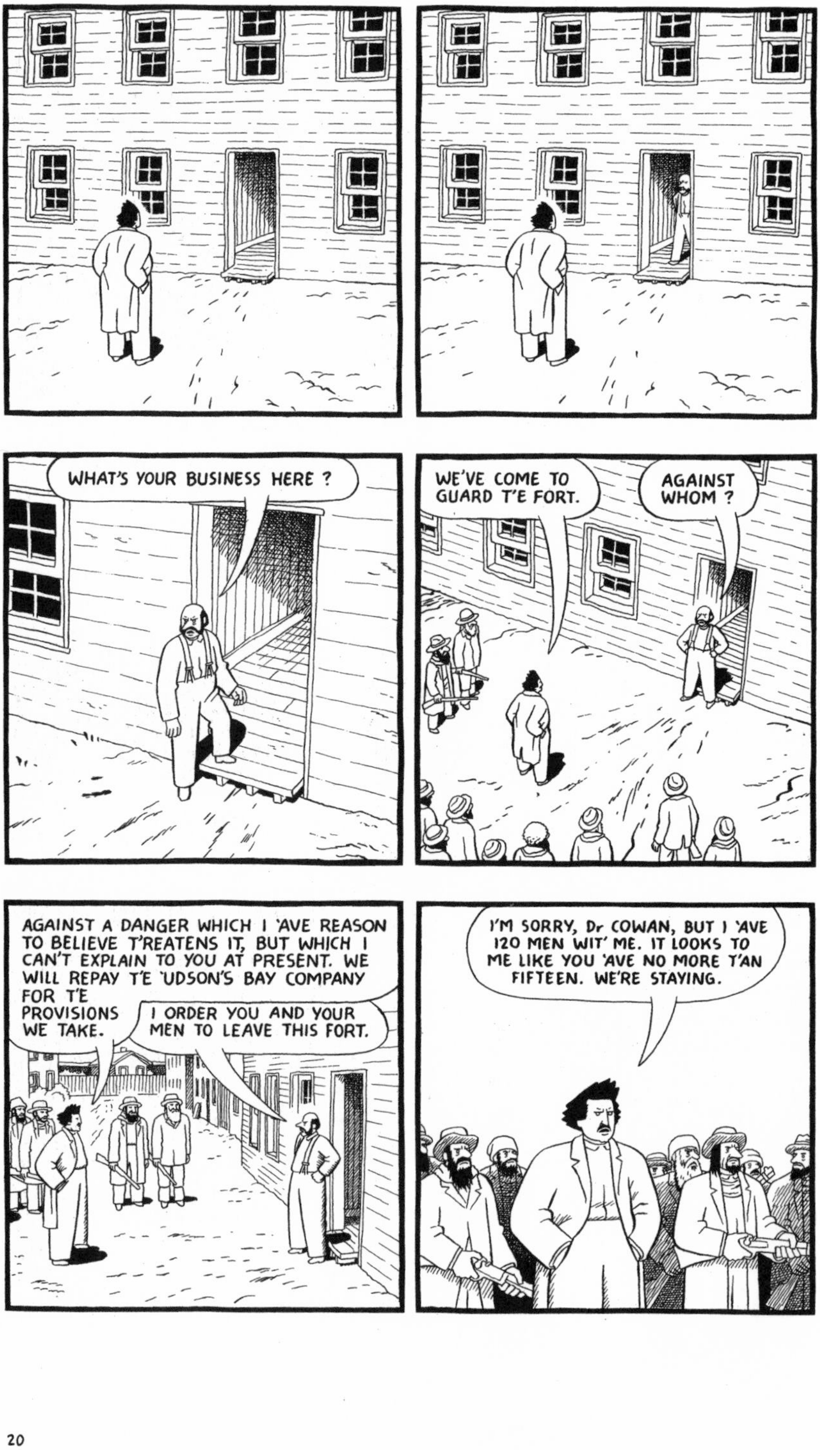
WHAT'S YOUR BUSINESS HERE ?
WE'VE COME TO GUARD T'E FORT.
AGAINST WHOM ?
AGAINST A DANGER WHICH I 'AVE REASON TO BELIEVE T'REATENS IT, BUT WHICH I CAN'T EXPLAIN TO YOU AT PRESENT. WE WILL REPAY T'E 'UDSON'S BAY COMPANY FOR T'E PROVISIONS WE TAKE.
I ORDER YOU AND YOUR MEN TO LEAVE THIS FORT.
I'M SORRY, Dr COWAN, BUT I 'AVE 120 MEN WIT' ME. IT LOOKS TO ME LIKE YOU 'AVE NO MORE T'AN FIFTEEN. WE'RE STAYING.

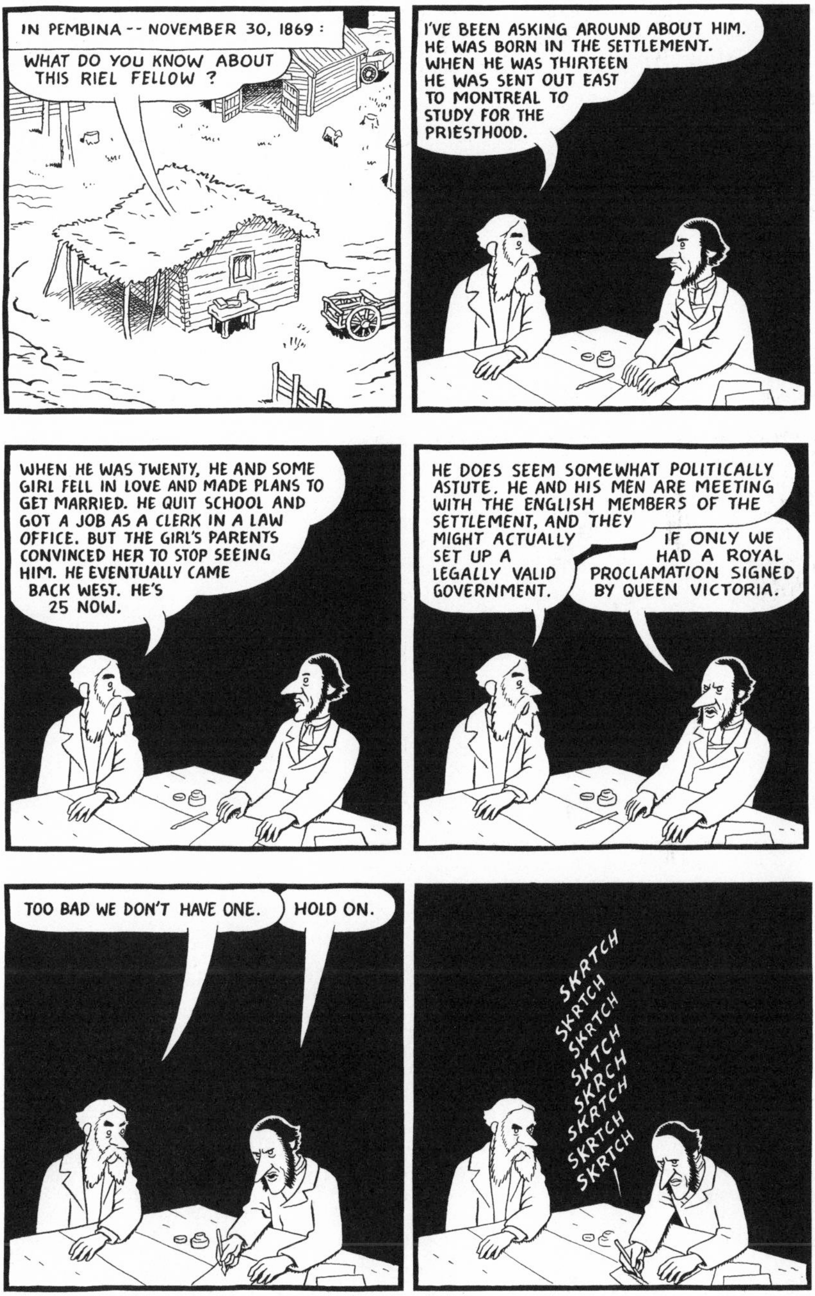
IN PEMBINA -- NOVEMBER 30, 1869 :
WHAT DO YOU KNOW ABOUT THIS RIEL FELLOW ?
I'VE BEEN ASKING AROUND ABOUT HIM. HE WAS BORN IN THE SETTLEMENT. WHEN HE WAS THIRTEEN HE WAS SENT OUT EAST TO MONTREAL TO STUDY FOR THE PRIESTHOOD.
WHEN HE WAS TWENTY, HE AND SOME GIRL FELL IN LOVE AND MADE PLANS TO GET MARRIED. HE QUIT SCHOOL AND GOT A JOB AS A CLERK IN A LAW OFFICE. BUT THE GIRL'S PARENTS CONVINCED HER TO STOP SEEING HIM. HE EVENTUALLY CAME BACK WEST. HE'S 25 NOW.
HE DOES SEEM SOMEWHAT POLITICALLY ASTUTE. HE AND HIS MEN ARE MEETING WITH THE ENGLISH MEMBERS OF THE SETTLEMENT, AND THEY MIGHT ACTUALLY SET UP A LEGALLY VALID GOVERNMENT.
IF ONLY WE HAD A ROYAL PROCLAMATION SIGNED BY QUEEN VICTORIA.
TOO BAD WE DON'T HAVE ONE.
HOLD ON.
SKRTCH
SKRTCH
SKRTCH
SKRTCH
SKTCH
SKRCH
SKRTCH
SKRTCH
SKRTCH

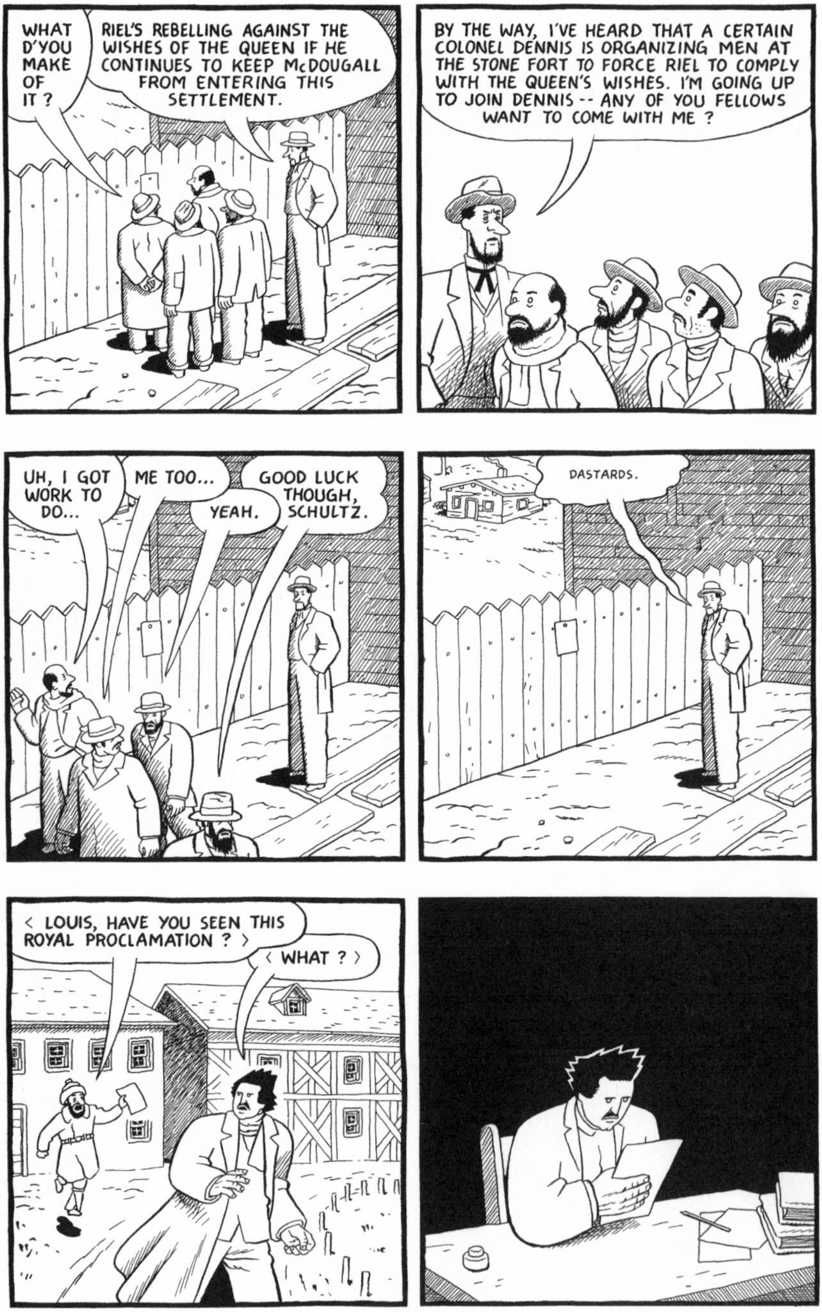
WHAT D'YOU MAKE OF IT ?
RIEL'S REBELLING AGAINST THE WISHES OF THE QUEEN IF HE CONTINUES TO KEEP McDOUGALL FROM ENTERING THIS SETTLEMENT.
BY THE WAY, I'VE HEARD THAT A CERTAIN COLONEL DENNIS IS ORGANIZING MEN AT THE STONE FORT TO FORCE RIEL TO COMPLY WITH THE QUEEN'S WISHES. I'M GOING UP TO JOIN DENNIS -- ANY OF YOU FELLOWS WANT TO COME WITH ME ?
UH, I GOT WORK TO DO...
ME TOO...
YEAH.
GOOD LUCK THOUGH, SCHULTZ.
DASTARDS.
< LOUIS, HAVE YOU SEEN THIS ROYAL PROCLAMATION ? >
< WHAT ? >

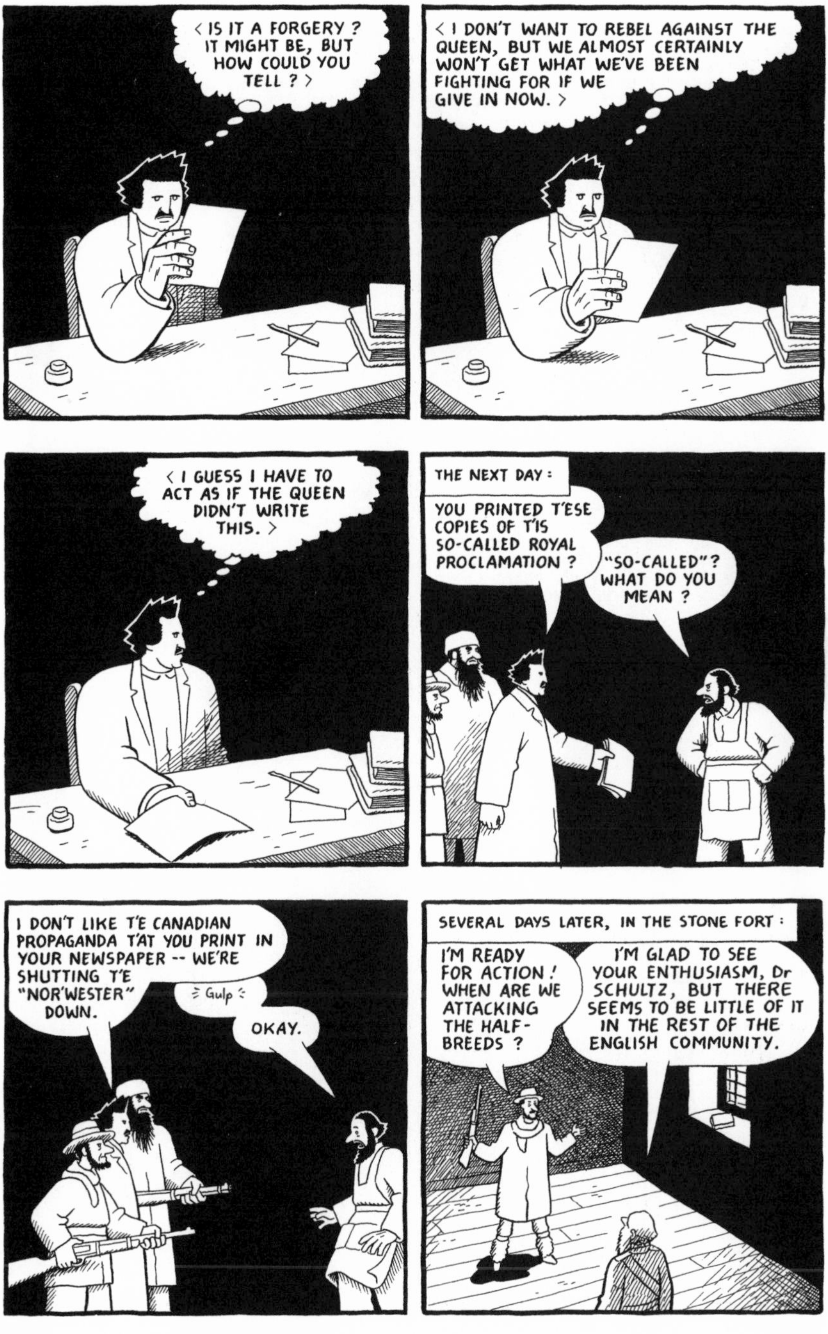
< IS IT A FORGERY ? IT MIGHT BE, BUT HOW COULD YOU TELL ? >
< I DON'T WANT TO REBEL AGAINST THE QUEEN, BUT WE ALMOST CERTAINLY WON'T GET WHAT WE'VE BEEN FIGHTING FOR IF WE GIVE IN NOW. >
< I GUESS I HAVE TO ACT AS IF THE QUEEN DIDN'T WRITE THIS. >
THE NEXT DAY :
YOU PRINTED T'ESE COPIES OF T'IS SO-CALLED ROYAL PROCLAMATION ?
"SO-CALLED"? WHAT DO YOU MEAN ?
I DON'T LIKE T'E CANADIAN PROPAGANDA T'AT YOU PRINT IN YOUR NEWSPAPER -- WE'RE SHUTTING T'E "NOR'WESTER" DOWN.
Gulp
OKAY.
SEVERAL DAYS LATER, IN THE STONE FORT :
I'M READY FOR ACTION ! WHEN ARE WE ATTACKING THE HALF-BREEDS ?
I'M GLAD TO SEE YOUR ENTHUSIASM, Dr SCHULTZ, BUT THERE SEEMS TO BE LITTLE OF IT IN THE REST OF THE ENGLISH COMMUNITY.

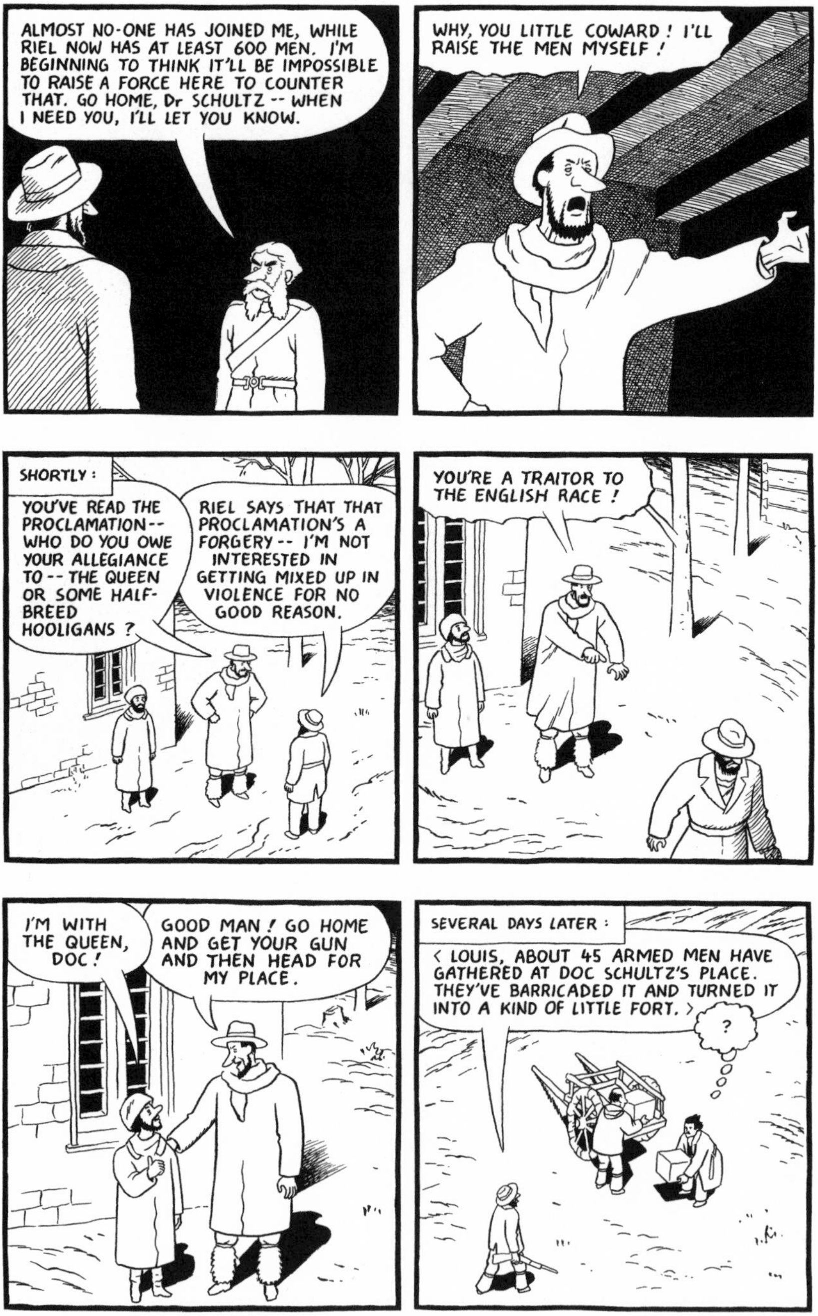
ALMOST NO-ONE HAS JOINED ME, WHILE RIEL NOW HAS AT LEAST 600 MEN. I'M BEGINNING TO THINK IT'LL BE IMPOSSIBLE TO RAISE A FORCE HERE TO COUNTER THAT. GO HOME, Dr SCHULTZ -- WHEN I NEED YOU, I'LL LET YOU KNOW.
WHY, YOU LITTLE COWARD! I'LL RAISE THE MEN MYSELF!
SHORTLY:
YOU'VE READ THE PROCLAMATION-- WHO DO YOU OWE YOUR ALLEGIANCE TO -- THE QUEEN OR SOME HALF-BREED HOOLIGANS?
RIEL SAYS THAT THAT PROCLAMATION'S A FORGERY -- I'M NOT INTERESTED IN GETTING MIXED UP IN VIOLENCE FOR NO GOOD REASON.
YOU'RE A TRAITOR TO THE ENGLISH RACE!
I'M WITH THE QUEEN, DOC!
GOOD MAN! GO HOME AND GET YOUR GUN AND THEN HEAD FOR MY PLACE.
SEVERAL DAYS LATER:
< LOUIS, ABOUT 45 ARMED MEN HAVE GATHERED AT DOC SCHULTZ'S PLACE. THEY'VE BARRICADED IT AND TURNED IT INTO A KIND OF LITTLE FORT. >
?

THEY'RE WILLING TO SURRENDER IF YOU AGREE TO MEET THESE DEMANDS.

TELL T'EM T'AT T'EIR LIVES WILL BE SPARED IF T'EY GIVE UP NOW. IF T'EY WILL NOT SURRENDER, T'EY SHOULD AT LEAST SEND OUT T'E WOMEN AND CHILDREN.

RIP

T'EY 'AVE FIFTEEN MINUTES TO DECIDE BEFORE WE START FIRING.

29

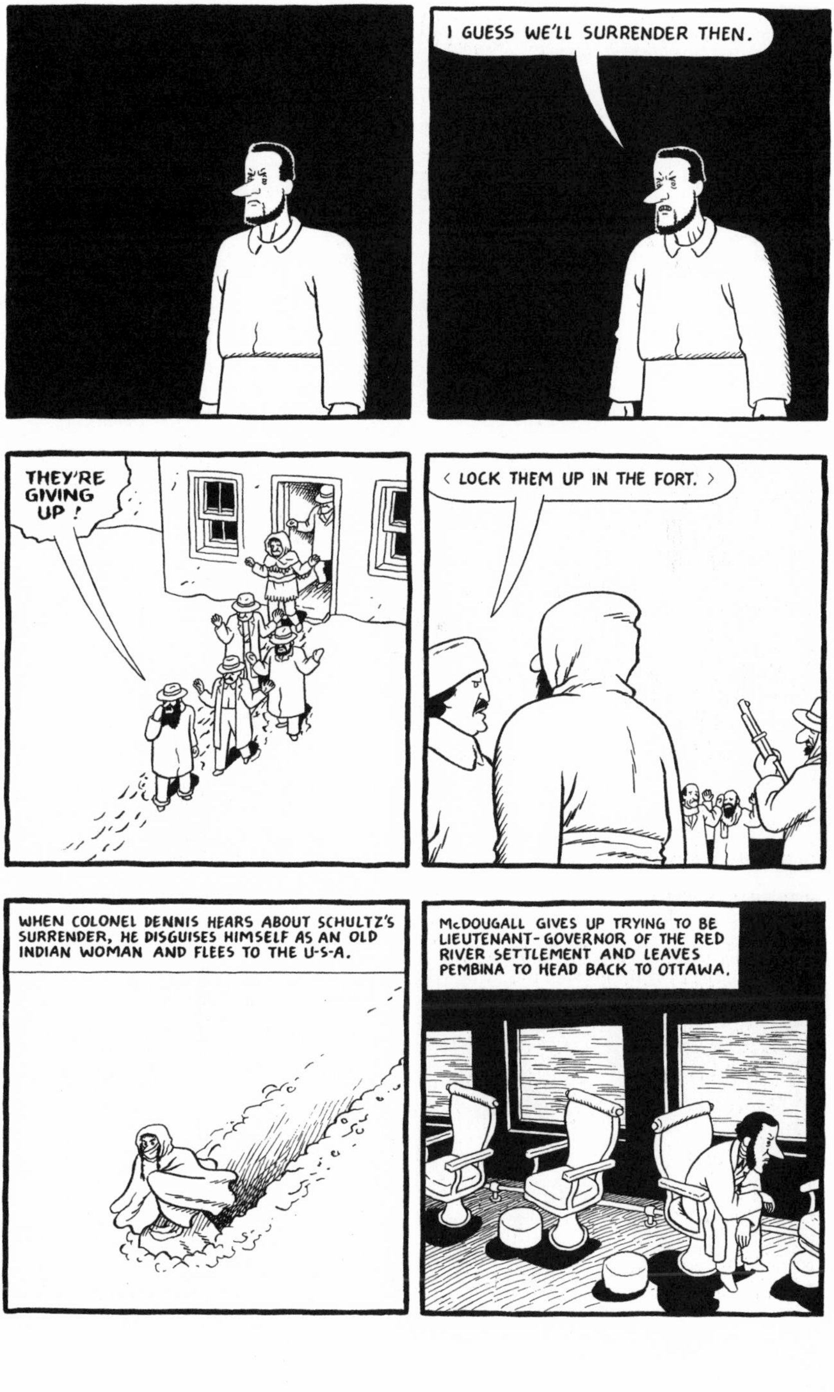
I GUESS WE'LL SURRENDER THEN.
THEY'RE GIVING UP!
< LOCK THEM UP IN THE FORT. >
WHEN COLONEL DENNIS HEARS ABOUT SCHULTZ'S SURRENDER, HE DISGUISES HIMSELF AS AN OLD INDIAN WOMAN AND FLEES TO THE U-S-A.
McDOUGALL GIVES UP TRYING TO BE LIEUTENANT-GOVERNOR OF THE RED RIVER SETTLEMENT AND LEAVES PEMBINA TO HEAD BACK TO OTTAWA.

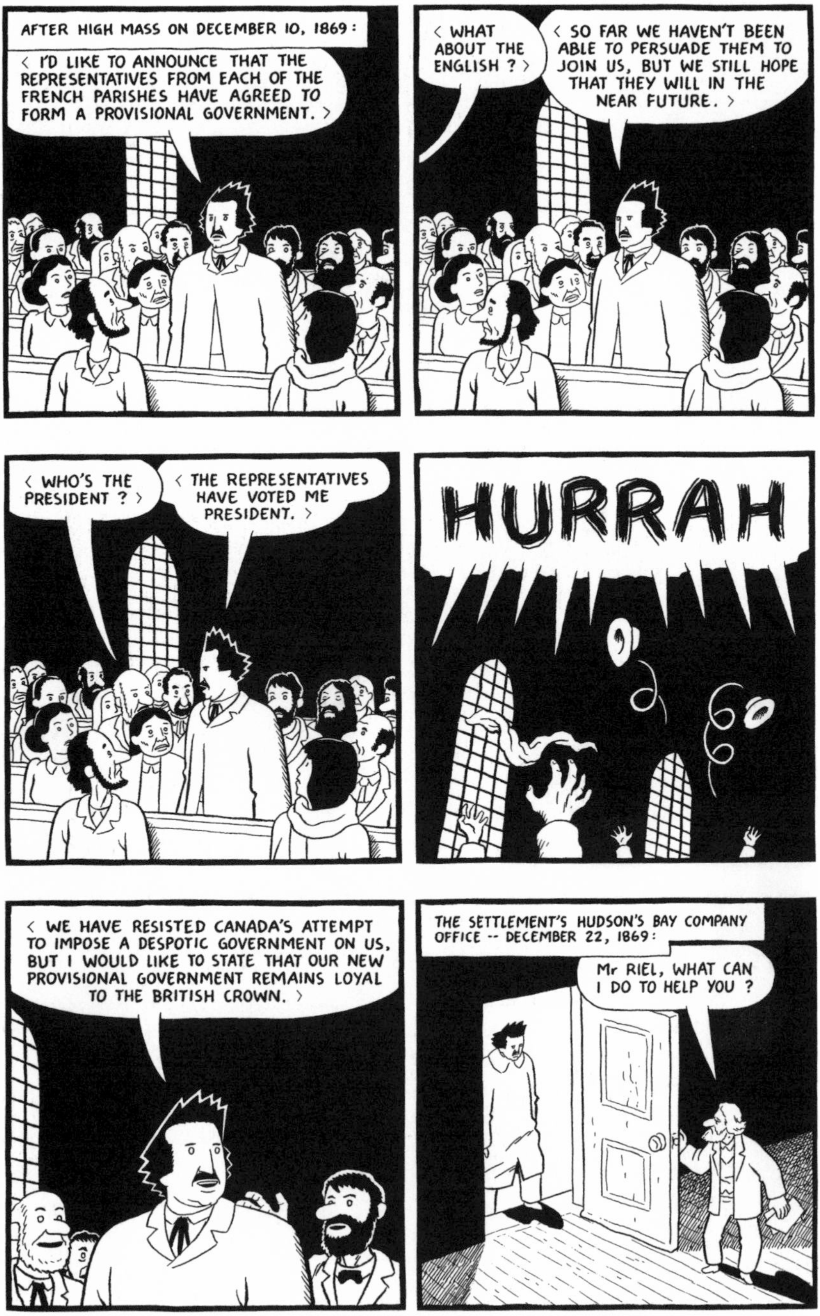
AFTER HIGH MASS ON DECEMBER 10, 1869:
< I'D LIKE TO ANNOUNCE THAT THE REPRESENTATIVES FROM EACH OF THE FRENCH PARISHES HAVE AGREED TO FORM A PROVISIONAL GOVERNMENT. >
< WHAT ABOUT THE ENGLISH ? >
< SO FAR WE HAVEN'T BEEN ABLE TO PERSUADE THEM TO JOIN US, BUT WE STILL HOPE THAT THEY WILL IN THE NEAR FUTURE. >
< WHO'S THE PRESIDENT ? >
< THE REPRESENTATIVES HAVE VOTED ME PRESIDENT. >
HURRAH
< WE HAVE RESISTED CANADA'S ATTEMPT TO IMPOSE A DESPOTIC GOVERNMENT ON US, BUT I WOULD LIKE TO STATE THAT OUR NEW PROVISIONAL GOVERNMENT REMAINS LOYAL TO THE BRITISH CROWN. >
THE SETTLEMENT'S HUDSON'S BAY COMPANY OFFICE -- DECEMBER 22, 1869:
Mr RIEL, WHAT CAN I DO TO HELP YOU ?

33

I PROPOSE T'AT WE SET UP A CONVENTION OF 40 -- T'E FRENCH WILL ELECT 20 REPRESENTATIVES, AND SO WILL T'E ENGLISH. TOGET'ER WE'LL DECIDE WHAT RIGHTS WE'RE ENTITLED TO --

-- AND WHAT'S MORE, GENTLEMEN, WE'LL GET T'OSE RIGHTS !

HURRAH

AFTER THE ELECTION OF THE CONVENTION OF 40 :

KNOCK KNOCK

MONSIEUR SMIT' OF T'E 'UDSON'S BAY COMPANY -- BONJOUR. T'IS IS A SURPRISE VISIT.

Mr NOLIN.

WOULD YOU LIKE TO COME IN ?

JUST FOR A MOMENT.

LET ME TAKE YOUR COAT.

NO, NO -- I'M NOT STAYING. I JUST CAME BY TO CONGRATULATE YOU ON YOUR ELECTION TO THE CONVENTION OF 40 --

34

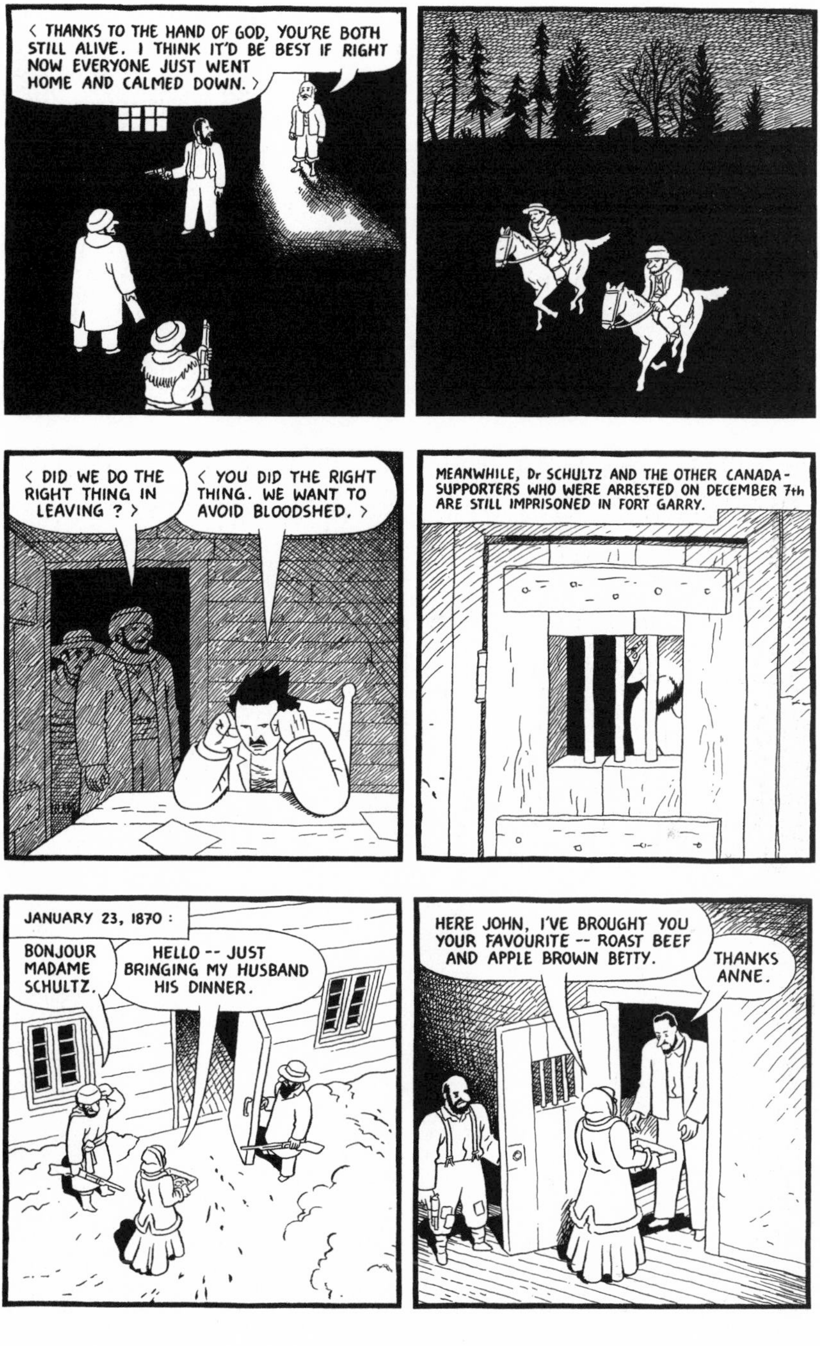
< THANKS TO THE HAND OF GOD, YOU'RE BOTH STILL ALIVE. I THINK IT'D BE BEST IF RIGHT NOW EVERYONE JUST WENT HOME AND CALMED DOWN. >
< DID WE DO THE RIGHT THING IN LEAVING ? >
< YOU DID THE RIGHT THING. WE WANT TO AVOID BLOODSHED. >
MEANWHILE, Dr SCHULTZ AND THE OTHER CANADA-SUPPORTERS WHO WERE ARRESTED ON DECEMBER 7th ARE STILL IMPRISONED IN FORT GARRY.
JANUARY 23, 1870 :
BONJOUR MADAME SCHULTZ.
HELLO -- JUST BRINGING MY HUSBAND HIS DINNER.
HERE JOHN, I'VE BROUGHT YOU YOUR FAVOURITE -- ROAST BEEF AND APPLE BROWN BETTY.
THANKS ANNE.

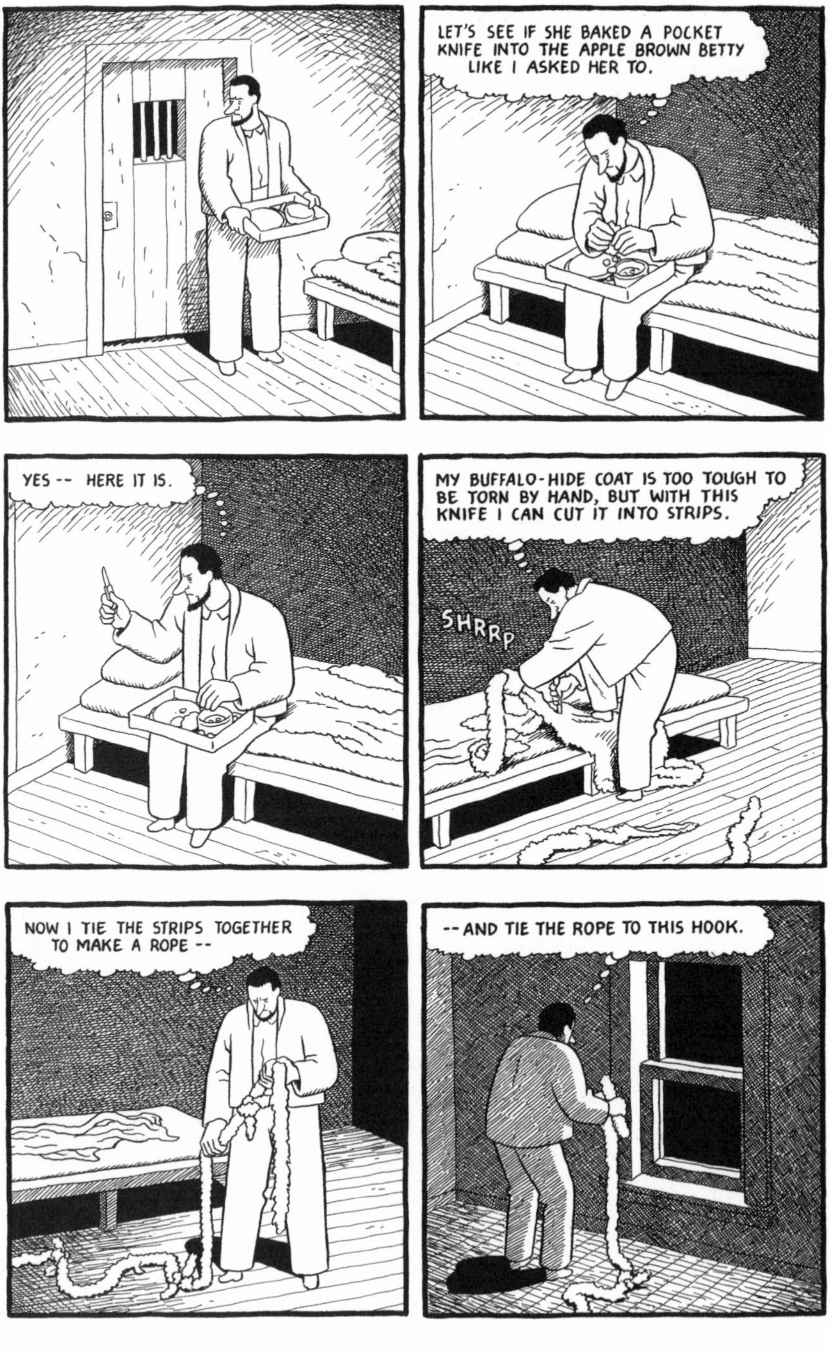
LET'S SEE IF SHE BAKED A POCKET KNIFE INTO THE APPLE BROWN BETTY LIKE I ASKED HER TO.
YES -- HERE IT IS.
MY BUFFALO-HIDE COAT IS TOO TOUGH TO BE TORN BY HAND, BUT WITH THIS KNIFE I CAN CUT IT INTO STRIPS.
SHRRP
NOW I TIE THE STRIPS TOGETHER TO MAKE A ROPE --
-- AND TIE THE ROPE TO THIS HOOK.

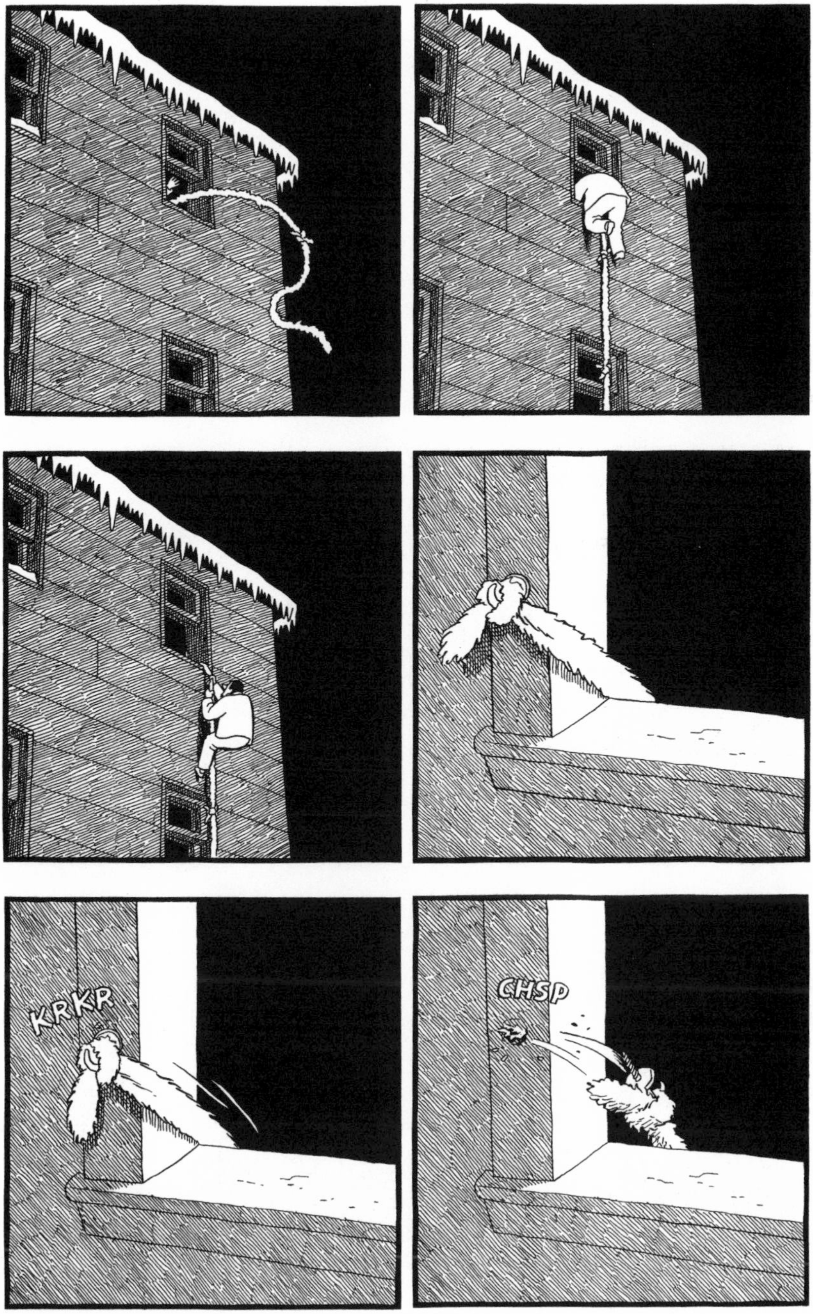
KRKR
CHSP

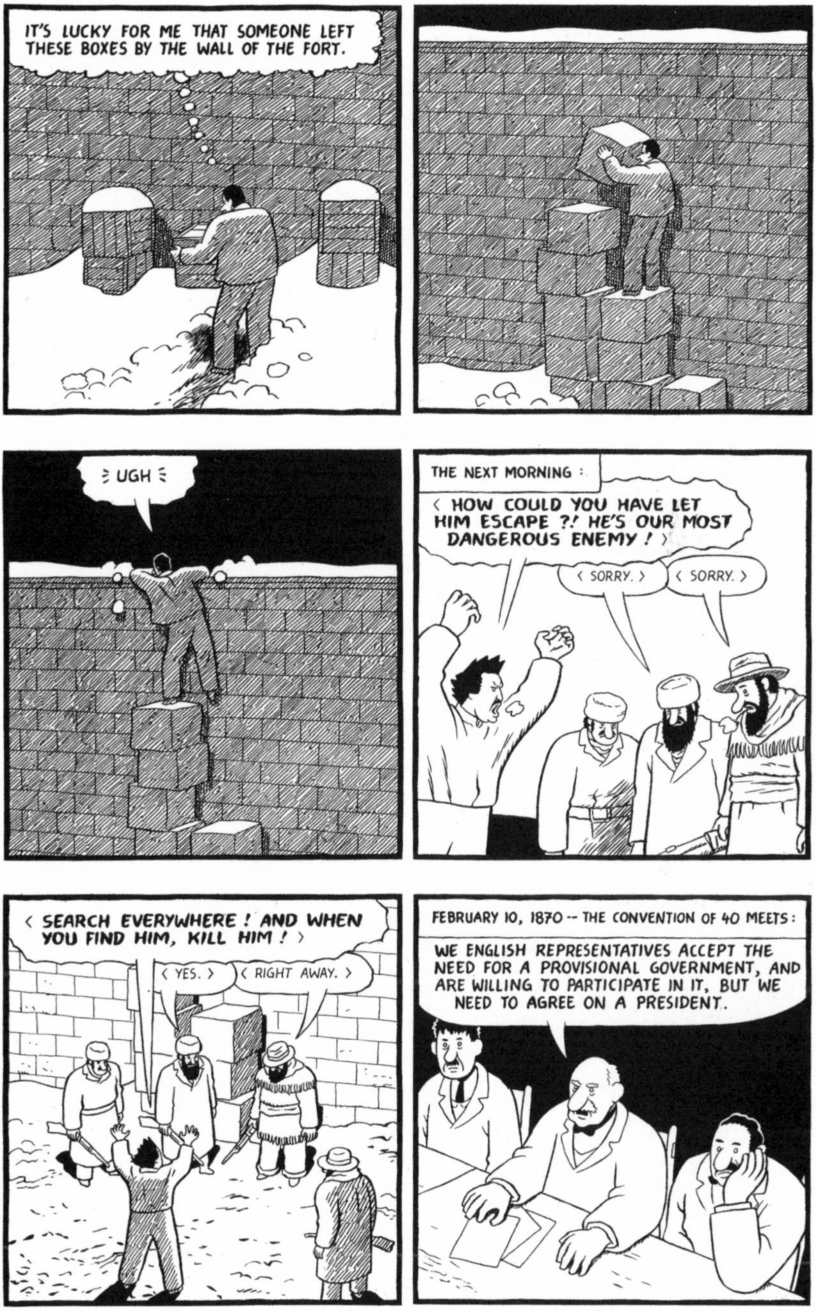

IT'S LUCKY FOR ME THAT SOMEONE LEFT THESE BOXES BY THE WALL OF THE FORT.
UGH
THE NEXT MORNING :
‹ HOW COULD YOU HAVE LET HIM ESCAPE ?! HE'S OUR MOST DANGEROUS ENEMY ! ›
‹ SORRY. ›
‹ SORRY. ›
‹ SEARCH EVERYWHERE ! AND WHEN YOU FIND HIM, KILL HIM ! ›
‹ YES. ›
‹ RIGHT AWAY. ›
FEBRUARY 10, 1870 -- THE CONVENTION OF 40 MEETS :
WE ENGLISH REPRESENTATIVES ACCEPT THE NEED FOR A PROVISIONAL GOVERNMENT, AND ARE WILLING TO PARTICIPATE IN IT, BUT WE NEED TO AGREE ON A PRESIDENT.

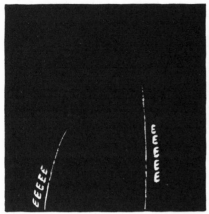

EEEEE EEEEE

PK PF

RIEL, IT MIGHT BE TIME TO START THINKING ABOUT LETTING THOSE PRISONERS IN FORT GARRY GO FREE.

NOT YET.

JOHN SUTHERLAND -- AN ENGLISH SETTLER

I'VE HEARD A RUMOUR THAT SCHULTZ IS NOW IN KILDONAN AND HAS MANAGED TO PUT TOGETHER AN ARMY OF OVER 300 MEN TO FREE THE PRISONERS.

SCHULTZ COULDN'T HAVE GOTTEN THAT MANY MEN MOTIVATED IF YOU DIDN'T HAVE ANY PRISONERS -- IT GIVES HIM A CAUSE TO RALLY AROUND.

LET ME T'INK ABOUT IT.

ON FEBRUARY 15, 1870, A MÉTIS NAMED NORBERT PARISIEN WANDERS THROUGH KILDONAN:

< SEEMS TO BE A BIG COMMOTION GOING ON HERE. >

create

46

47

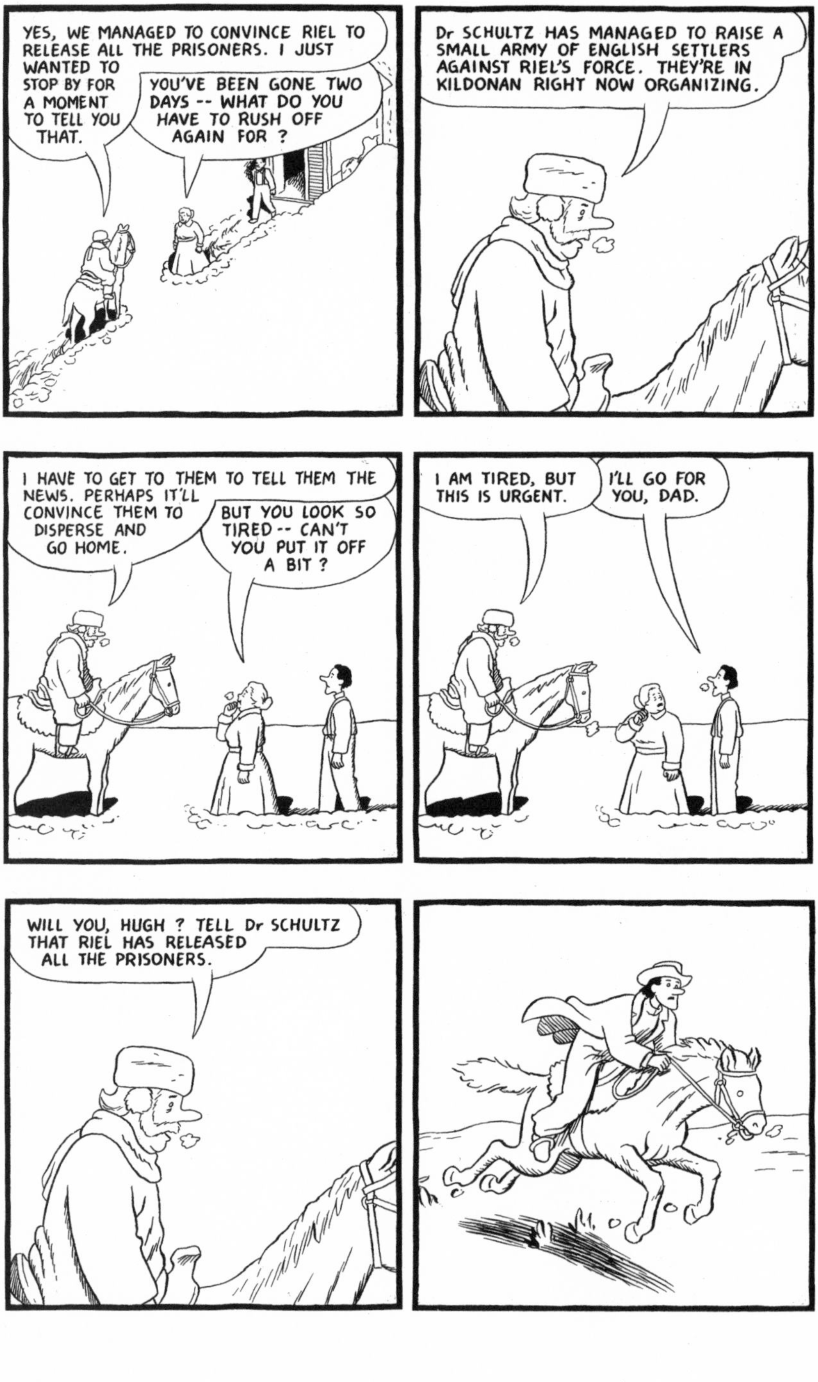
YES, WE MANAGED TO CONVINCE RIEL TO RELEASE ALL THE PRISONERS. I JUST WANTED TO STOP BY FOR A MOMENT TO TELL YOU THAT.
YOU'VE BEEN GONE TWO DAYS -- WHAT DO YOU HAVE TO RUSH OFF AGAIN FOR ?
Dr SCHULTZ HAS MANAGED TO RAISE A SMALL ARMY OF ENGLISH SETTLERS AGAINST RIEL'S FORCE. THEY'RE IN KILDONAN RIGHT NOW ORGANIZING.
I HAVE TO GET TO THEM TO TELL THEM THE NEWS. PERHAPS IT'LL CONVINCE THEM TO DISPERSE AND GO HOME.
BUT YOU LOOK SO TIRED -- CAN'T YOU PUT IT OFF A BIT ?
I AM TIRED, BUT THIS IS URGENT.
I'LL GO FOR YOU, DAD.
WILL YOU, HUGH ? TELL Dr SCHULTZ THAT RIEL HAS RELEASED ALL THE PRISONERS.

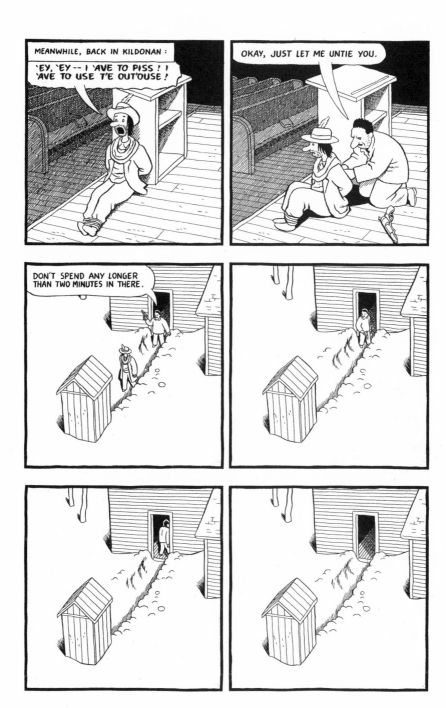

49

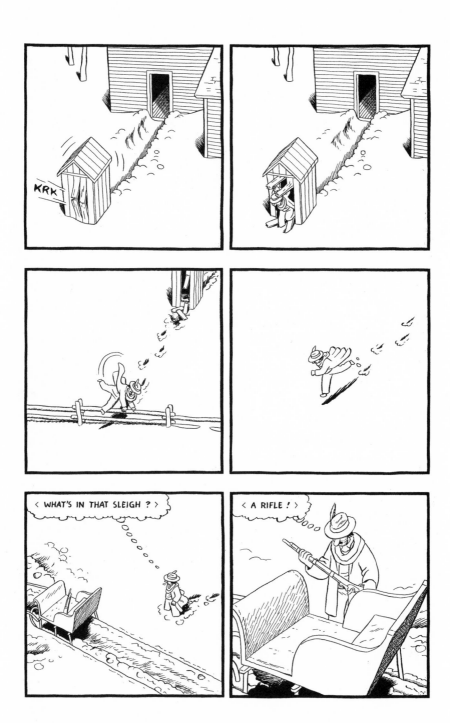

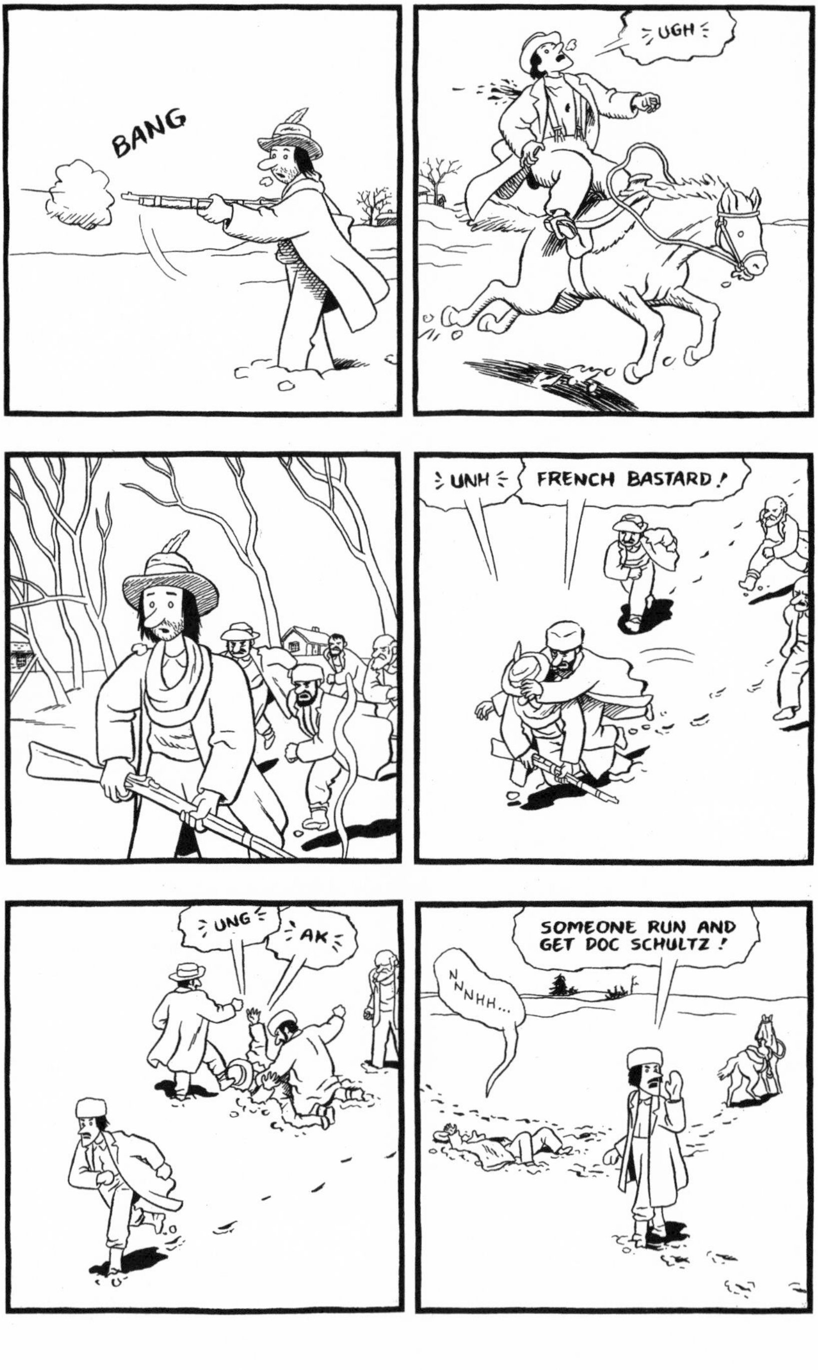
BANG
UGH
UNH
FRENCH BASTARD!
UNG
AK
NNNHH...
SOMEONE RUN AND GET DOC SCHULTZ!

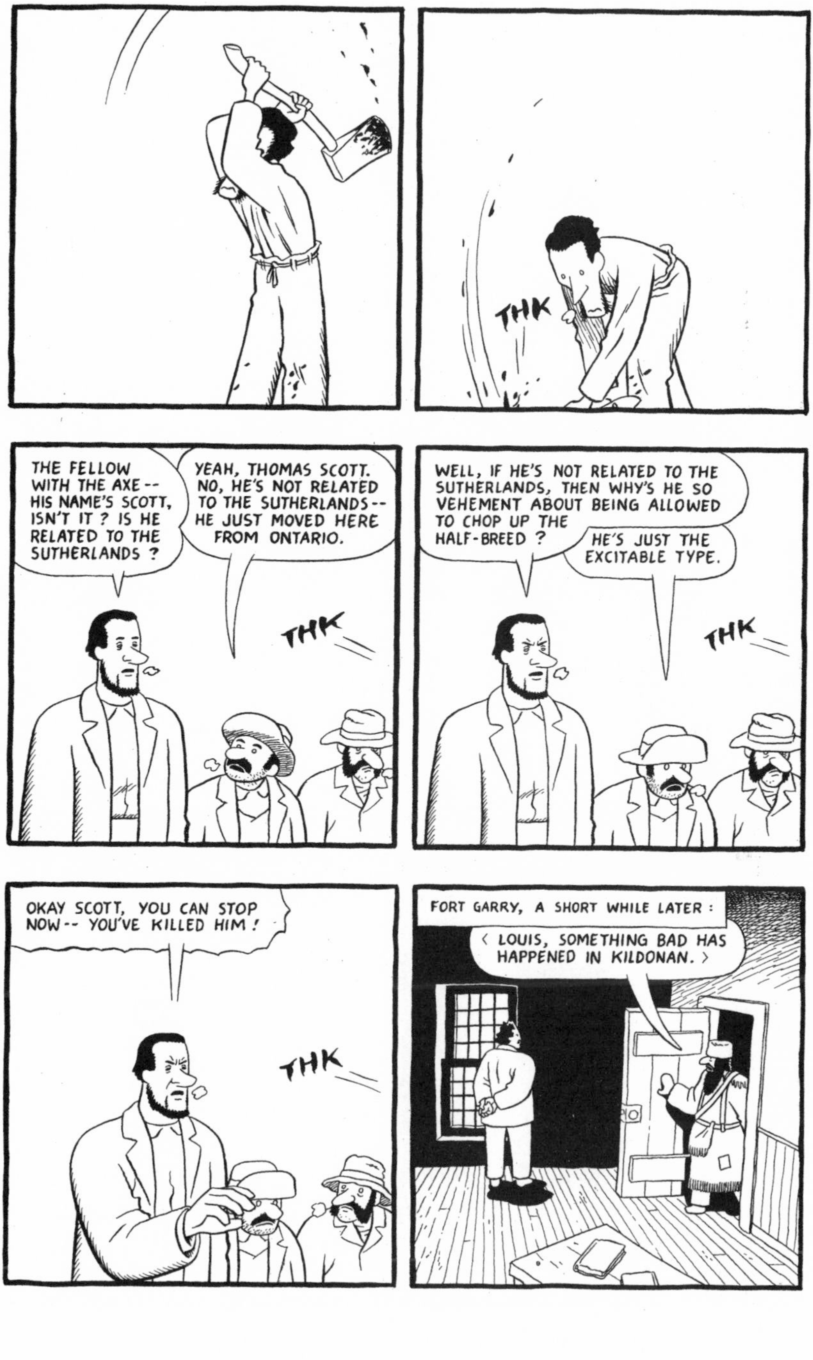
THK
THE FELLOW WITH THE AXE -- HIS NAME'S SCOTT, ISN'T IT ? IS HE RELATED TO THE SUTHERLANDS ?
YEAH, THOMAS SCOTT. NO, HE'S NOT RELATED TO THE SUTHERLANDS -- HE JUST MOVED HERE FROM ONTARIO.
THK
WELL, IF HE'S NOT RELATED TO THE SUTHERLANDS, THEN WHY'S HE SO VEHEMENT ABOUT BEING ALLOWED TO CHOP UP THE HALF-BREED ?
HE'S JUST THE EXCITABLE TYPE.
THK
OKAY SCOTT, YOU CAN STOP NOW -- YOU'VE KILLED HIM !
THK
FORT GARRY, A SHORT WHILE LATER :
‹ LOUIS, SOMETHING BAD HAS HAPPENED IN KILDONAN. ›

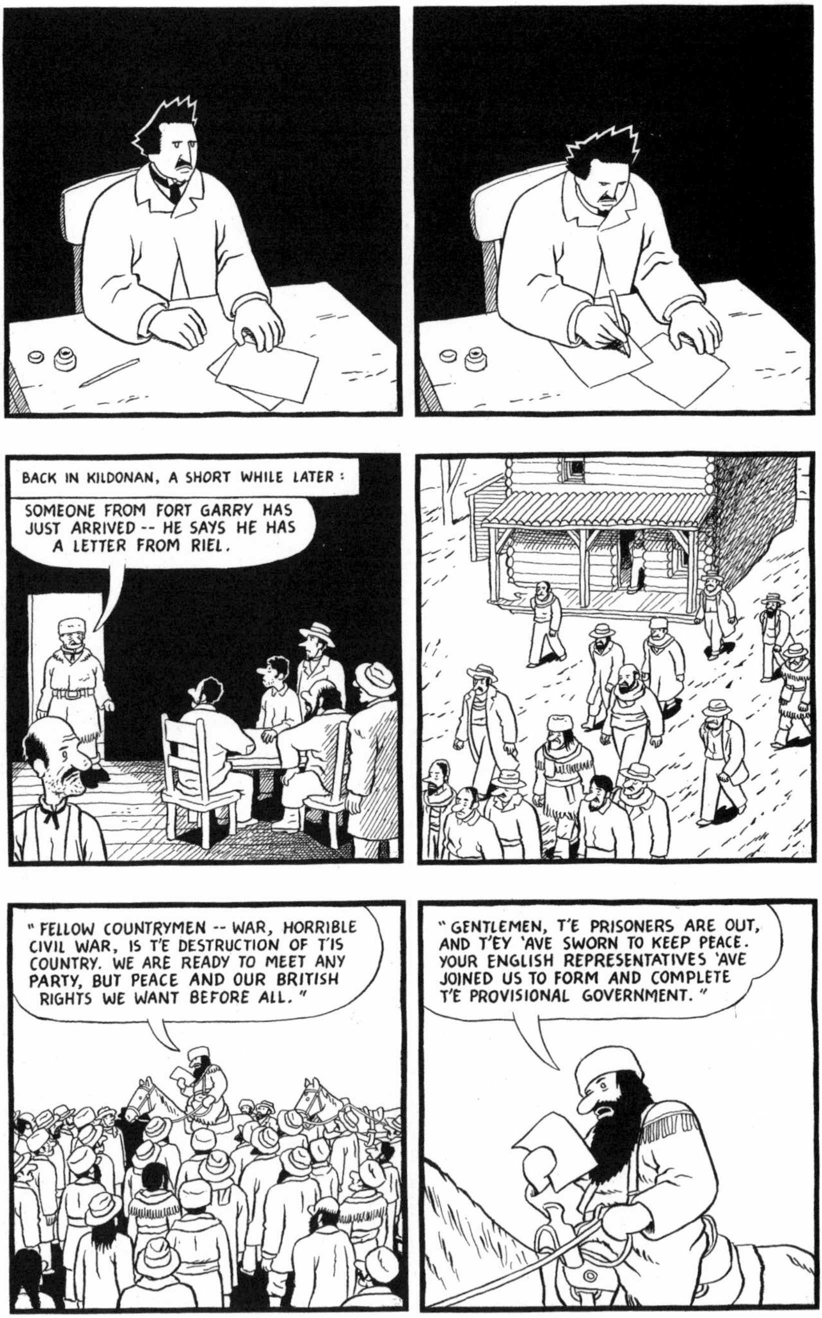
BACK IN KILDONAN, A SHORT WHILE LATER:
SOMEONE FROM FORT GARRY HAS JUST ARRIVED -- HE SAYS HE HAS A LETTER FROM RIEL.
" FELLOW COUNTRYMEN -- WAR, HORRIBLE CIVIL WAR, IS T'E DESTRUCTION OF T'IS COUNTRY. WE ARE READY TO MEET ANY PARTY, BUT PEACE AND OUR BRITISH RIGHTS WE WANT BEFORE ALL."
" GENTLEMEN, T'E PRISONERS ARE OUT, AND T'EY 'AVE SWORN TO KEEP PEACE. YOUR ENGLISH REPRESENTATIVES 'AVE JOINED US TO FORM AND COMPLETE T'E PROVISIONAL GOVERNMENT."

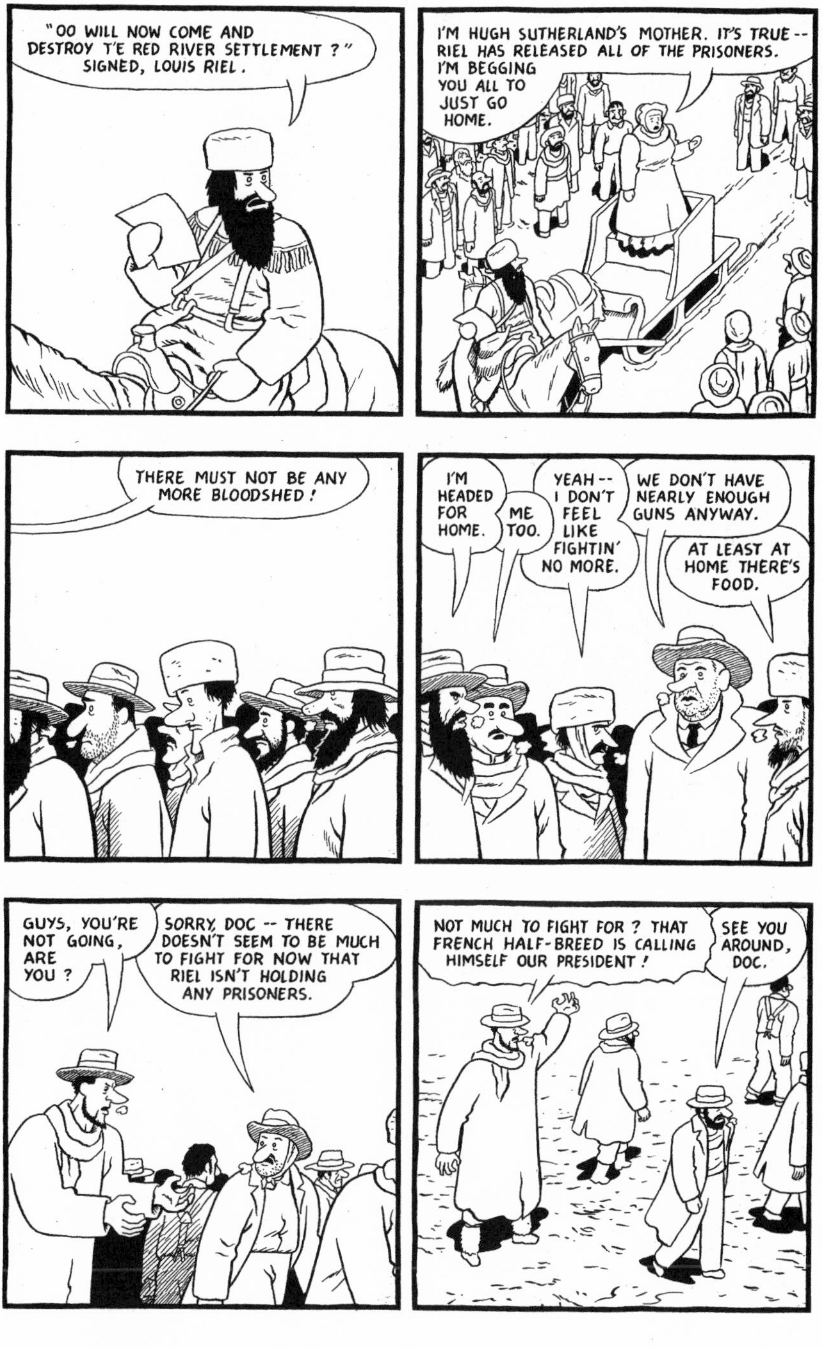
"OO WILL NOW COME AND DESTROY T'E RED RIVER SETTLEMENT ?" SIGNED, LOUIS RIEL.
I'M HUGH SUTHERLAND'S MOTHER. IT'S TRUE -- RIEL HAS RELEASED ALL OF THE PRISONERS. I'M BEGGING YOU ALL TO JUST GO HOME.
THERE MUST NOT BE ANY MORE BLOODSHED!
I'M HEADED FOR HOME.
ME TOO.
YEAH -- I DON'T FEEL LIKE FIGHTIN' NO MORE.
WE DON'T HAVE NEARLY ENOUGH GUNS ANYWAY.
AT LEAST AT HOME THERE'S FOOD.
GUYS, YOU'RE NOT GOING, ARE YOU ?
SORRY, DOC -- THERE DOESN'T SEEM TO BE MUCH TO FIGHT FOR NOW THAT RIEL ISN'T HOLDING ANY PRISONERS.
NOT MUCH TO FIGHT FOR ? THAT FRENCH HALF-BREED IS CALLING HIMSELF OUR PRESIDENT!
SEE YOU AROUND, DOC.

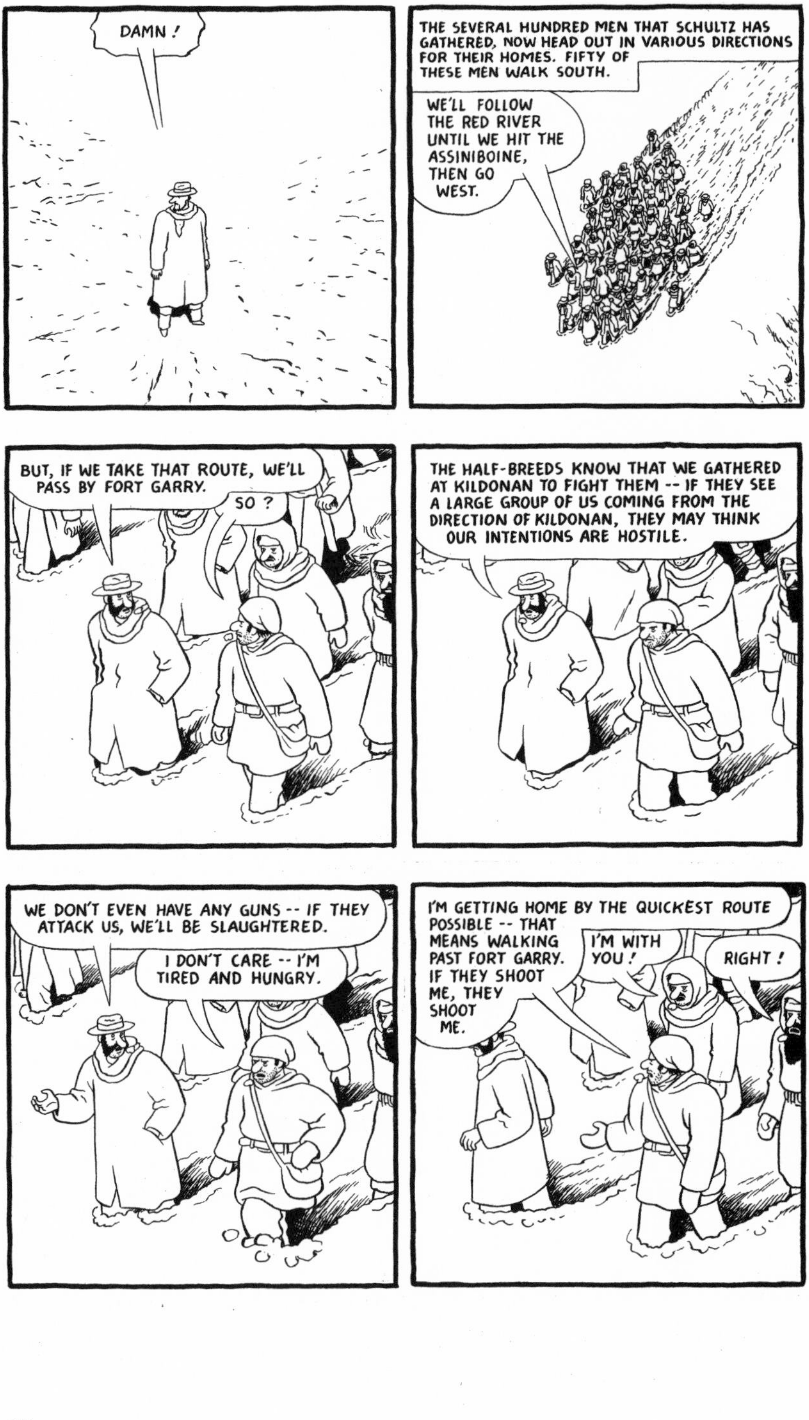
DAMN !
THE SEVERAL HUNDRED MEN THAT SCHULTZ HAS GATHERED, NOW HEAD OUT IN VARIOUS DIRECTIONS FOR THEIR HOMES. FIFTY OF THESE MEN WALK SOUTH.
WE'LL FOLLOW THE RED RIVER UNTIL WE HIT THE ASSINIBOINE, THEN GO WEST.
BUT, IF WE TAKE THAT ROUTE, WE'LL PASS BY FORT GARRY.
SO ?
THE HALF-BREEDS KNOW THAT WE GATHERED AT KILDONAN TO FIGHT THEM -- IF THEY SEE A LARGE GROUP OF US COMING FROM THE DIRECTION OF KILDONAN, THEY MAY THINK OUR INTENTIONS ARE HOSTILE.
WE DON'T EVEN HAVE ANY GUNS -- IF THEY ATTACK US, WE'LL BE SLAUGHTERED.
I DON'T CARE -- I'M TIRED AND HUNGRY.
I'M GETTING HOME BY THE QUICKEST ROUTE POSSIBLE -- THAT MEANS WALKING PAST FORT GARRY. IF THEY SHOOT ME, THEY SHOOT ME.
I'M WITH YOU !
RIGHT !

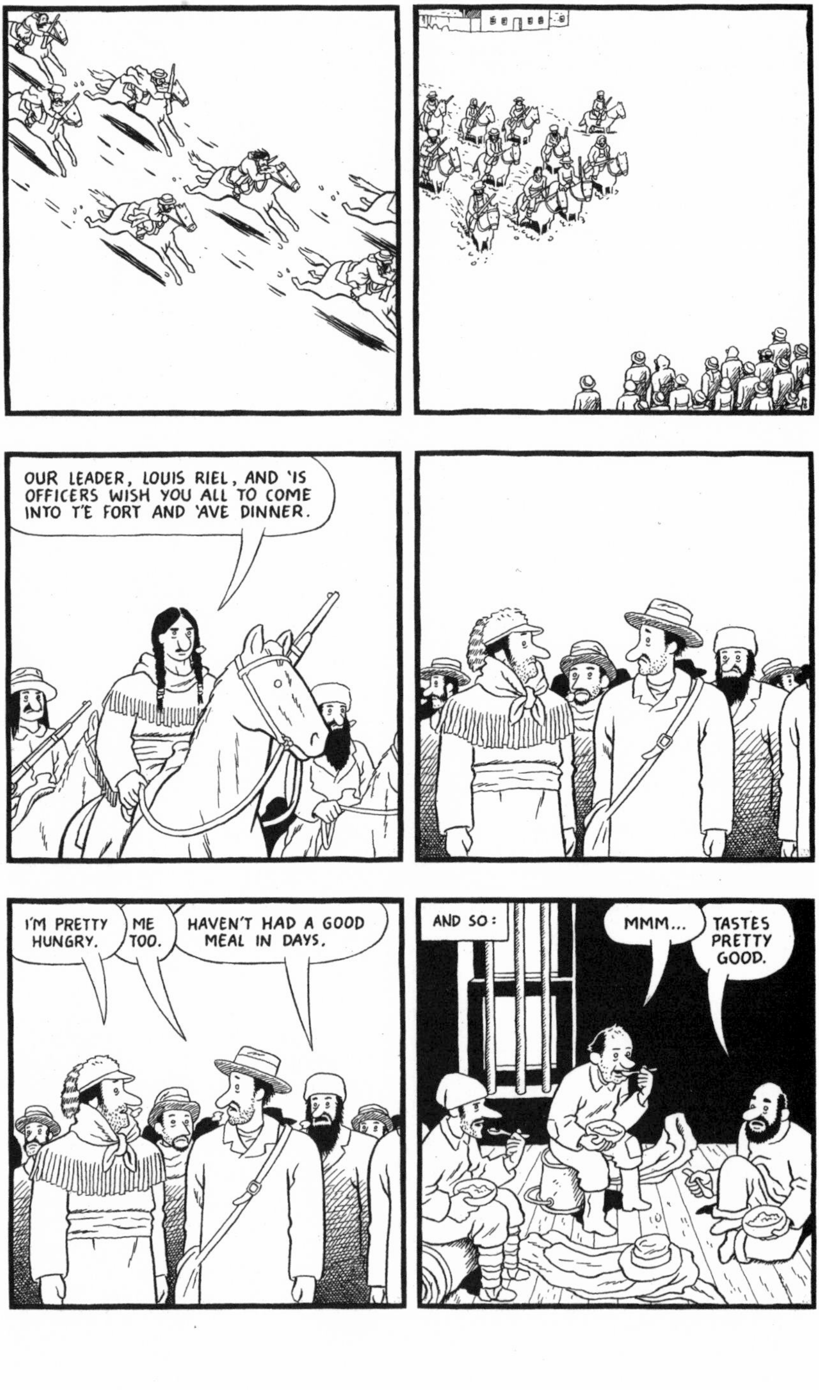
OUR LEADER, LOUIS RIEL, AND 'IS OFFICERS WISH YOU ALL TO COME INTO T'E FORT AND 'AVE DINNER.
I'M PRETTY HUNGRY.
ME TOO.
HAVEN'T HAD A GOOD MEAL IN DAYS.
AND SO:
MMM...
TASTES PRETTY GOOD.

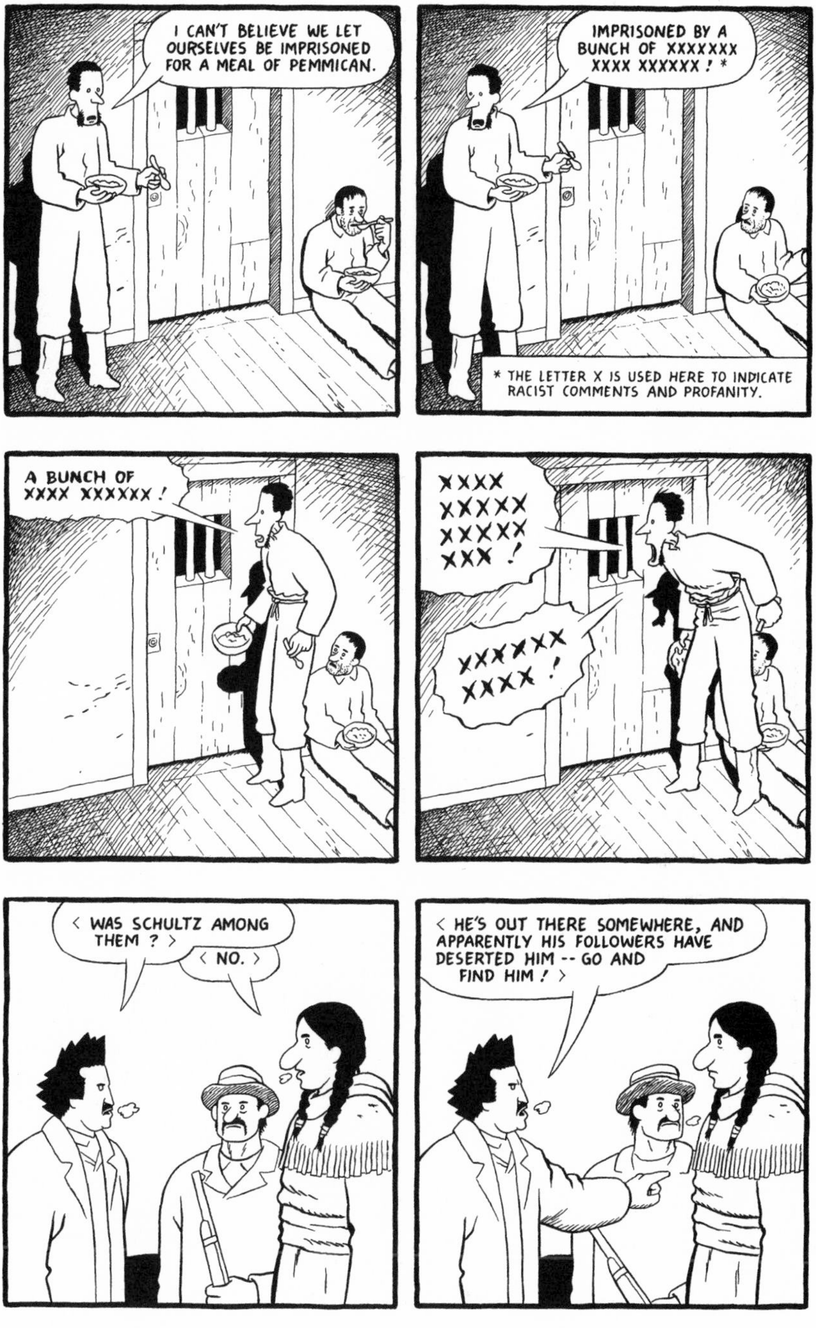
I CAN'T BELIEVE WE LET OURSELVES BE IMPRISONED FOR A MEAL OF PEMMICAN.
IMPRISONED BY A BUNCH OF XXXXXXX XXXX XXXXXX ! *
* THE LETTER X IS USED HERE TO INDICATE RACIST COMMENTS AND PROFANITY.
A BUNCH OF XXXX XXXXXX !
XXXX XXXXX XXXXX XXX !
XXXXXX XXXX !
< WAS SCHULTZ AMONG THEM ? >
< NO. >
< HE'S OUT THERE SOMEWHERE, AND APPARENTLY HIS FOLLOWERS HAVE DESERTED HIM -- GO AND FIND HIM ! >

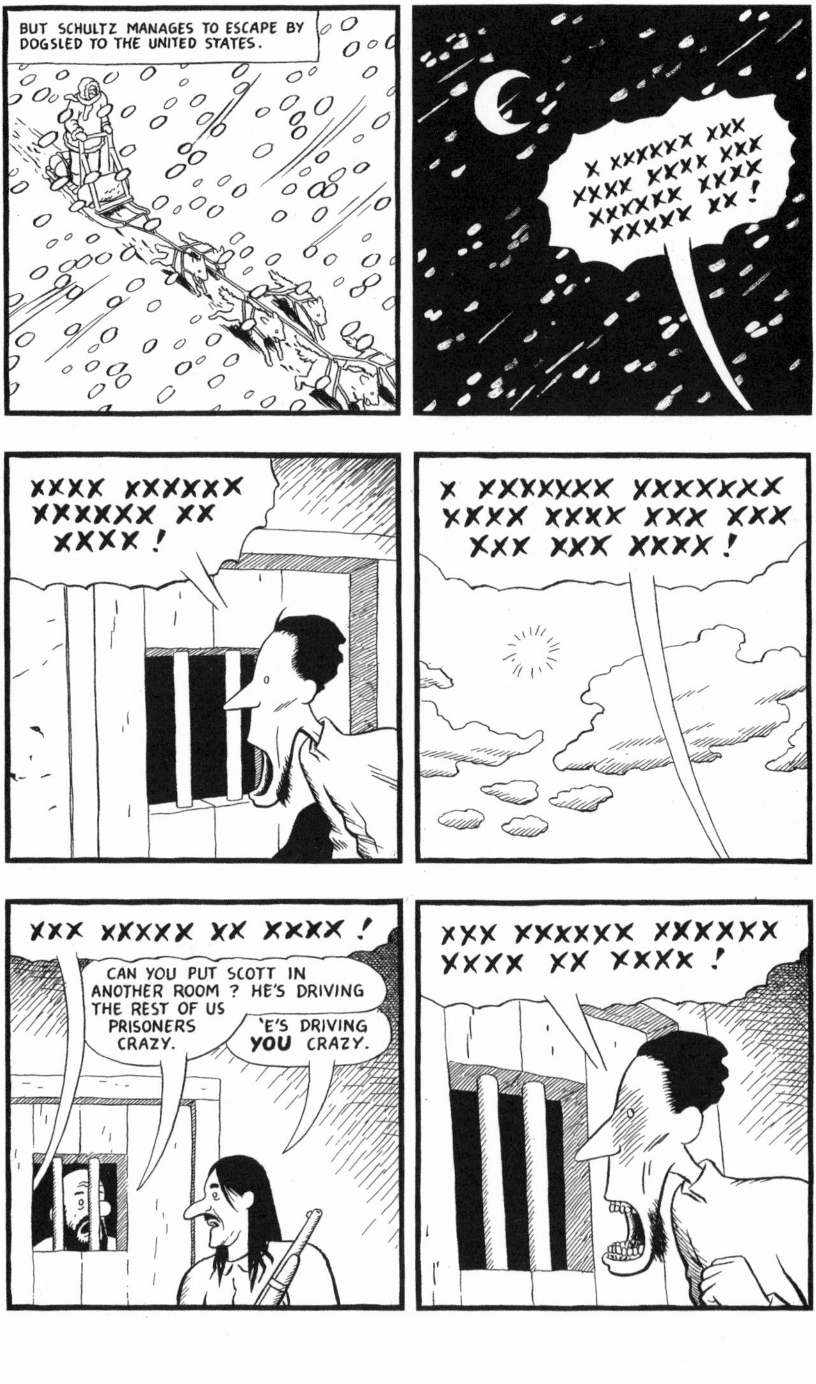

BUT SCHULTZ MANAGES TO ESCAPE BY DOGSLED TO THE UNITED STATES.
X XXXXXX XXX XXXX XXXX XXX XXXXXX XXXX XXXXX XX !
XXXX XXXXXX XXXXXX XX XXXX !
X XXXXXXX XXXXXXX XXXX XXXX XXX XXX XXX XXX XXXX !
XXX XXXXX XX XXXX !
CAN YOU PUT SCOTT IN ANOTHER ROOM ? HE'S DRIVING THE REST OF US PRISONERS CRAZY.
'E'S DRIVING **YOU** CRAZY.
XXX XXXXXX XXXXXX XXXX XX XXXX !

XXXXX XX XXXX XXXXX XX XXX XXXX!
XXXX XX XXX XXXX XX XXXX XXXX!
XXXXXX XXX XX XXX XX X XXXXX!
XXX XXX XX XXXXX XXX X XX XXXX!
URG
OW

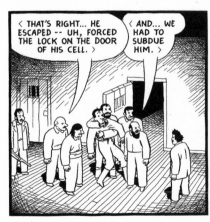

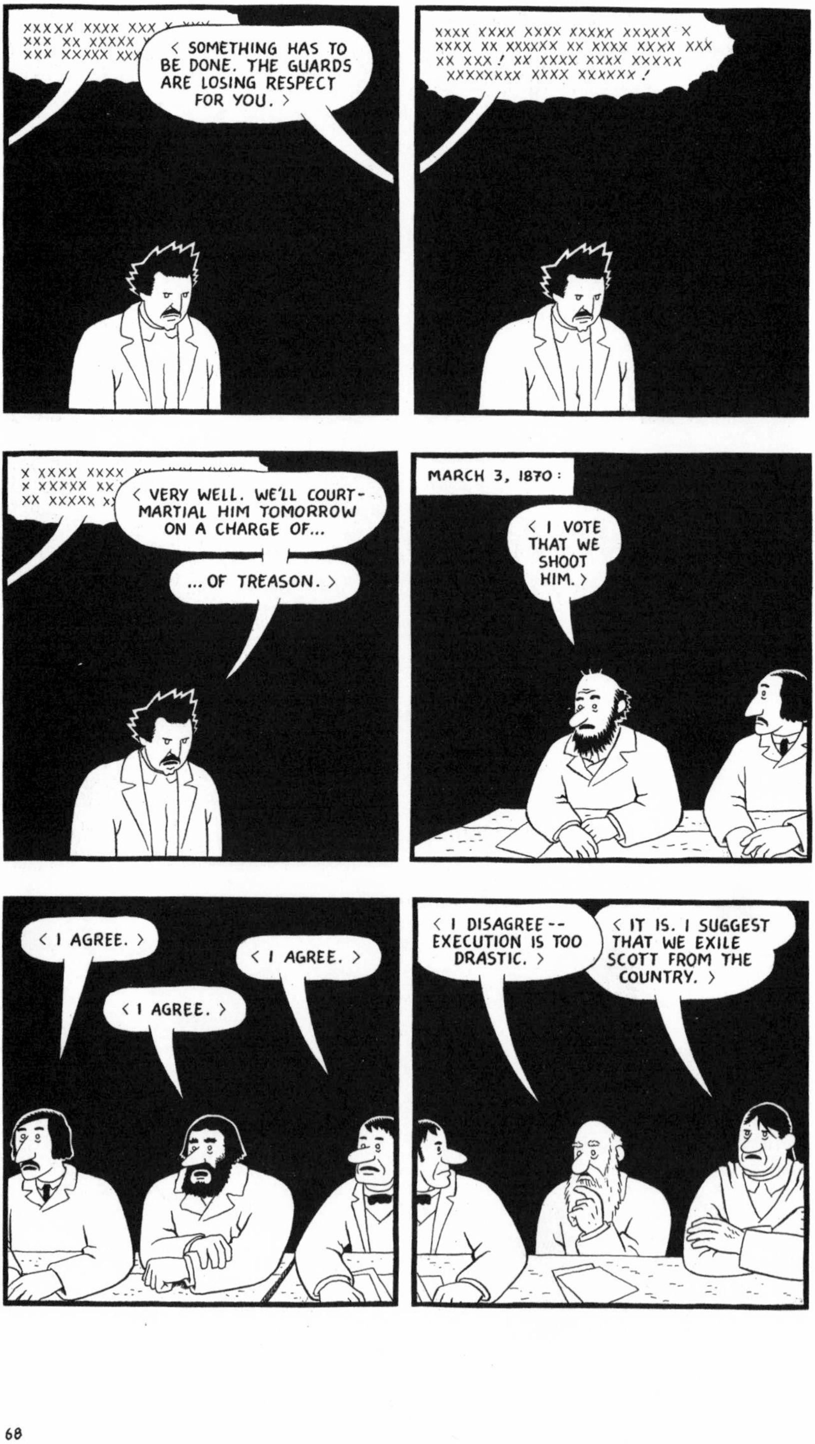
< SOMETHING HAS TO BE DONE. THE GUARDS ARE LOSING RESPECT FOR YOU. >
< VERY WELL. WE'LL COURT-MARTIAL HIM TOMORROW ON A CHARGE OF...
... OF TREASON. >
MARCH 3, 1870:
< I VOTE THAT WE SHOOT HIM. >
< I AGREE. >
< I AGREE. >
< I AGREE. >
< I DISAGREE -- EXECUTION IS TOO DRASTIC. >
< IT IS. I SUGGEST THAT WE EXILE SCOTT FROM THE COUNTRY. >

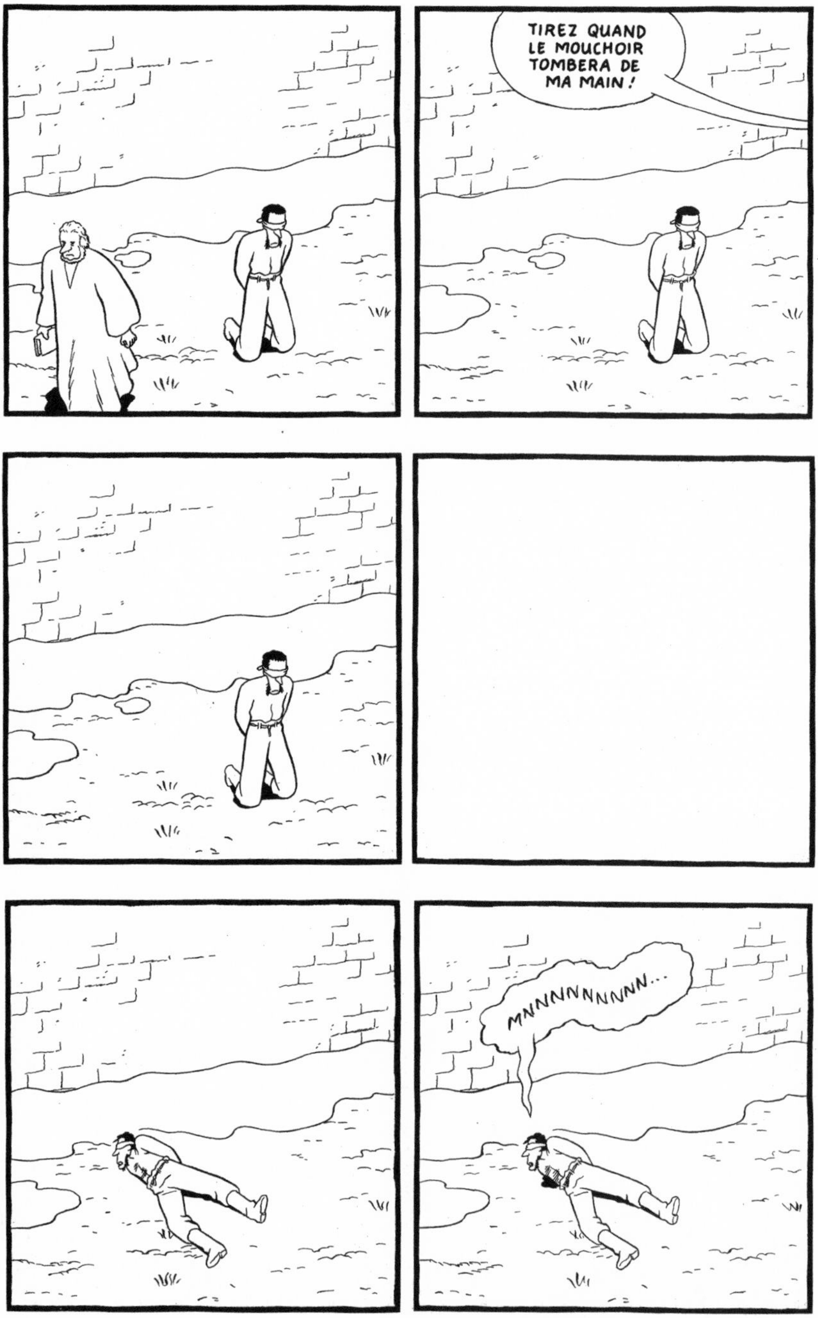
TIREZ QUAND LE MOUCHOIR TOMBERA DE MA MAIN !
MNNNNNNNNN...

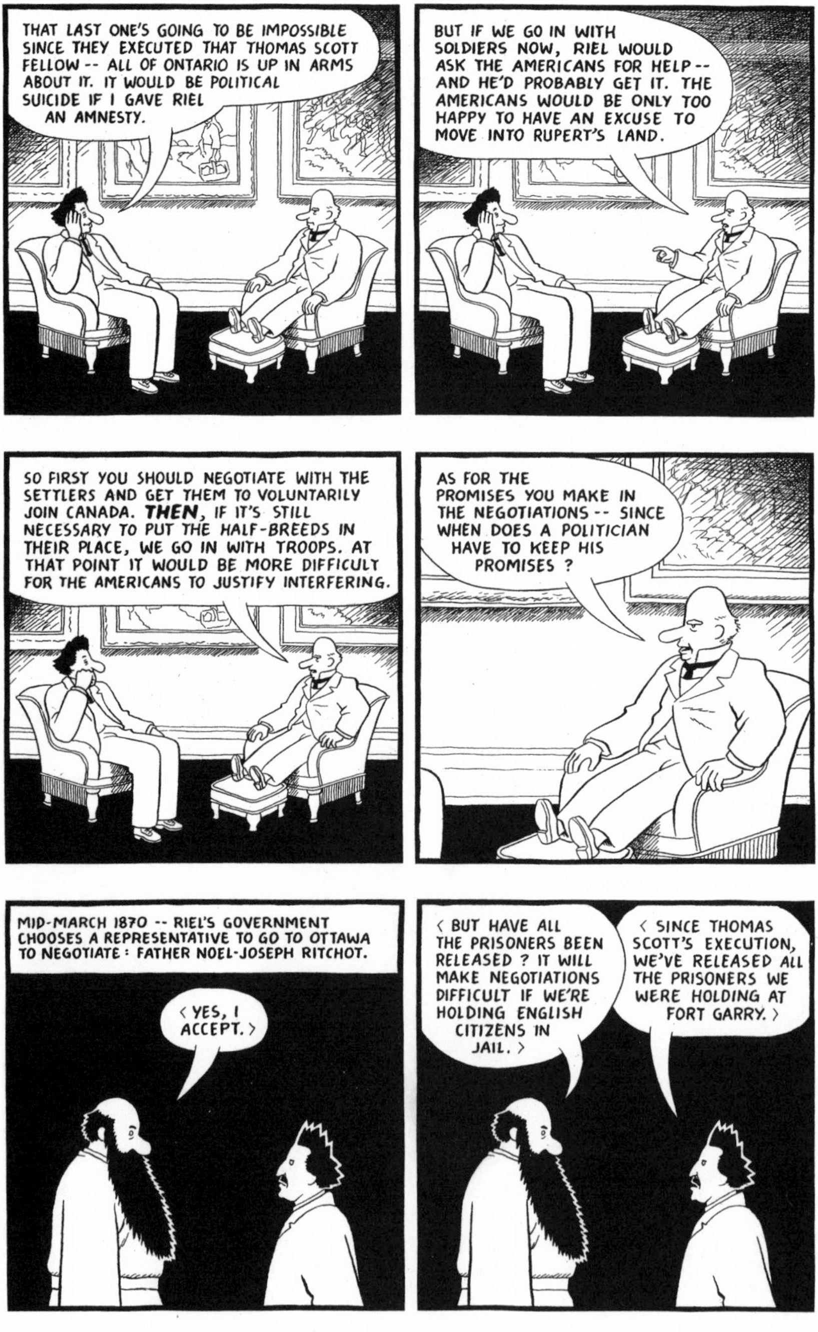
THAT LAST ONE'S GOING TO BE IMPOSSIBLE SINCE THEY EXECUTED THAT THOMAS SCOTT FELLOW -- ALL OF ONTARIO IS UP IN ARMS ABOUT IT. IT WOULD BE POLITICAL SUICIDE IF I GAVE RIEL AN AMNESTY.
BUT IF WE GO IN WITH SOLDIERS NOW, RIEL WOULD ASK THE AMERICANS FOR HELP -- AND HE'D PROBABLY GET IT. THE AMERICANS WOULD BE ONLY TOO HAPPY TO HAVE AN EXCUSE TO MOVE INTO RUPERT'S LAND.
SO FIRST YOU SHOULD NEGOTIATE WITH THE SETTLERS AND GET THEM TO VOLUNTARILY JOIN CANADA. THEN, IF IT'S STILL NECESSARY TO PUT THE HALF-BREEDS IN THEIR PLACE, WE GO IN WITH TROOPS. AT THAT POINT IT WOULD BE MORE DIFFICULT FOR THE AMERICANS TO JUSTIFY INTERFERING.
AS FOR THE PROMISES YOU MAKE IN THE NEGOTIATIONS -- SINCE WHEN DOES A POLITICIAN HAVE TO KEEP HIS PROMISES ?
MID-MARCH 1870 -- RIEL'S GOVERNMENT CHOOSES A REPRESENTATIVE TO GO TO OTTAWA TO NEGOTIATE : FATHER NOEL-JOSEPH RITCHOT.
< YES, I ACCEPT. >
< BUT HAVE ALL THE PRISONERS BEEN RELEASED ? IT WILL MAKE NEGOTIATIONS DIFFICULT IF WE'RE HOLDING ENGLISH CITIZENS IN JAIL. >
< SINCE THOMAS SCOTT'S EXECUTION, WE'VE RELEASED ALL THE PRISONERS WE WERE HOLDING AT FORT GARRY. >

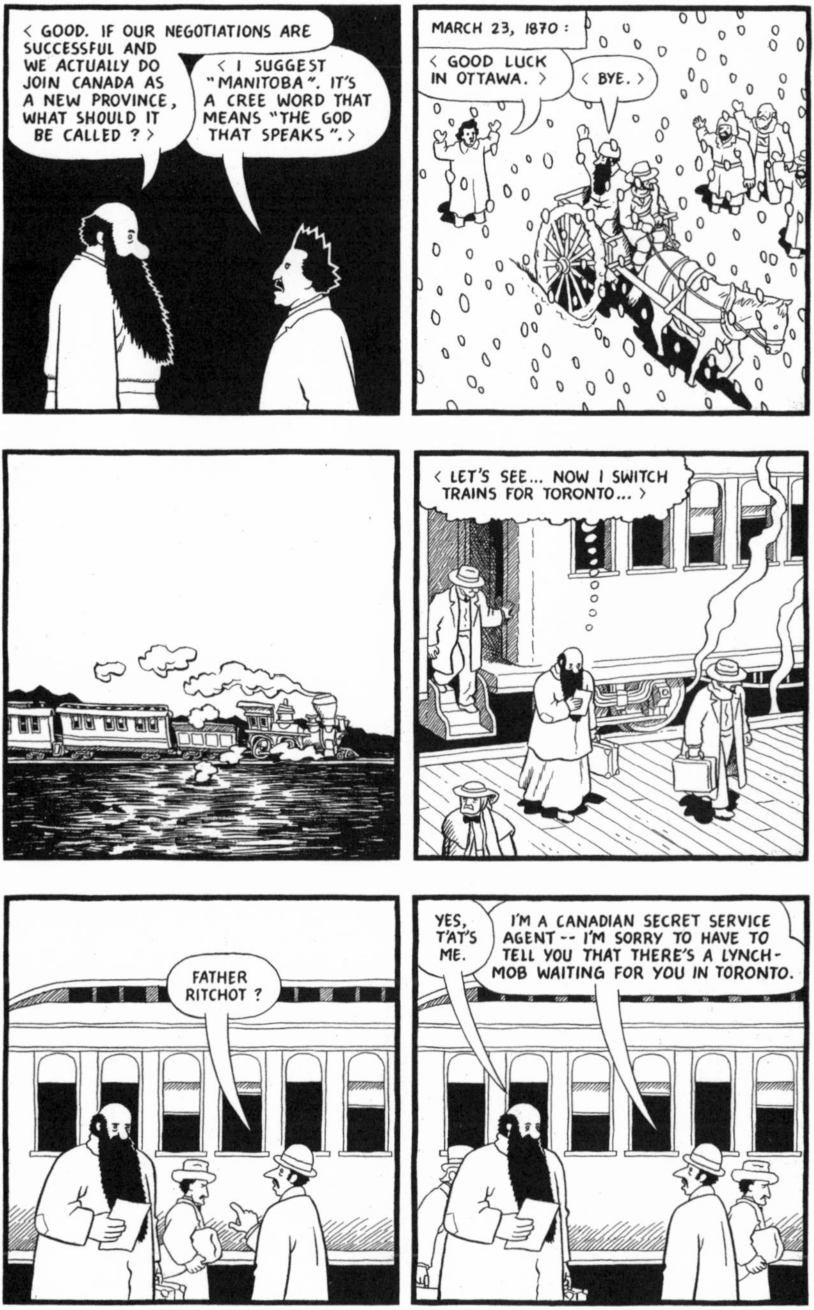
< GOOD. IF OUR NEGOTIATIONS ARE SUCCESSFUL AND WE ACTUALLY DO JOIN CANADA AS A NEW PROVINCE, WHAT SHOULD IT BE CALLED ? >
< I SUGGEST "MANITOBA". IT'S A CREE WORD THAT MEANS "THE GOD THAT SPEAKS". >
MARCH 23, 1870 :
< GOOD LUCK IN OTTAWA. >
< BYE. >
< LET'S SEE... NOW I SWITCH TRAINS FOR TORONTO... >
FATHER RITCHOT ?
YES, T'AT'S ME.
I'M A CANADIAN SECRET SERVICE AGENT -- I'M SORRY TO HAVE TO TELL YOU THAT THERE'S A LYNCH-MOB WAITING FOR YOU IN TORONTO.

I ASSURE YOU THAT IT'S A FRIENDLY EXPEDITION. THESE TROOPS ARE TO ACT ONLY AS A KIND OF POLICE FORCE TO KEEP THE INDIANS PEACEFUL AND AS A SHOW OF STRENGTH FOR THE AMERICANS.

JUNE 17, 1870 -- FATHER RITCHOT ARRIVES BACK IN THE RED RIVER SETTLEMENT TO A 21-GUN SALUTE.

< SO WHAT ARE THE DETAILS ? DID WE GET EVERYTHING WE ASKED FOR ? >

< WE NOW LIVE IN A CANADIAN PROVINCE CALLED MANITOBA. >

< WE'LL HAVE AN ELECTED PROVINCIAL GOVERNMENT AS WELL AS ELECTED REPRESEN-TATIVES IN THE FEDERAL GOVERNMENT IN OTTAWA. EVERYONE RETAINS THE RIGHT TO THE LAND THEY ALREADY OCCUPY, AND 1,400,000 ACRES WILL BE RESERVED FOR THE MÉTIS TO POSSESS IN THE FUTURE. >

< IF WE MAKE SURE THAT THOSE 1,400,000 ACRES ARE ALONG THE RED AND ASSINIBOINE RIVERS, THEN WE'LL HAVE THE BEST LAND IN THE PROVINCE. >

< EXACTLY ! >

80

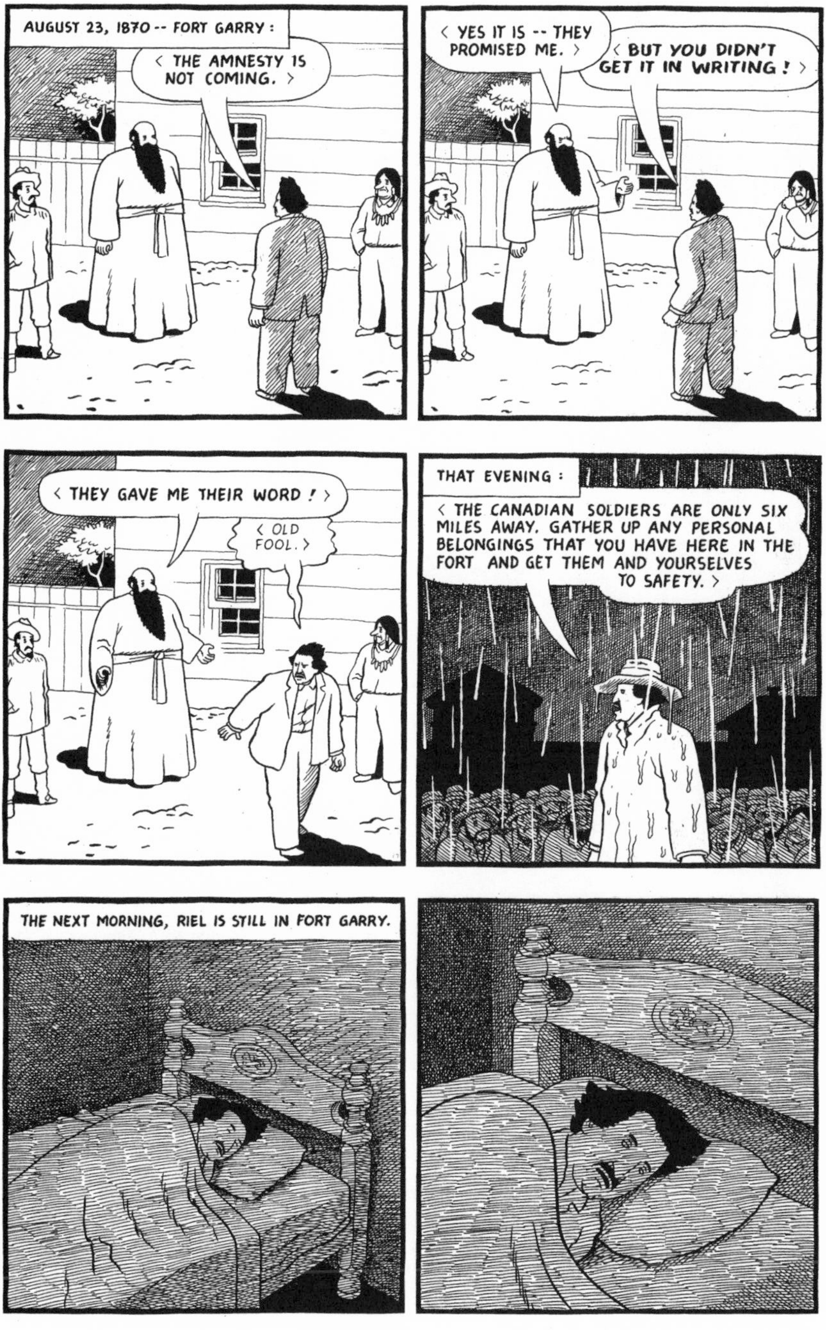
AUGUST 23, 1870 -- FORT GARRY :
< THE AMNESTY IS NOT COMING. >
< YES IT IS -- THEY PROMISED ME. >
< BUT YOU DIDN'T GET IT IN WRITING ! >
< THEY GAVE ME THEIR WORD ! >
< OLD FOOL. >
THAT EVENING :
< THE CANADIAN SOLDIERS ARE ONLY SIX MILES AWAY. GATHER UP ANY PERSONAL BELONGINGS THAT YOU HAVE HERE IN THE FORT AND GET THEM AND YOURSELVES TO SAFETY. >
THE NEXT MORNING, RIEL IS STILL IN FORT GARRY.

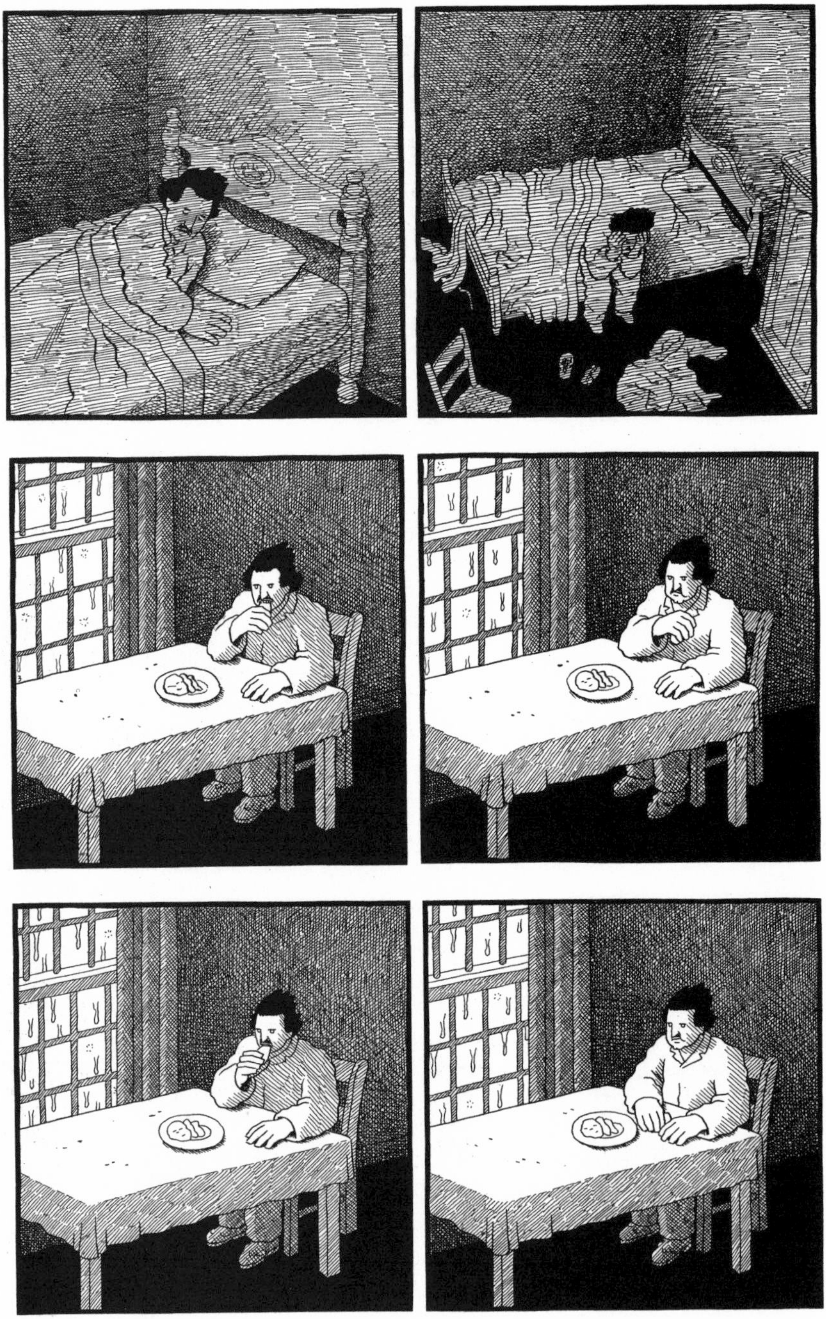

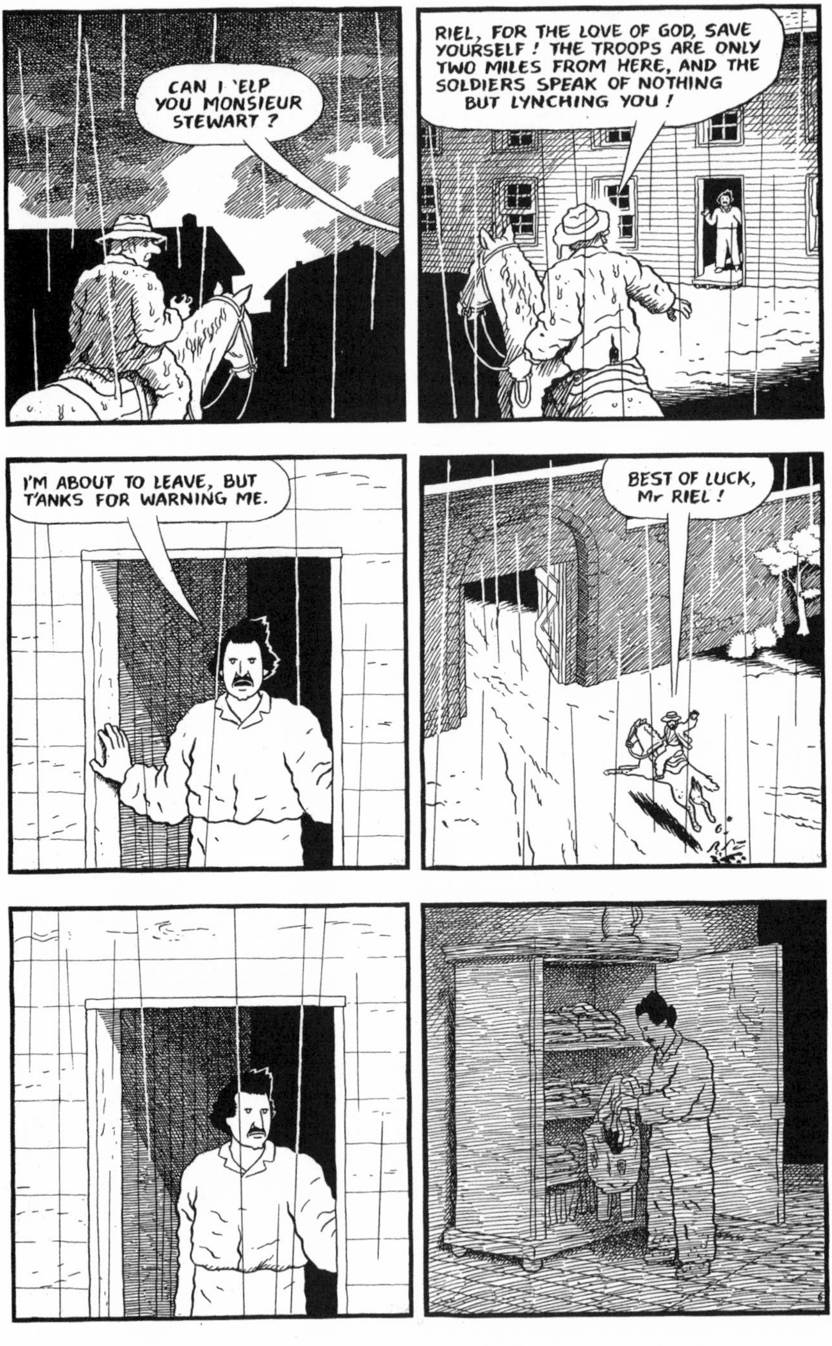
CAN I 'ELP YOU MONSIEUR STEWART ?
RIEL, FOR THE LOVE OF GOD, SAVE YOURSELF ! THE TROOPS ARE ONLY TWO MILES FROM HERE, AND THE SOLDIERS SPEAK OF NOTHING BUT LYNCHING YOU !
I'M ABOUT TO LEAVE, BUT T'ANKS FOR WARNING ME.
BEST OF LUCK, Mr RIEL !

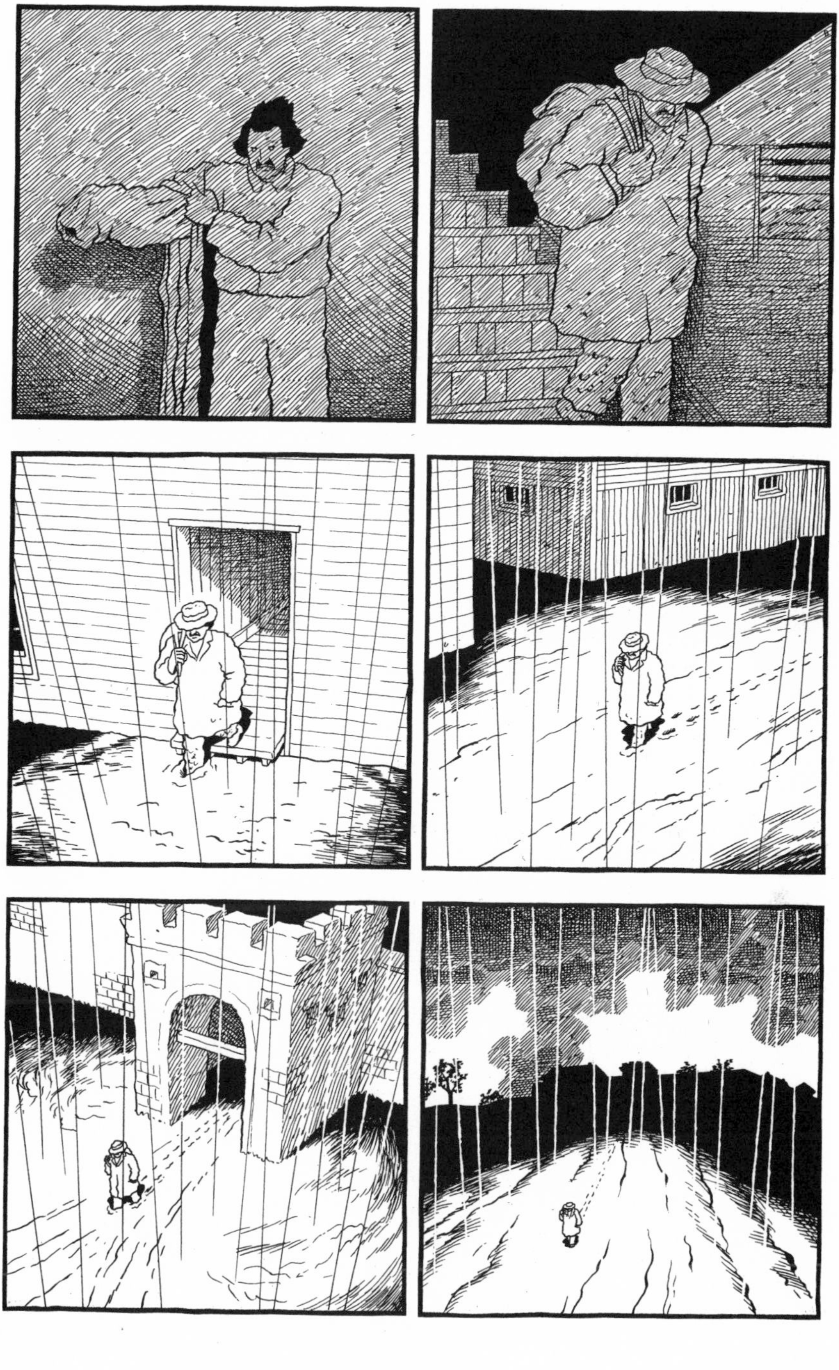

PART TWO

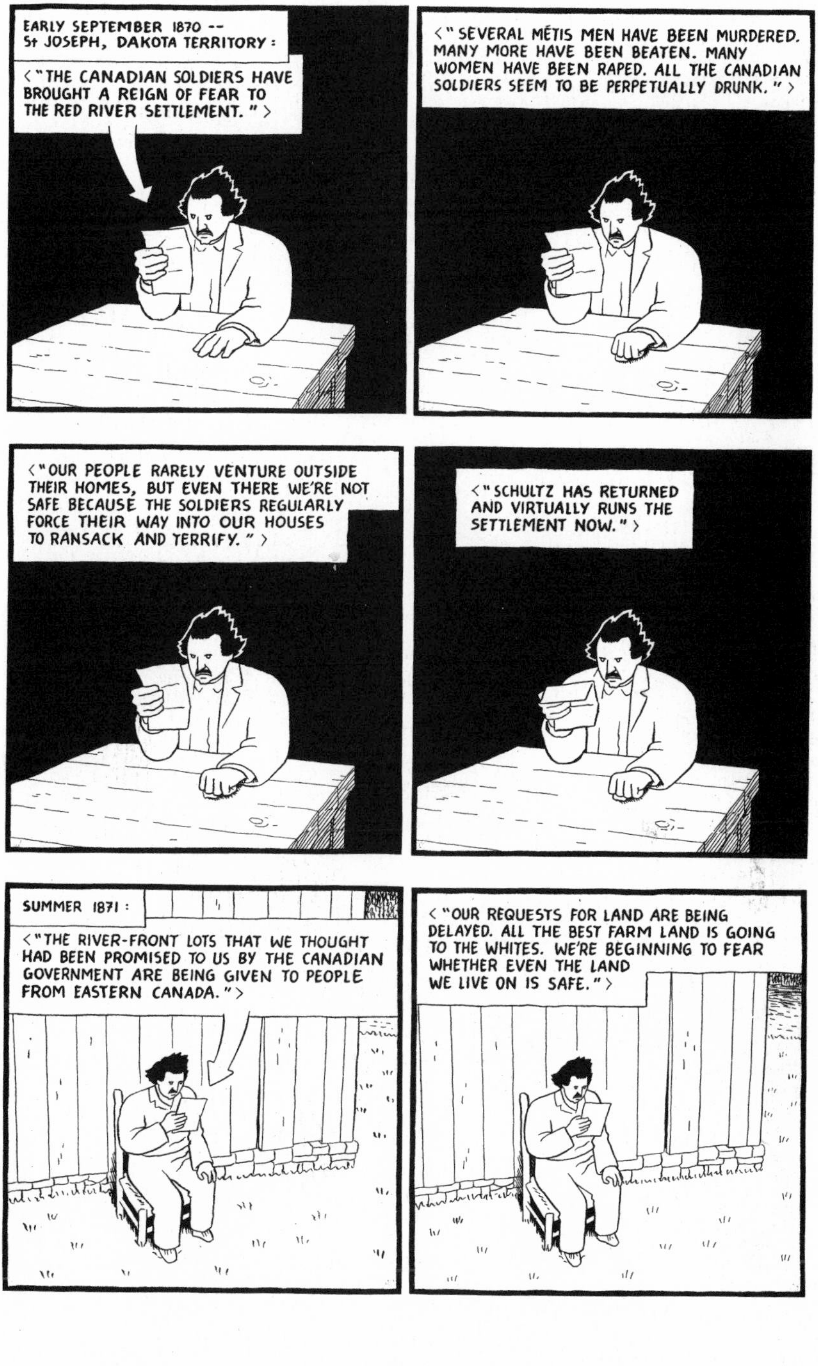
EARLY SEPTEMBER 1870 -- St JOSEPH, DAKOTA TERRITORY :
<"THE CANADIAN SOLDIERS HAVE BROUGHT A REIGN OF FEAR TO THE RED RIVER SETTLEMENT.">
<"SEVERAL MÉTIS MEN HAVE BEEN MURDERED. MANY MORE HAVE BEEN BEATEN. MANY WOMEN HAVE BEEN RAPED. ALL THE CANADIAN SOLDIERS SEEM TO BE PERPETUALLY DRUNK.">
<"OUR PEOPLE RARELY VENTURE OUTSIDE THEIR HOMES, BUT EVEN THERE WE'RE NOT SAFE BECAUSE THE SOLDIERS REGULARLY FORCE THEIR WAY INTO OUR HOUSES TO RANSACK AND TERRIFY.">
<"SCHULTZ HAS RETURNED AND VIRTUALLY RUNS THE SETTLEMENT NOW.">
SUMMER 1871 :
<"THE RIVER-FRONT LOTS THAT WE THOUGHT HAD BEEN PROMISED TO US BY THE CANADIAN GOVERNMENT ARE BEING GIVEN TO PEOPLE FROM EASTERN CANADA.">
<"OUR REQUESTS FOR LAND ARE BEING DELAYED. ALL THE BEST FARM LAND IS GOING TO THE WHITES. WE'RE BEGINNING TO FEAR WHETHER EVEN THE LAND WE LIVE ON IS SAFE.">

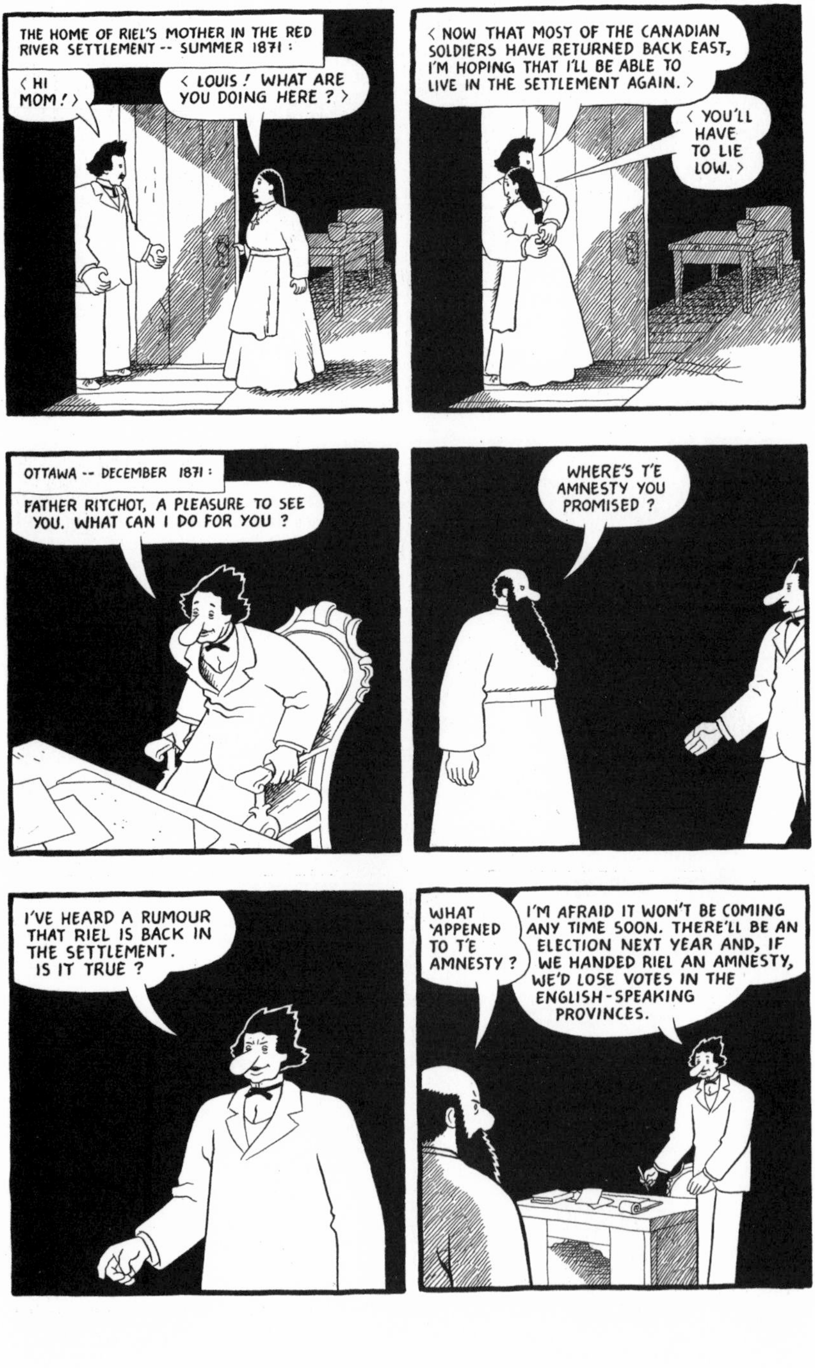
THE HOME OF RIEL'S MOTHER IN THE RED RIVER SETTLEMENT -- SUMMER 1871 :
< HI MOM ! >
< LOUIS ! WHAT ARE YOU DOING HERE ? >
< NOW THAT MOST OF THE CANADIAN SOLDIERS HAVE RETURNED BACK EAST, I'M HOPING THAT I'LL BE ABLE TO LIVE IN THE SETTLEMENT AGAIN. >
< YOU'LL HAVE TO LIE LOW. >
OTTAWA -- DECEMBER 1871 :
FATHER RITCHOT, A PLEASURE TO SEE YOU. WHAT CAN I DO FOR YOU ?
WHERE'S T'E AMNESTY YOU PROMISED ?
I'VE HEARD A RUMOUR THAT RIEL IS BACK IN THE SETTLEMENT. IS IT TRUE ?
WHAT 'APPENED TO T'E AMNESTY ?
I'M AFRAID IT WON'T BE COMING ANY TIME SOON. THERE'LL BE AN ELECTION NEXT YEAR AND, IF WE HANDED RIEL AN AMNESTY, WE'D LOSE VOTES IN THE ENGLISH-SPEAKING PROVINCES.

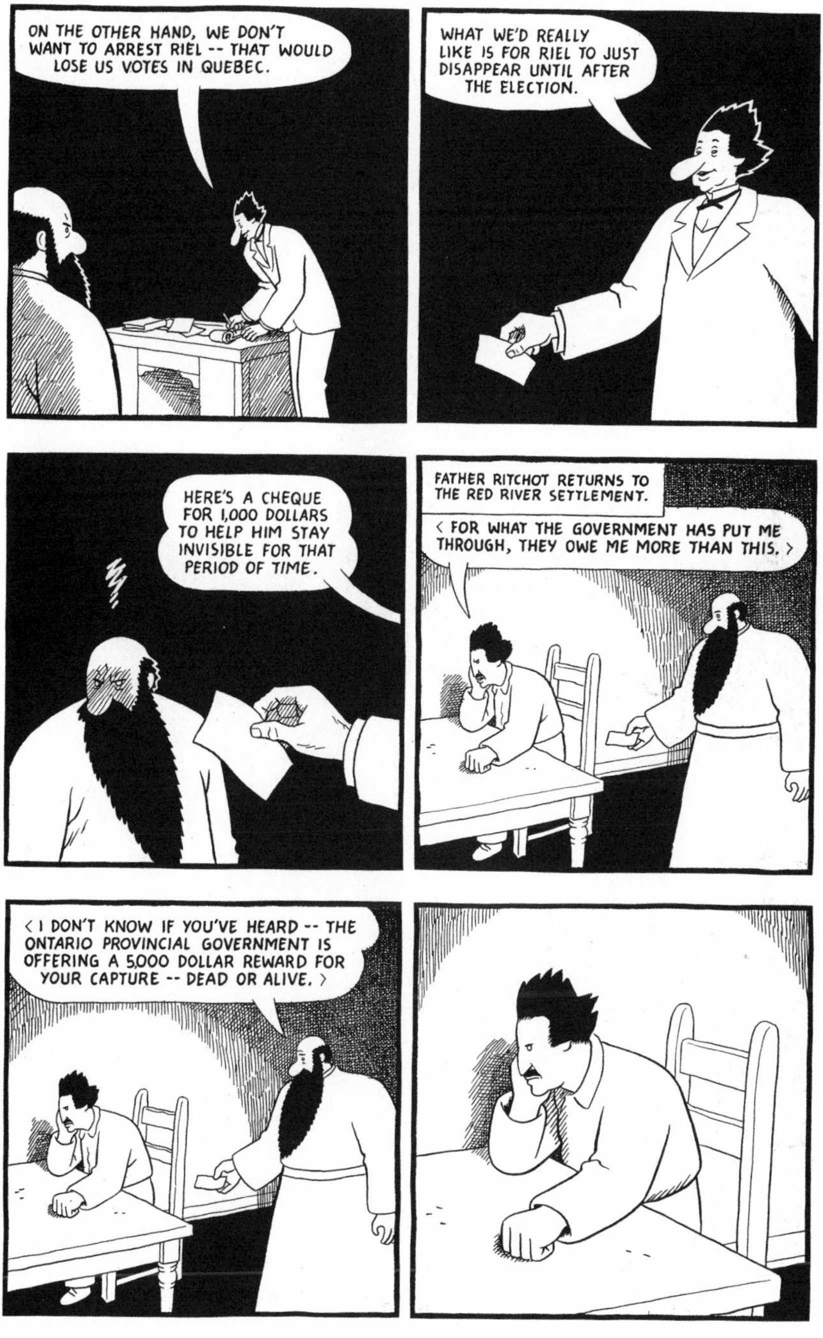
ON THE OTHER HAND, WE DON'T WANT TO ARREST RIEL -- THAT WOULD LOSE US VOTES IN QUEBEC.
WHAT WE'D REALLY LIKE IS FOR RIEL TO JUST DISAPPEAR UNTIL AFTER THE ELECTION.
HERE'S A CHEQUE FOR 1,000 DOLLARS TO HELP HIM STAY INVISIBLE FOR THAT PERIOD OF TIME.
FATHER RITCHOT RETURNS TO THE RED RIVER SETTLEMENT.
< FOR WHAT THE GOVERNMENT HAS PUT ME THROUGH, THEY OWE ME MORE THAN THIS. >
< I DON'T KNOW IF YOU'VE HEARD -- THE ONTARIO PROVINCIAL GOVERNMENT IS OFFERING A 5,000 DOLLAR REWARD FOR YOUR CAPTURE -- DEAD OR ALIVE. >

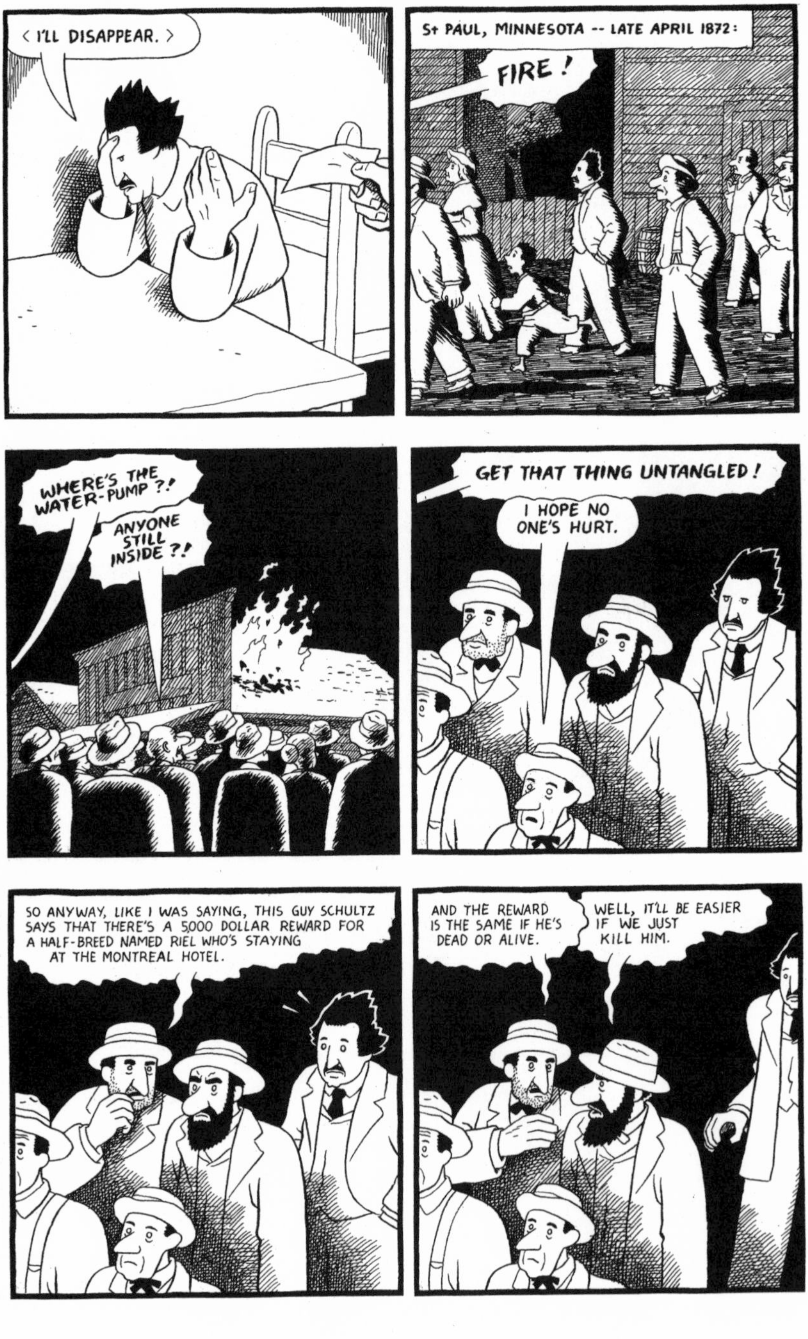
< I'LL DISAPPEAR. >
St PAUL, MINNESOTA -- LATE APRIL 1872:
FIRE!
WHERE'S THE WATER-PUMP ?!
ANYONE STILL INSIDE ?!
GET THAT THING UNTANGLED!
I HOPE NO ONE'S HURT.
SO ANYWAY, LIKE I WAS SAYING, THIS GUY SCHULTZ SAYS THAT THERE'S A 5,000 DOLLAR REWARD FOR A HALF-BREED NAMED RIEL WHO'S STAYING AT THE MONTREAL HOTEL.
AND THE REWARD IS THE SAME IF HE'S DEAD OR ALIVE.
WELL, IT'LL BE EASIER IF WE JUST KILL HIM.

93

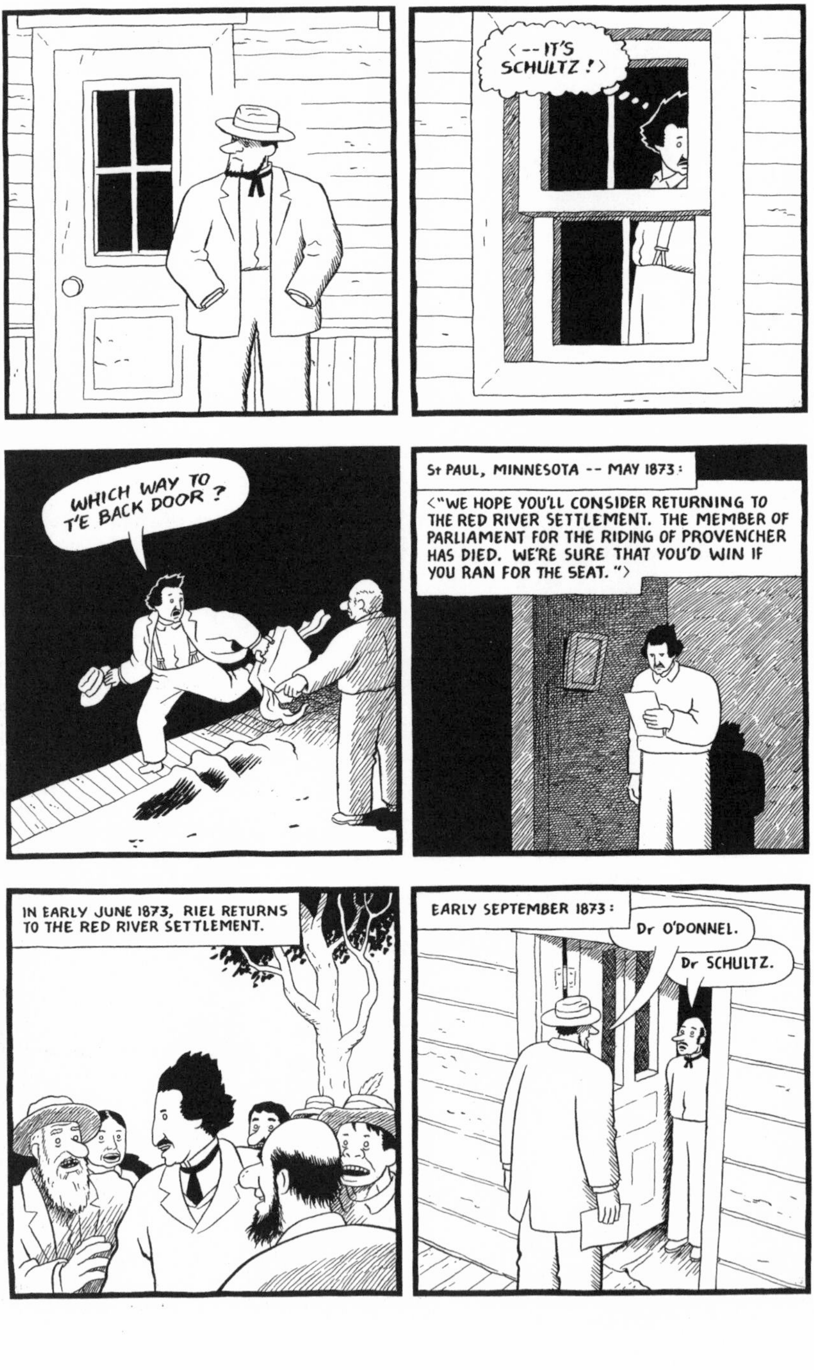

<--IT'S SCHULTZ!>
WHICH WAY TO T'E BACK DOOR?
St PAUL, MINNESOTA -- MAY 1873:
<"WE HOPE YOU'LL CONSIDER RETURNING TO THE RED RIVER SETTLEMENT. THE MEMBER OF PARLIAMENT FOR THE RIDING OF PROVENCHER HAS DIED. WE'RE SURE THAT YOU'D WIN IF YOU RAN FOR THE SEAT.">
IN EARLY JUNE 1873, RIEL RETURNS TO THE RED RIVER SETTLEMENT.
EARLY SEPTEMBER 1873:
Dr O'DONNEL.
Dr SCHULTZ.

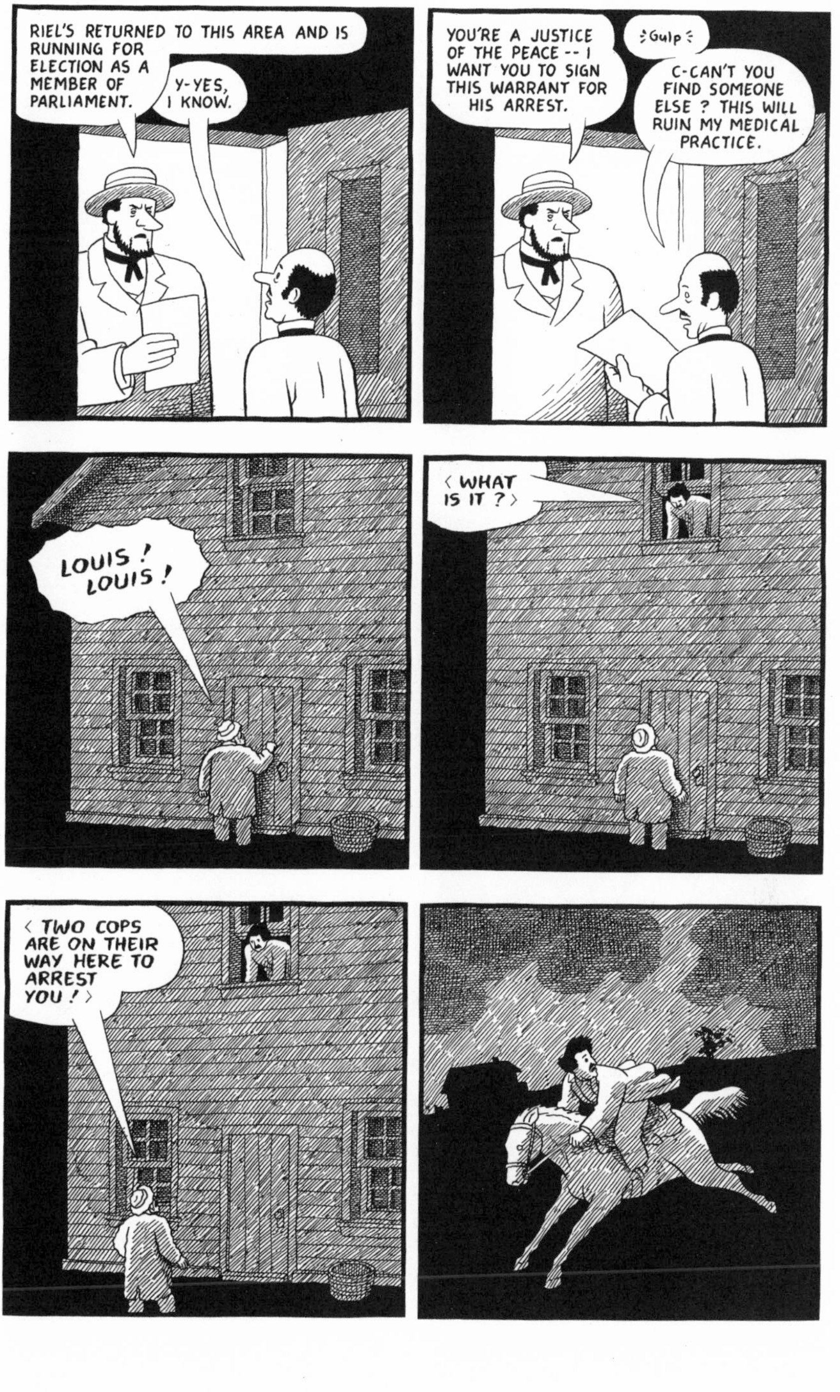
RIEL'S RETURNED TO THIS AREA AND IS RUNNING FOR ELECTION AS A MEMBER OF PARLIAMENT.
Y-YES, I KNOW.
YOU'RE A JUSTICE OF THE PEACE -- I WANT YOU TO SIGN THIS WARRANT FOR HIS ARREST.
Gulp
C-CAN'T YOU FIND SOMEONE ELSE ? THIS WILL RUIN MY MEDICAL PRACTICE.
LOUIS ! LOUIS !
< WHAT IS IT ? >
< TWO COPS ARE ON THEIR WAY HERE TO ARREST YOU ! >

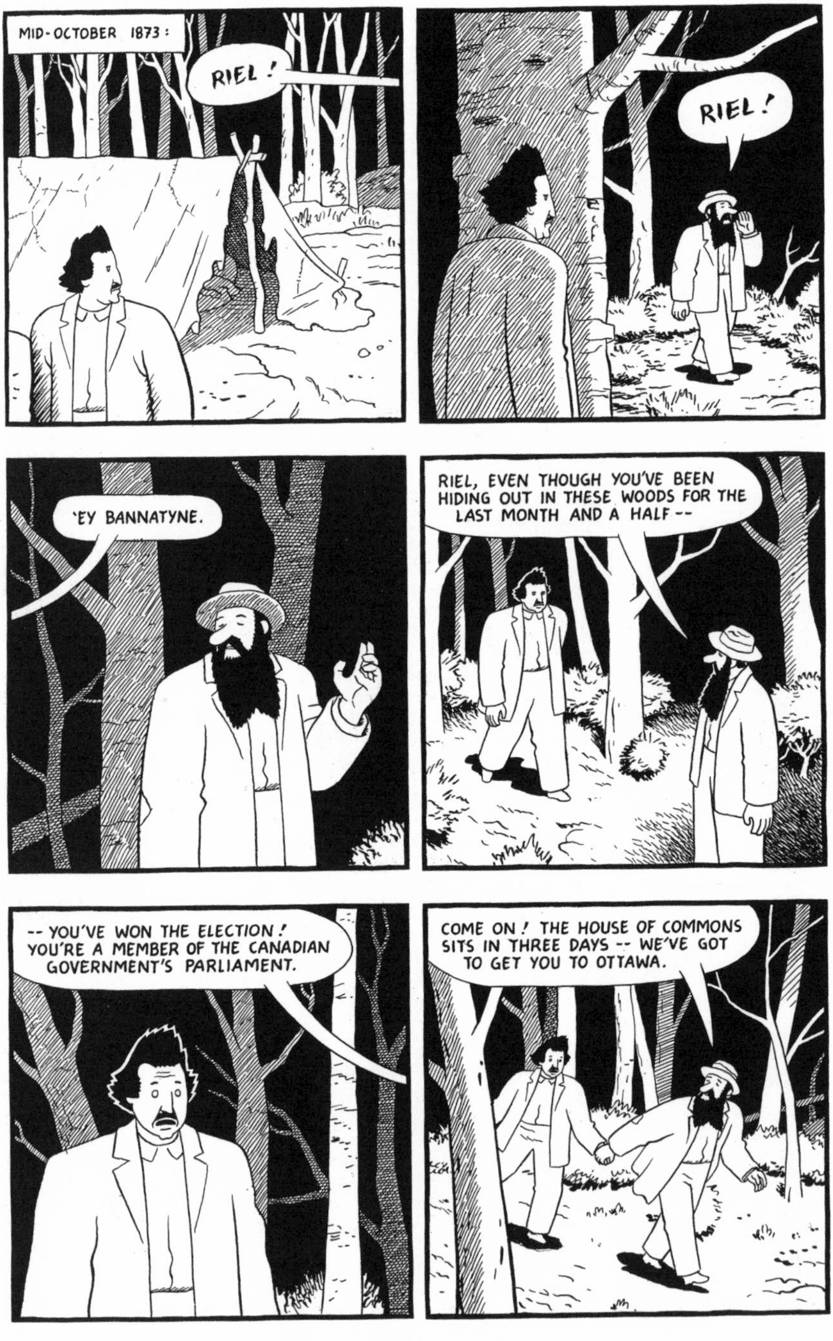

MID-OCTOBER 1873:
RIEL!
RIEL!
'EY BANNATYNE.
RIEL, EVEN THOUGH YOU'VE BEEN HIDING OUT IN THESE WOODS FOR THE LAST MONTH AND A HALF --
-- YOU'VE WON THE ELECTION! YOU'RE A MEMBER OF THE CANADIAN GOVERNMENT'S PARLIAMENT.
COME ON! THE HOUSE OF COMMONS SITS IN THREE DAYS -- WE'VE GOT TO GET YOU TO OTTAWA.

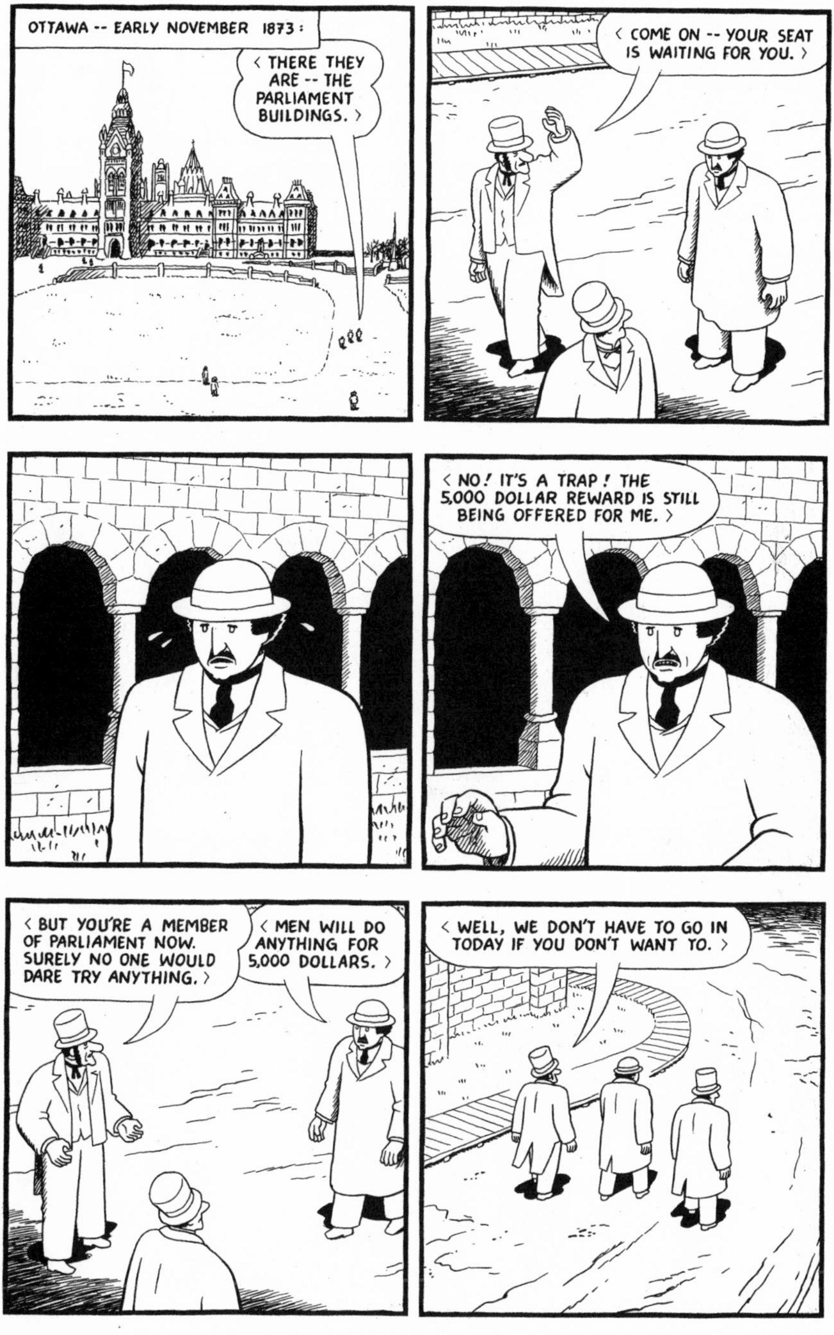
OTTAWA -- EARLY NOVEMBER 1873:
< THERE THEY ARE -- THE PARLIAMENT BUILDINGS. >
< COME ON -- YOUR SEAT IS WAITING FOR YOU. >
< NO! IT'S A TRAP! THE 5,000 DOLLAR REWARD IS STILL BEING OFFERED FOR ME. >
< BUT YOU'RE A MEMBER OF PARLIAMENT NOW. SURELY NO ONE WOULD DARE TRY ANYTHING. >
< MEN WILL DO ANYTHING FOR 5,000 DOLLARS. >
< WELL, WE DON'T HAVE TO GO IN TODAY IF YOU DON'T WANT TO. >

〈 HE'S BEEN ON THE RUN FOR SEVERAL YEARS NOW. MAYBE HE SHOULD JUST REST FOR AWHILE. 〉

RIEL RESTS -- HE STAYS IN THE HOMES OF FRIENDS OR OF PEOPLE WHO SUPPORT THE MÉTIS CAUSE.

PLATTSBURGH, NEW YORK -- NOVEMBER 1873:

KEESEVILLE, NEW YORK -- DECEMBER 1873:

MONTREAL -- EARLY JANUARY 1874:

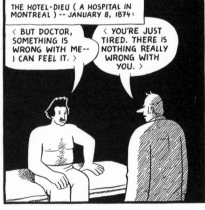

THE HOTEL-DIEU (A HOSPITAL IN MONTREAL) -- JANUARY 8, 1874:

〈 BUT DOCTOR, SOMETHING IS WRONG WITH ME-- I CAN FEEL IT. 〉

〈 YOU'RE JUST TIRED. THERE IS NOTHING REALLY WRONG WITH YOU. 〉

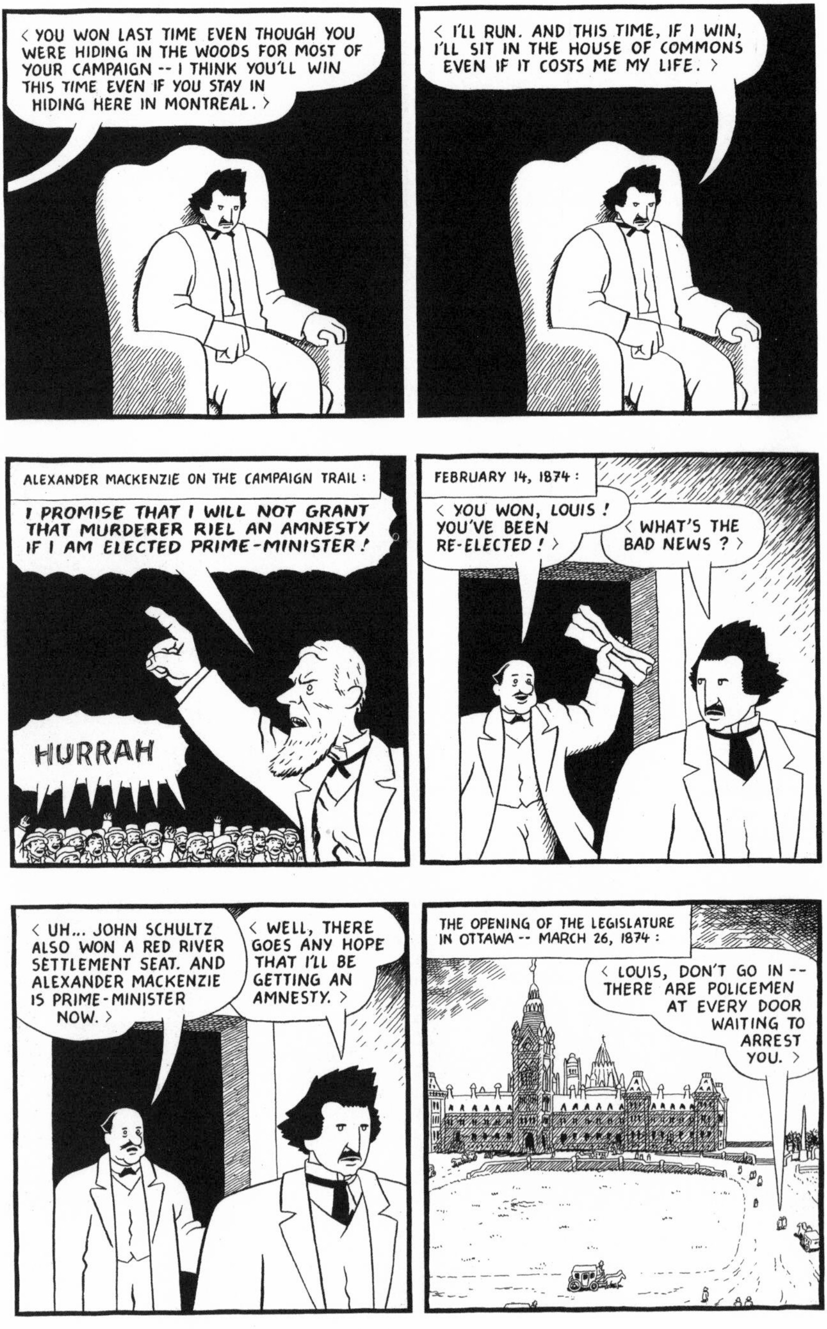
< YOU WON LAST TIME EVEN THOUGH YOU WERE HIDING IN THE WOODS FOR MOST OF YOUR CAMPAIGN -- I THINK YOU'LL WIN THIS TIME EVEN IF YOU STAY IN HIDING HERE IN MONTREAL. >
< I'LL RUN. AND THIS TIME, IF I WIN, I'LL SIT IN THE HOUSE OF COMMONS EVEN IF IT COSTS ME MY LIFE. >
ALEXANDER MACKENZIE ON THE CAMPAIGN TRAIL :
I PROMISE THAT I WILL NOT GRANT THAT MURDERER RIEL AN AMNESTY IF I AM ELECTED PRIME-MINISTER !
HURRAH
FEBRUARY 14, 1874 :
< YOU WON, LOUIS ! YOU'VE BEEN RE-ELECTED ! >
< WHAT'S THE BAD NEWS ? >
< UH... JOHN SCHULTZ ALSO WON A RED RIVER SETTLEMENT SEAT. AND ALEXANDER MACKENZIE IS PRIME-MINISTER NOW. >
< WELL, THERE GOES ANY HOPE THAT I'LL BE GETTING AN AMNESTY. >
THE OPENING OF THE LEGISLATURE IN OTTAWA -- MARCH 26, 1874 :
< LOUIS, DON'T GO IN -- THERE ARE POLICEMEN AT EVERY DOOR WAITING TO ARREST YOU. >

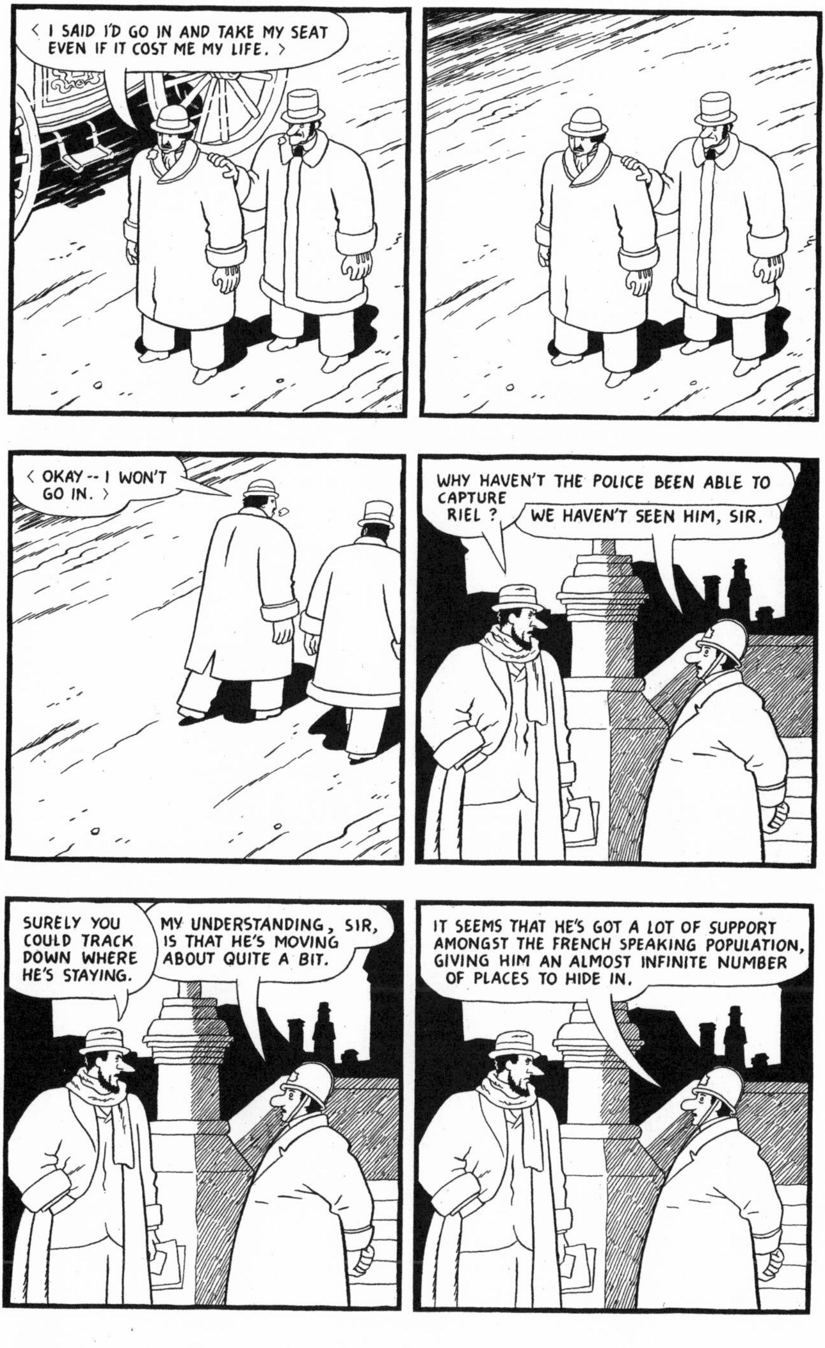
< I SAID I'D GO IN AND TAKE MY SEAT EVEN IF IT COST ME MY LIFE. >
< OKAY -- I WON'T GO IN. >
WHY HAVEN'T THE POLICE BEEN ABLE TO CAPTURE RIEL ?
WE HAVEN'T SEEN HIM, SIR.
SURELY YOU COULD TRACK DOWN WHERE HE'S STAYING.
MY UNDERSTANDING, SIR, IS THAT HE'S MOVING ABOUT QUITE A BIT.
IT SEEMS THAT HE'S GOT A LOT OF SUPPORT AMONGST THE FRENCH SPEAKING POPULATION, GIVING HIM AN ALMOST INFINITE NUMBER OF PLACES TO HIDE IN.

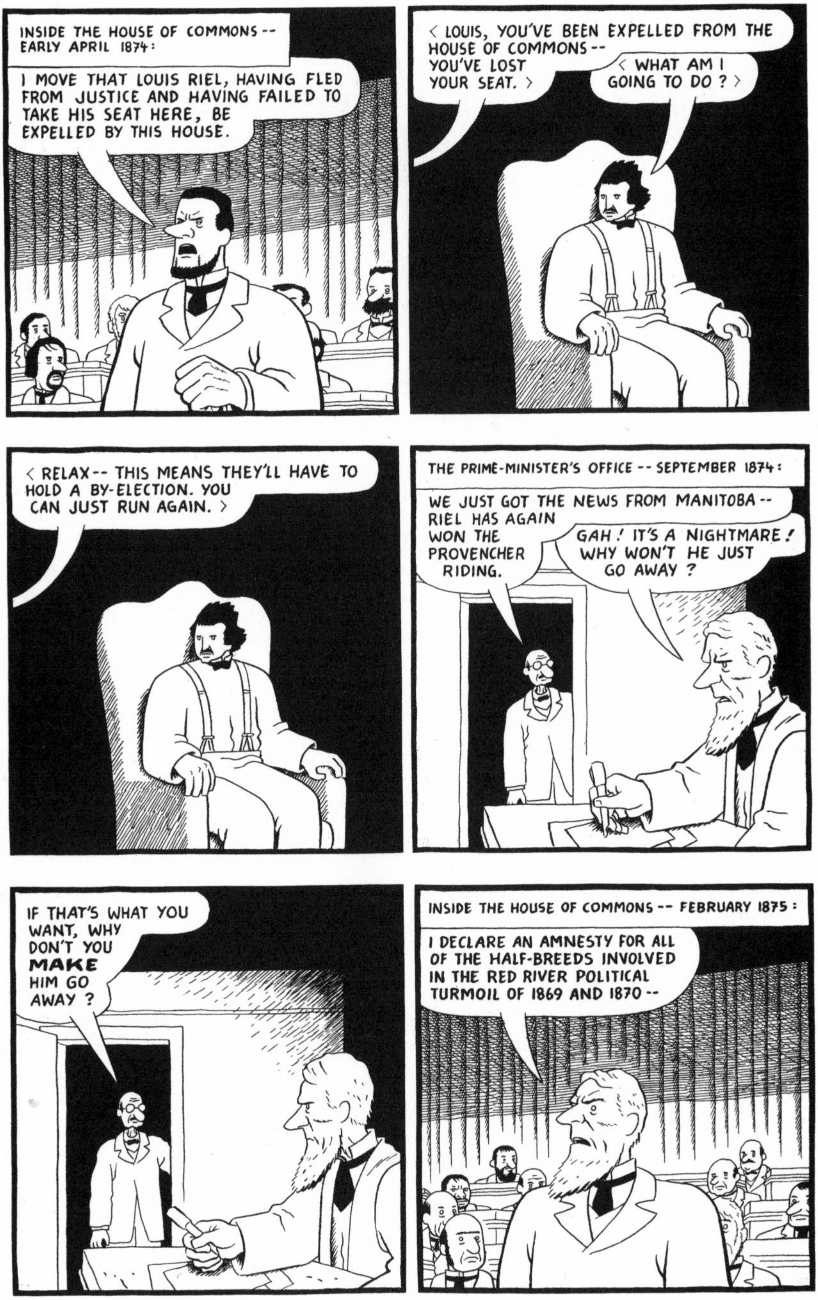

INSIDE THE HOUSE OF COMMONS -- EARLY APRIL 1874:
I MOVE THAT LOUIS RIEL, HAVING FLED FROM JUSTICE AND HAVING FAILED TO TAKE HIS SEAT HERE, BE EXPELLED BY THIS HOUSE.
< LOUIS, YOU'VE BEEN EXPELLED FROM THE HOUSE OF COMMONS -- YOU'VE LOST YOUR SEAT. >
< WHAT AM I GOING TO DO ? >
< RELAX -- THIS MEANS THEY'LL HAVE TO HOLD A BY-ELECTION. YOU CAN JUST RUN AGAIN. >
THE PRIME-MINISTER'S OFFICE -- SEPTEMBER 1874:
WE JUST GOT THE NEWS FROM MANITOBA -- RIEL HAS AGAIN WON THE PROVENCHER RIDING.
GAH! IT'S A NIGHTMARE! WHY WON'T HE JUST GO AWAY ?
IF THAT'S WHAT YOU WANT, WHY DON'T YOU **MAKE** HIM GO AWAY ?
INSIDE THE HOUSE OF COMMONS -- FEBRUARY 1875:
I DECLARE AN AMNESTY FOR ALL OF THE HALF-BREEDS INVOLVED IN THE RED RIVER POLITICAL TURMOIL OF 1869 AND 1870 --

--ALL EXCEPT LOUIS RIEL.

AN AMNESTY WILL BE GRANTED TO LOUIS RIEL, CONDITIONAL ON A FIVE YEAR BANISHMENT FROM CANADA.

IN DECEMBER 1875, RIEL MEETS WITH AMERICAN PRESIDENT ULYSSES S. GRANT AT THE WHITE HOUSE IN WASHINGTON, D.C.

I HOPE YOUR EXILE IN OUR COUNTRY ISN'T PROVING TO BE TOO DREADFUL.

NO, NOT AT ALL. T'E AMERICANS ARE VERY GENEROUS PEOPLE, ALT'OUGH I DO MISS MY 'OME.

OF COURSE. HOW CAN I HELP YOU ?

T'ERE ARE ALMOST 5,000 INDIANS AND 'ALF BREEDS IN MANITOBA AND T'E NORT'-WEST, AND T'EY 'AVE ALL BECOME VERY DISILLUSIONED AND UN'APPY WIT' T'E CANADIAN GOVERN-MENT AND 'OW IT'S INTERPRETING TREATIES AND T'E MANITOBA ACT.

I AM CONVINCED T'AT I COULD RAISE A MILITARY FORCE SUFFICIENT TO COMPEL T'E CANADIAN GOVERNMENT TO RECONSIDER IT'S RELATIONSHIP TO T'E NORT'-WEST.

WHY TELL ME THIS ?

WE NEED MONEY AND A PROMISE T'AT YOU WILL NOT LET CANADIAN TROOPS TRAVEL OVER AMERICAN SOIL TO OUR TERRITORY.

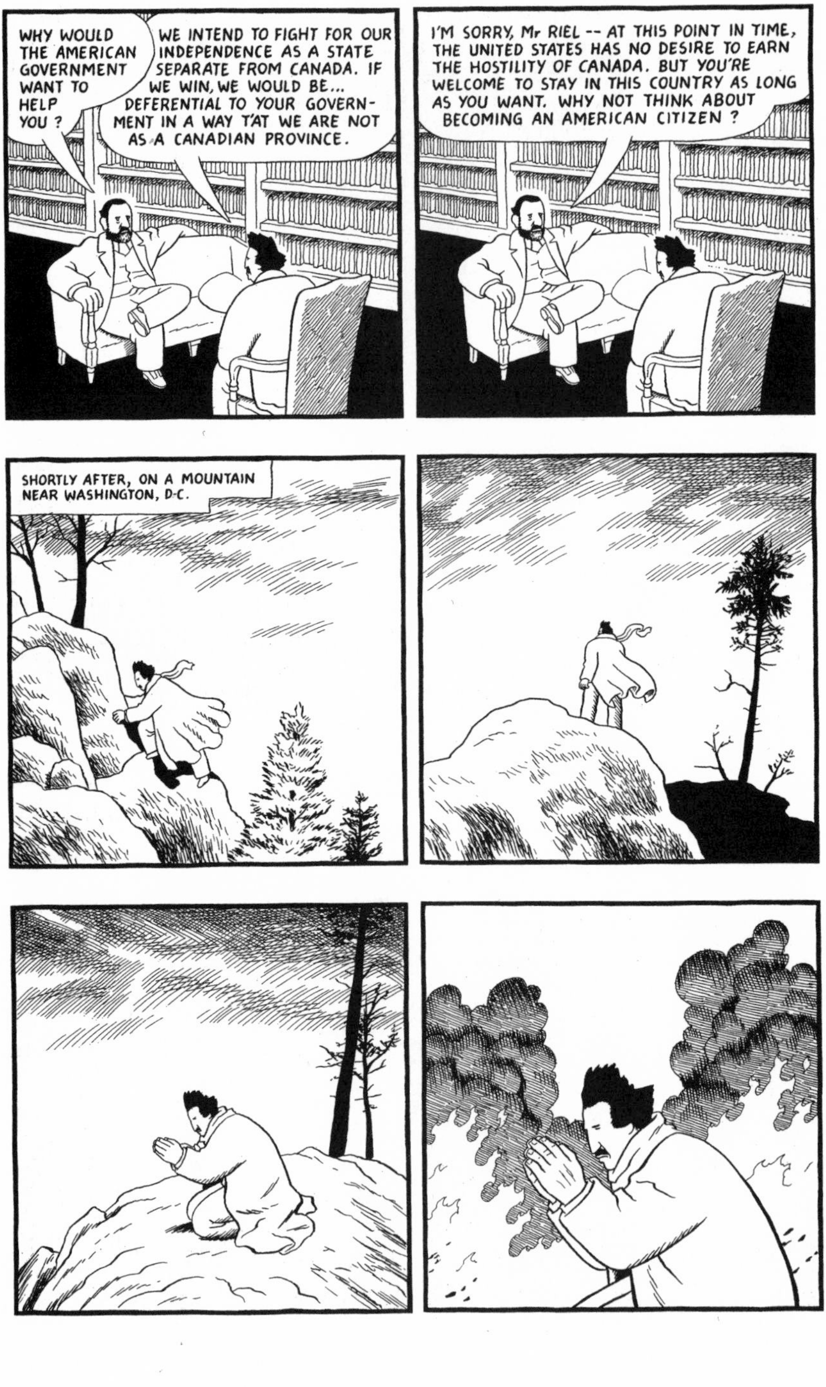
WHY WOULD THE AMERICAN GOVERNMENT WANT TO HELP YOU ?
WE INTEND TO FIGHT FOR OUR INDEPENDENCE AS A STATE SEPARATE FROM CANADA. IF WE WIN, WE WOULD BE... DEFERENTIAL TO YOUR GOVERNMENT IN A WAY T'AT WE ARE NOT AS A CANADIAN PROVINCE.
I'M SORRY, Mr RIEL -- AT THIS POINT IN TIME, THE UNITED STATES HAS NO DESIRE TO EARN THE HOSTILITY OF CANADA. BUT YOU'RE WELCOME TO STAY IN THIS COUNTRY AS LONG AS YOU WANT. WHY NOT THINK ABOUT BECOMING AN AMERICAN CITIZEN ?
SHORTLY AFTER, ON A MOUNTAIN NEAR WASHINGTON, D.C.

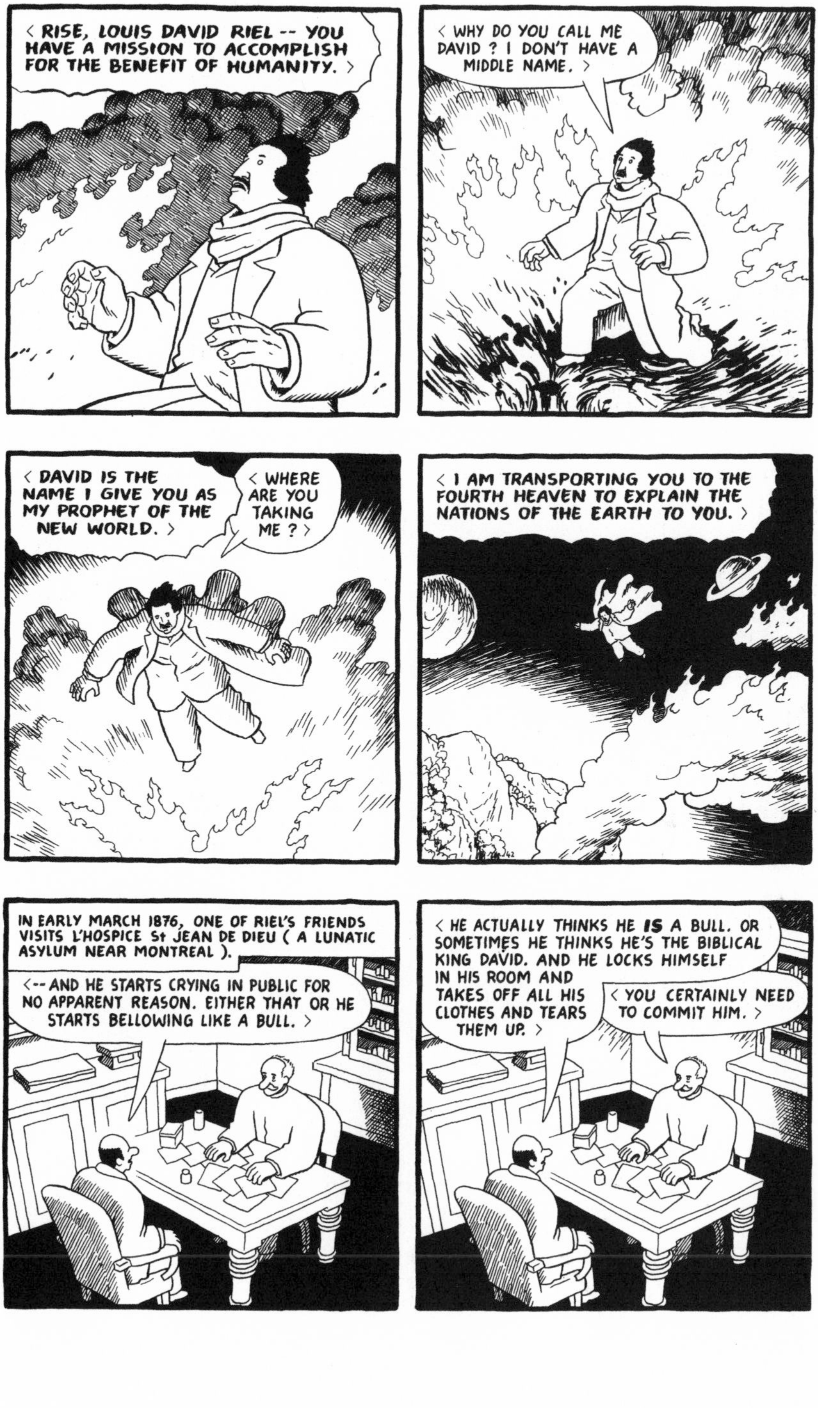
< RISE, LOUIS DAVID RIEL -- YOU HAVE A MISSION TO ACCOMPLISH FOR THE BENEFIT OF HUMANITY. >
< WHY DO YOU CALL ME DAVID ? I DON'T HAVE A MIDDLE NAME. >
< DAVID IS THE NAME I GIVE YOU AS MY PROPHET OF THE NEW WORLD. >
< WHERE ARE YOU TAKING ME ? >
< I AM TRANSPORTING YOU TO THE FOURTH HEAVEN TO EXPLAIN THE NATIONS OF THE EARTH TO YOU. >
IN EARLY MARCH 1876, ONE OF RIEL'S FRIENDS VISITS L'HOSPICE St JEAN DE DIEU (A LUNATIC ASYLUM NEAR MONTREAL).
<-- AND HE STARTS CRYING IN PUBLIC FOR NO APPARENT REASON. EITHER THAT OR HE STARTS BELLOWING LIKE A BULL. >
< HE ACTUALLY THINKS HE **IS** A BULL. OR SOMETIMES HE THINKS HE'S THE BIBLICAL KING DAVID. AND HE LOCKS HIMSELF IN HIS ROOM AND TAKES OFF ALL HIS CLOTHES AND TEARS THEM UP. >
< YOU CERTAINLY NEED TO COMMIT HIM. >

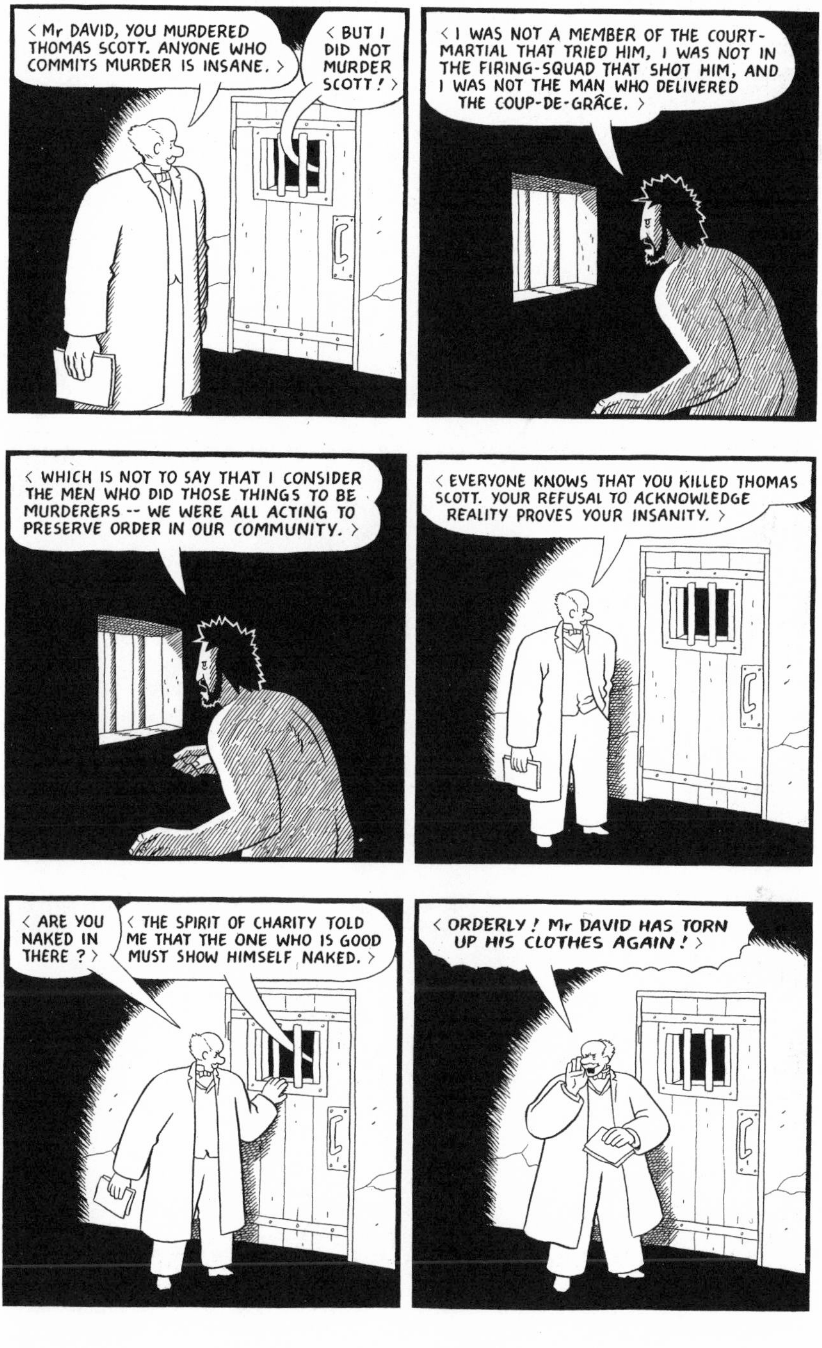
< Mr DAVID, YOU MURDERED THOMAS SCOTT. ANYONE WHO COMMITS MURDER IS INSANE. >
< BUT I DID NOT MURDER SCOTT! >
< I WAS NOT A MEMBER OF THE COURT-MARTIAL THAT TRIED HIM, I WAS NOT IN THE FIRING-SQUAD THAT SHOT HIM, AND I WAS NOT THE MAN WHO DELIVERED THE COUP-DE-GRÂCE. >
< WHICH IS NOT TO SAY THAT I CONSIDER THE MEN WHO DID THOSE THINGS TO BE MURDERERS -- WE WERE ALL ACTING TO PRESERVE ORDER IN OUR COMMUNITY. >
< EVERYONE KNOWS THAT YOU KILLED THOMAS SCOTT. YOUR REFUSAL TO ACKNOWLEDGE REALITY PROVES YOUR INSANITY. >
< ARE YOU NAKED IN THERE ? >
< THE SPIRIT OF CHARITY TOLD ME THAT THE ONE WHO IS GOOD MUST SHOW HIMSELF NAKED. >
< ORDERLY! Mr DAVID HAS TORN UP HIS CLOTHES AGAIN! >

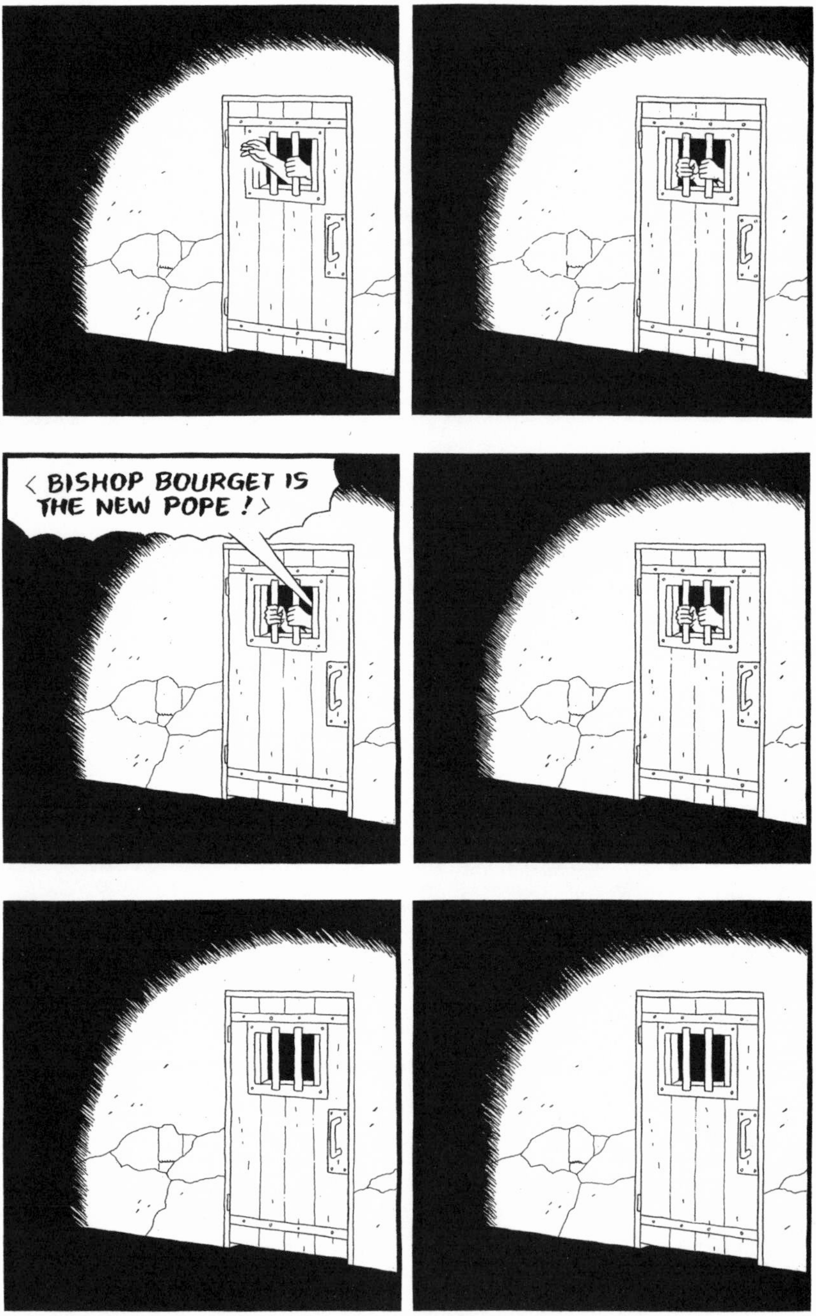
< BISHOP BOURGET IS THE NEW POPE ! >

SECOND
MAP SECTION

In the 1870 Manitoba Act, the
Canadian government had promised
to give 1,400,000 acres to the Métis.
Riel and Father Ritchot had hoped
that this land would be along the
Red and Assiniboine Rivers, ensuring
the development of a strong and
prosperous Métis community, and had
expected that the Métis would be
allowed to select their own lots. The
government at first appeared undecided
about how to hand out the land and
delayed the distribution. During this
period of delay, many of the river-
front lots that the Métis would have
wanted were given to immigrants from
Ontario. After a few years, the
government finally settled on a distribution scheme for the 1,400,000 acres.
Instead of letting the Métis choose the
land that they wanted, the government
chose the lots, which, rather than
being river-front lots, ended up being
interior prarie-land unconnected to
waterways -- land that the Métis
considered to be inferior. These lots
were then distributed by lottery. Since
this land wasn't suited to the form of
agriculture that they were used to,
the Métis had no interest in it and
sold it to land-speculators.

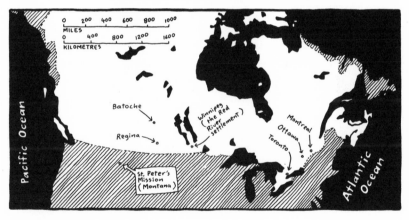

☐ Canada

▨ Not Canada

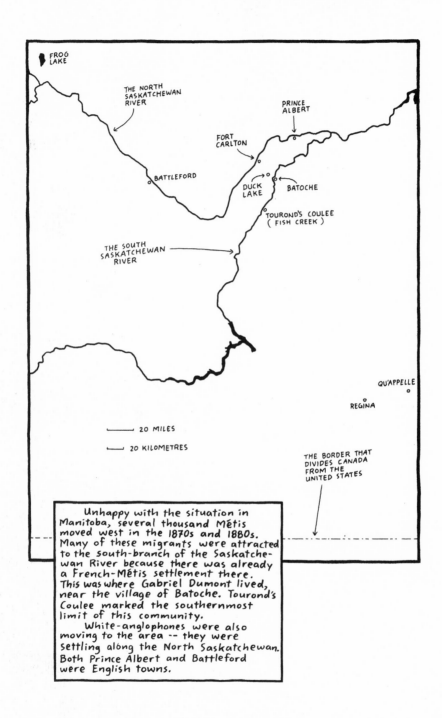

FROG
LAKE

THE NORTH
SASKATCHEWAN
RIVER

PRINCE
ALBERT

FORT
CARLTON

BATTLEFORD

DUCK
LAKE

BATOCHE

TOUROND'S COULEE
(FISH CREEK)

THE SOUTH
SASKATCHEWAN
RIVER

QU'APPELLE

REGINA

20 MILES

20 KILOMETRES

THE BORDER THAT
DIVIDES CANADA
FROM THE
UNITED STATES

Unhappy with the situation in
Manitoba, several thousand Métis
moved west in the 1870s and 1880s.
Many of these migrants were attracted
to the south-branch of the Saskatchewan River because there was already
a French-Métis settlement there.
This was where Gabriel Dumont lived,
near the village of Batoche. Tourond's
Coulee marked the southernmost
limit of this community.
  White-anglophones were also
moving to the area -- they were
settling along the North Saskatchewan.
Both Prince Albert and Battleford
were English towns.

PART THREE

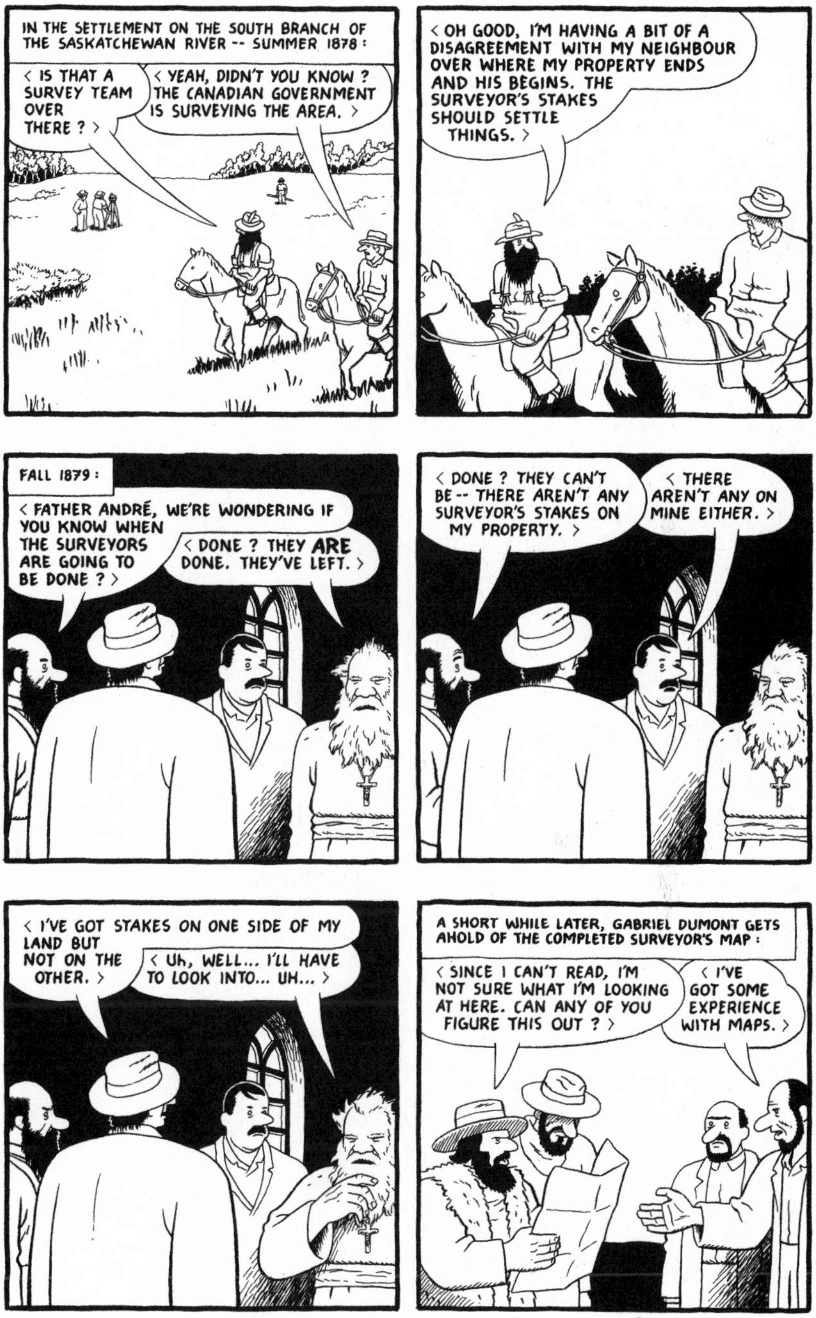
IN THE SETTLEMENT ON THE SOUTH BRANCH OF THE SASKATCHEWAN RIVER -- SUMMER 1878 :
< IS THAT A SURVEY TEAM OVER THERE ? >
< YEAH, DIDN'T YOU KNOW ? THE CANADIAN GOVERNMENT IS SURVEYING THE AREA. >
< OH GOOD, I'M HAVING A BIT OF A DISAGREEMENT WITH MY NEIGHBOUR OVER WHERE MY PROPERTY ENDS AND HIS BEGINS. THE SURVEYOR'S STAKES SHOULD SETTLE THINGS. >
FALL 1879 :
< FATHER ANDRÉ, WE'RE WONDERING IF YOU KNOW WHEN THE SURVEYORS ARE GOING TO BE DONE ? >
< DONE ? THEY ARE DONE. THEY'VE LEFT. >
< DONE ? THEY CAN'T BE -- THERE AREN'T ANY SURVEYOR'S STAKES ON MY PROPERTY. >
< THERE AREN'T ANY ON MINE EITHER. >
< I'VE GOT STAKES ON ONE SIDE OF MY LAND BUT NOT ON THE OTHER. >
< Uh, WELL... I'LL HAVE TO LOOK INTO... UH... >
A SHORT WHILE LATER, GABRIEL DUMONT GETS AHOLD OF THE COMPLETED SURVEYOR'S MAP :
< SINCE I CAN'T READ, I'M NOT SURE WHAT I'M LOOKING AT HERE. CAN ANY OF YOU FIGURE THIS OUT ? >
< I'VE GOT SOME EXPERIENCE WITH MAPS. >

< LET'S
SEE...
mmm... >

< WHEN THEY BEGAN THE SURVEY IN 1878, THEY WERE DIVIDING THE LOTS THE WAY WE ACTUALLY SET THEM UP -- >

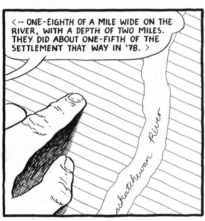

<-- ONE-EIGHTH OF A MILE WIDE ON THE RIVER, WITH A DEPTH OF TWO MILES. THEY DID ABOUT ONE-FIFTH OF THE SETTLEMENT THAT WAY IN '78. >

Saskatchewan River

< BUT THEN, WHEN THEY RESUMED WORK THIS SUMMER, THEY STARTED TO DIVIDE THE LAND IN THE ENGLISH WAY -- SQUARE LOTS -- A HALF-MILE BY A HALF-MILE. >

< WHY WOULD THEY DO THAT? THEY CAN SEE THE WAY OUR FARMS ARE LAID OUT. >

< THEY'RE TRYING TO FORCE US TO USE THEIR SYSTEM. >

< IT'S A LOUSY SYSTEM. MORE PEOPLE HAVE ACCESS TO THE WATER OUR WAY. >

< AND YOU'RE CLOSER TO YOUR NEIGH-BOURS. >

< WE HAVE A RIGHT TO SET UP OUR COMMUNITY THE WAY WE WANT IT. >

< THEY HAVE NO RESPECT FOR OUR WAY OF DOING THINGS. WE'LL HAVE TO MAKE THEM DO THE SURVEY OVER. >

DUMONT VISITS THE DOMINION LANDS OFFICE IN PRINCE ALBERT:

I'M SORRY, RESURVEYING THE AREA WOULD COST TOO MUCH.

< HE SAYS RESURVEYING WILL BE TOO EXPENSIVE. >

< BUT HOW CAN WE CLAIM TITLE TO OUR LAND WITHOUT A PROPER SURVEY? >

< AND THAT REMINDS ME, WHY DO WE HAVE TO WAIT THREE YEARS TO GET TITLE TO OUR LAND? >

'E WANTS TO KNOW WHY WE 'AVE TO WAIT T'REE YEARS FOR A PATENT.

EVERYONE WHO APPLIES FOR LAND THROUGH THE GOVERNMENT'S HOMESTEADING PROGRAM HAS TO WAIT THREE YEARS. THE SAME RULE APPLIES TO ENGLISH-SPEAKING WHITES TOO.

< HE SAYS THAT THE WHITES ALSO HAVE TO WAIT THREE YEARS. >

< YES, BUT **OUR** ANCESTORS **OWNED** THIS LAND -- THE RULES SHOULD BE DIFFERENT FOR THOSE OF US WITH INDIAN BLOOD. >

< IN THE OLD DAYS, IF WE WANTED TO SETTLE ON UNOCCUPIED LAND, WE'D JUST DO IT -- NO REGISTRATION FEE, NO PROVING TO GOVERN-MENT-INSPECTORS THAT WE'D FULFILLED ANY KIND OF "SETTLEMENT DUTIES", NO WAITING THREE YEARS FOR PATENT. >

IN 1881, GOVERNOR-GENERAL LORD LORNE VISITS BATOCHE:

WELL, I'LL CERTAINLY BRING THESE MATTERS TO THE ATTENTION OF THE PRIME-MINISTER.

T'ERE'S ANOT'ER T'ING WE WANT DEALT WIT'.

T'E MÉTIS IN MANITOBA RECEIVED LAND-GRANTS T'ROUGH T'E MANITOBA ACT -- T'OSE LAND-GRANTS WERE INTENDED TO EXTINGUISH T'E RIGHTS OF T'E MANITOBA MÉTIS AS DESCENDANTS OF INDIANS.

T'E MÉTIS OO DIDN'T LIVE IN MANITOBA ARE ALSO DESCENDED FROM INDIANS -- IF T'E MANI-TOBA MÉTIS GOT LAND, T'E MÉTIS LIVING OUTSIDE MANITOBA SHOULD GET LAND TOO.

LAND BEYOND WHAT THEY'RE ALREADY LIVING ON?

YES -- LIKE T'E MANITOBA LAND-GRANTS. IT'S ONLY FAIR.

WELL... I'LL... SEE WHAT I CAN DO.

MAY 24, 1884:

‹ LORD LORNE PROMISED TO TAKE OUR GRIEVANCES TO OTTAWA. WELL, THAT WAS MANY YEARS AGO, AND IN SPITE OF ALL THE LETTERS AND PETITIONS THAT WE'VE SENT SINCE THEN, WE'VE NOTHING TO SHOW FOR IT. ›

125

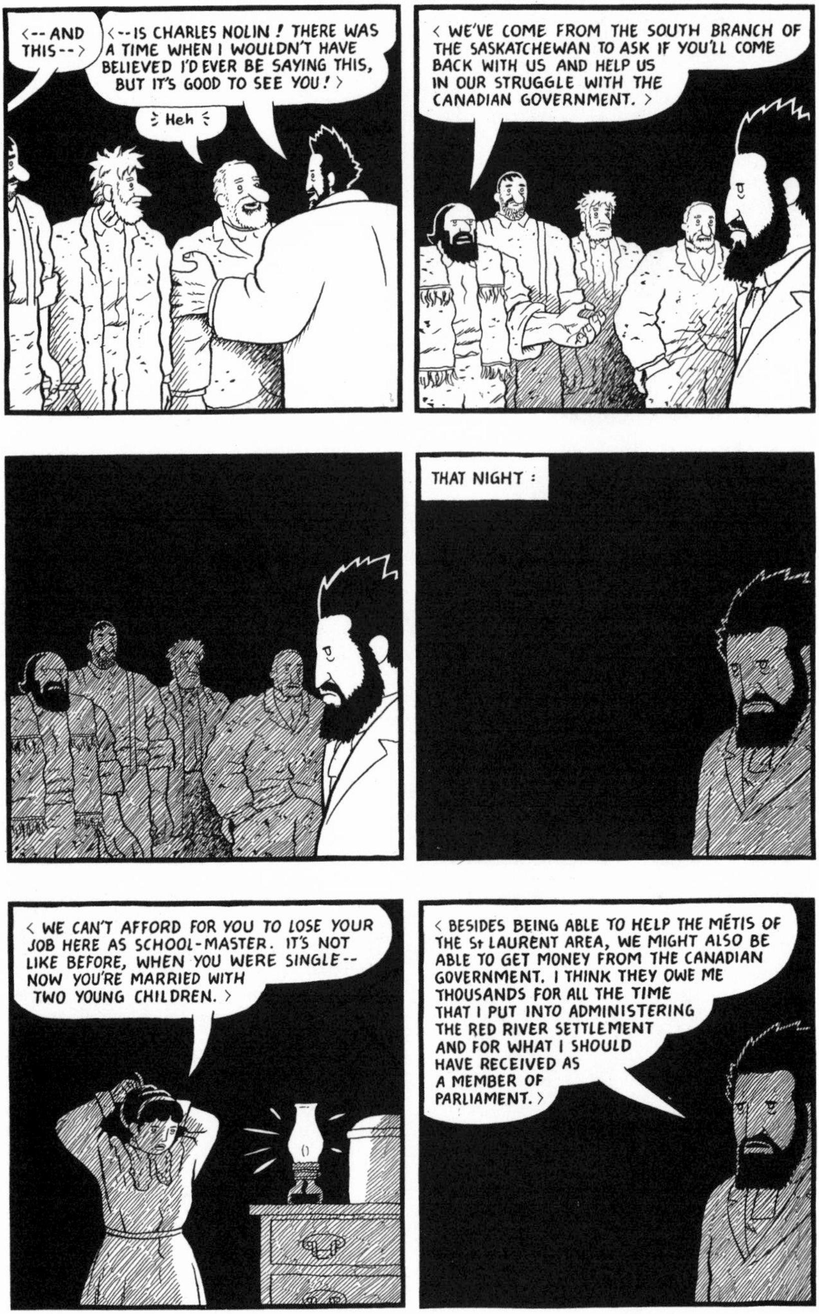

< -- AND THIS -- >
< -- IS CHARLES NOLIN ! THERE WAS A TIME WHEN I WOULDN'T HAVE BELIEVED I'D EVER BE SAYING THIS, BUT IT'S GOOD TO SEE YOU ! >
Heh
< WE'VE COME FROM THE SOUTH BRANCH OF THE SASKATCHEWAN TO ASK IF YOU'LL COME BACK WITH US AND HELP US IN OUR STRUGGLE WITH THE CANADIAN GOVERNMENT. >
THAT NIGHT :
< WE CAN'T AFFORD FOR YOU TO LOSE YOUR JOB HERE AS SCHOOL-MASTER. IT'S NOT LIKE BEFORE, WHEN YOU WERE SINGLE -- NOW YOU'RE MARRIED WITH TWO YOUNG CHILDREN. >
< BESIDES BEING ABLE TO HELP THE MÉTIS OF THE St LAURENT AREA, WE MIGHT ALSO BE ABLE TO GET MONEY FROM THE CANADIAN GOVERNMENT. I THINK THEY OWE ME THOUSANDS FOR ALL THE TIME THAT I PUT INTO ADMINISTERING THE RED RIVER SETTLEMENT AND FOR WHAT I SHOULD HAVE RECEIVED AS A MEMBER OF PARLIAMENT. >

129

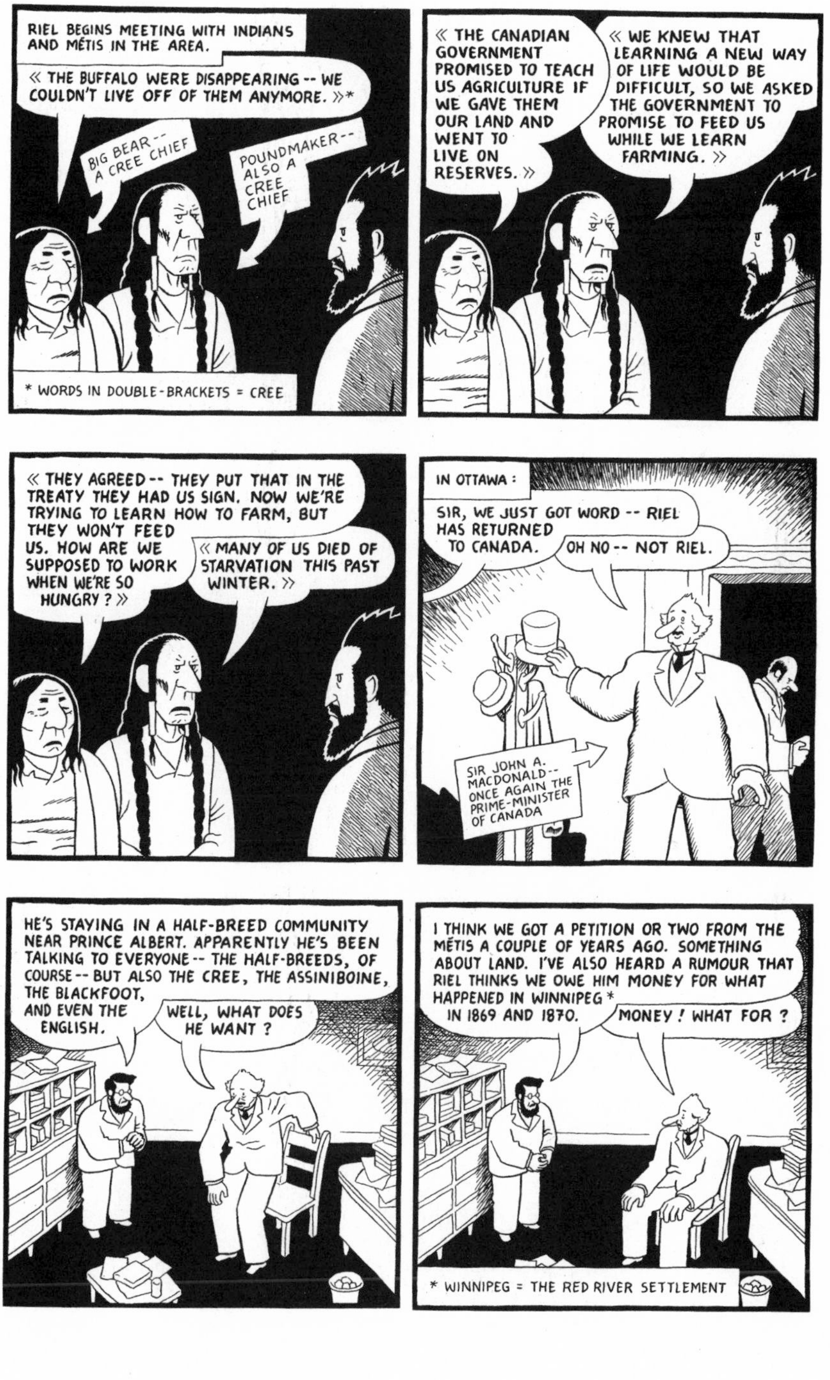
RIEL BEGINS MEETING WITH INDIANS AND MÉTIS IN THE AREA.
« THE BUFFALO WERE DISAPPEARING -- WE COULDN'T LIVE OFF OF THEM ANYMORE. »*
BIG BEAR -- A CREE CHIEF
POUNDMAKER -- ALSO A CREE CHIEF
* WORDS IN DOUBLE-BRACKETS = CREE
« THE CANADIAN GOVERNMENT PROMISED TO TEACH US AGRICULTURE IF WE GAVE THEM OUR LAND AND WENT TO LIVE ON RESERVES. »
« WE KNEW THAT LEARNING A NEW WAY OF LIFE WOULD BE DIFFICULT, SO WE ASKED THE GOVERNMENT TO PROMISE TO FEED US WHILE WE LEARN FARMING. »
« THEY AGREED -- THEY PUT THAT IN THE TREATY THEY HAD US SIGN. NOW WE'RE TRYING TO LEARN HOW TO FARM, BUT THEY WON'T FEED US. HOW ARE WE SUPPOSED TO WORK WHEN WE'RE SO HUNGRY? »
« MANY OF US DIED OF STARVATION THIS PAST WINTER. »
IN OTTAWA:
SIR, WE JUST GOT WORD -- RIEL HAS RETURNED TO CANADA.
OH NO -- NOT RIEL.
SIR JOHN A. MACDONALD -- ONCE AGAIN THE PRIME-MINISTER OF CANADA
HE'S STAYING IN A HALF-BREED COMMUNITY NEAR PRINCE ALBERT. APPARENTLY HE'S BEEN TALKING TO EVERYONE -- THE HALF-BREEDS, OF COURSE -- BUT ALSO THE CREE, THE ASSINIBOINE, THE BLACKFOOT, AND EVEN THE ENGLISH.
WELL, WHAT DOES HE WANT?
I THINK WE GOT A PETITION OR TWO FROM THE MÉTIS A COUPLE OF YEARS AGO. SOMETHING ABOUT LAND. I'VE ALSO HEARD A RUMOUR THAT RIEL THINKS WE OWE HIM MONEY FOR WHAT HAPPENED IN WINNIPEG* IN 1869 AND 1870.
MONEY! WHAT FOR?
* WINNIPEG = THE RED RIVER SETTLEMENT

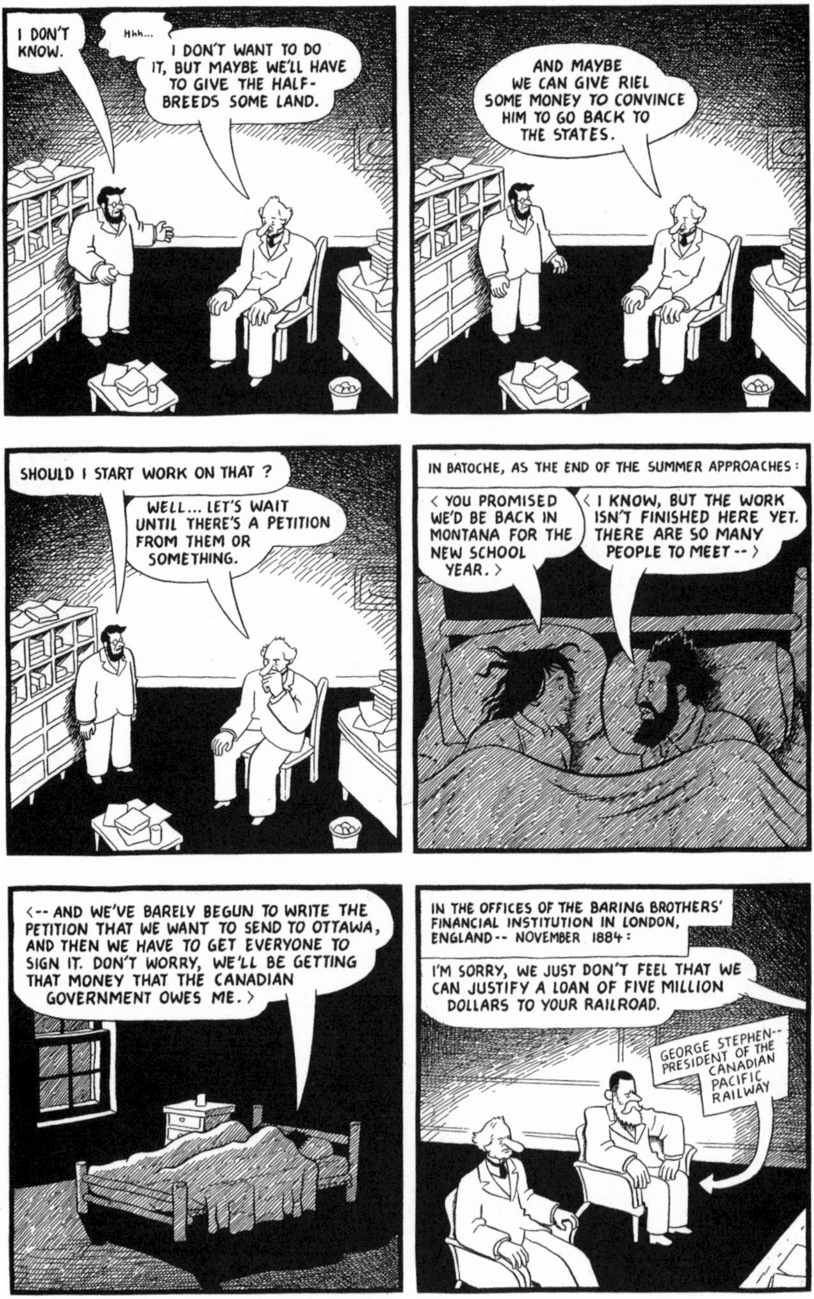
I DON'T KNOW.
Hhh...
I DON'T WANT TO DO IT, BUT MAYBE WE'LL HAVE TO GIVE THE HALF-BREEDS SOME LAND.
AND MAYBE WE CAN GIVE RIEL SOME MONEY TO CONVINCE HIM TO GO BACK TO THE STATES.
SHOULD I START WORK ON THAT ?
WELL... LET'S WAIT UNTIL THERE'S A PETITION FROM THEM OR SOMETHING.
IN BATOCHE, AS THE END OF THE SUMMER APPROACHES:
< YOU PROMISED WE'D BE BACK IN MONTANA FOR THE NEW SCHOOL YEAR. >
< I KNOW, BUT THE WORK ISN'T FINISHED HERE YET. THERE ARE SO MANY PEOPLE TO MEET -- >
<-- AND WE'VE BARELY BEGUN TO WRITE THE PETITION THAT WE WANT TO SEND TO OTTAWA, AND THEN WE HAVE TO GET EVERYONE TO SIGN IT. DON'T WORRY, WE'LL BE GETTING THAT MONEY THAT THE CANADIAN GOVERNMENT OWES ME. >
IN THE OFFICES OF THE BARING BROTHERS' FINANCIAL INSTITUTION IN LONDON, ENGLAND -- NOVEMBER 1884:
I'M SORRY, WE JUST DON'T FEEL THAT WE CAN JUSTIFY A LOAN OF FIVE MILLION DOLLARS TO YOUR RAILROAD.
GEORGE STEPHEN-- PRESIDENT OF THE CANADIAN PACIFIC RAILWAY

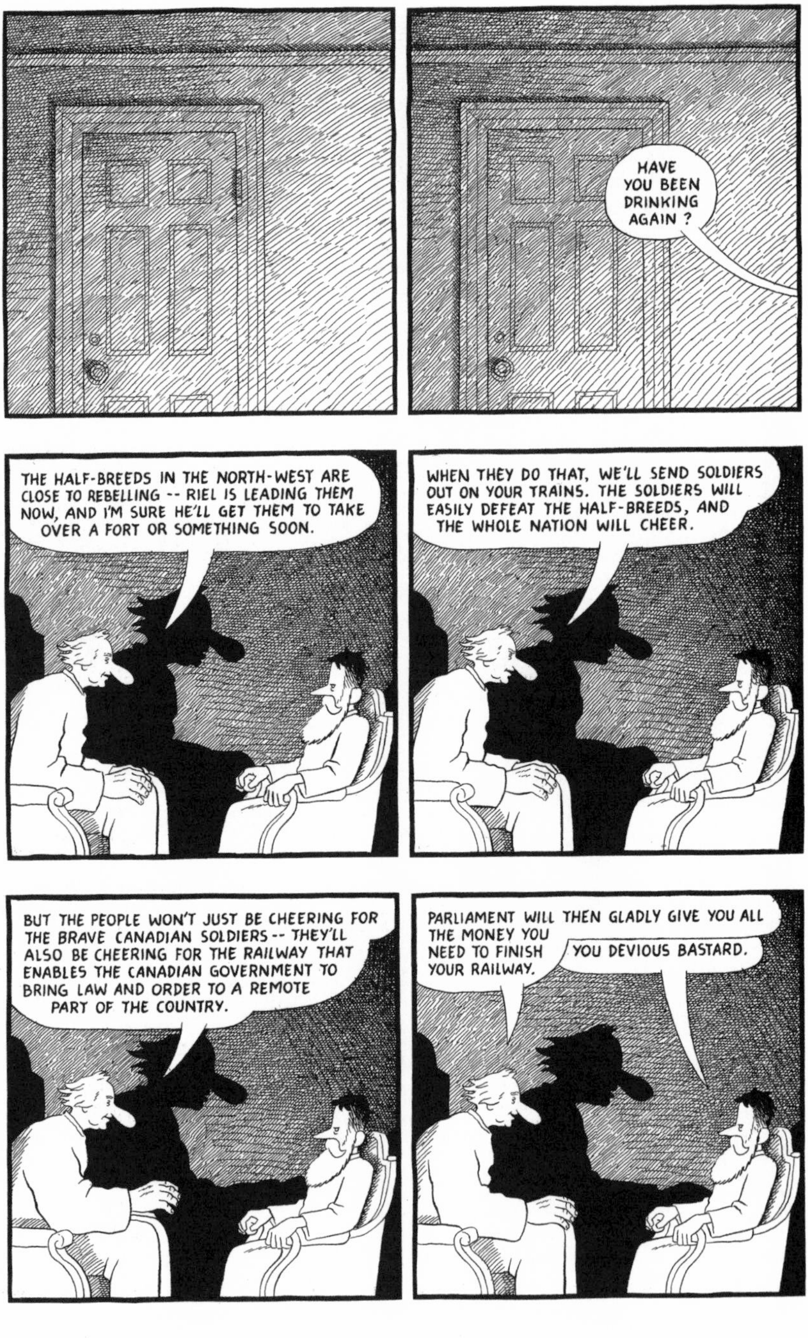
HAVE YOU BEEN DRINKING AGAIN ?
THE HALF-BREEDS IN THE NORTH-WEST ARE CLOSE TO REBELLING -- RIEL IS LEADING THEM NOW, AND I'M SURE HE'LL GET THEM TO TAKE OVER A FORT OR SOMETHING SOON.
WHEN THEY DO THAT, WE'LL SEND SOLDIERS OUT ON YOUR TRAINS. THE SOLDIERS WILL EASILY DEFEAT THE HALF-BREEDS, AND THE WHOLE NATION WILL CHEER.
BUT THE PEOPLE WON'T JUST BE CHEERING FOR THE BRAVE CANADIAN SOLDIERS -- THEY'LL ALSO BE CHEERING FOR THE RAILWAY THAT ENABLES THE CANADIAN GOVERNMENT TO BRING LAW AND ORDER TO A REMOTE PART OF THE COUNTRY.
PARLIAMENT WILL THEN GLADLY GIVE YOU ALL THE MONEY YOU NEED TO FINISH YOUR RAILWAY.
YOU DEVIOUS BASTARD.

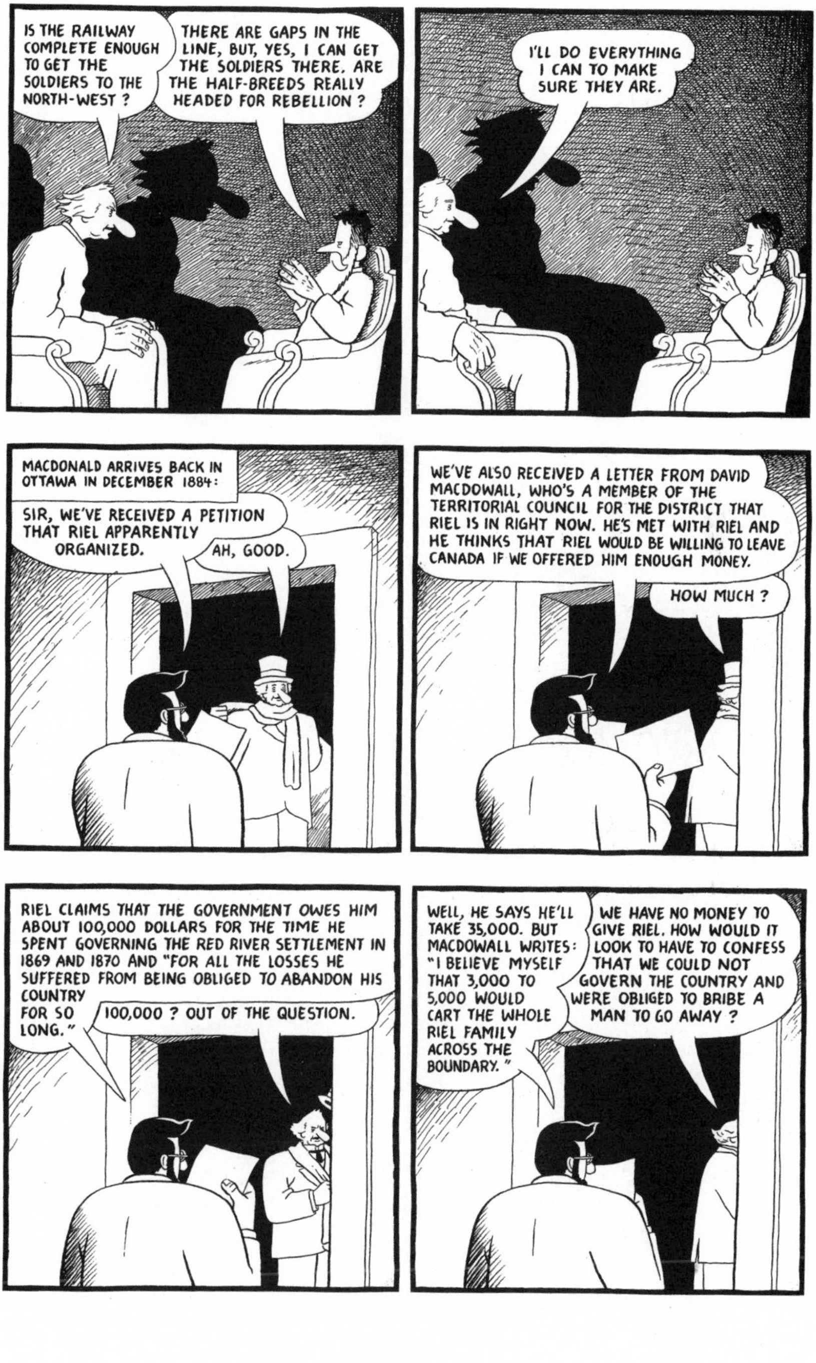
IS THE RAILWAY COMPLETE ENOUGH TO GET THE SOLDIERS TO THE NORTH-WEST ?
THERE ARE GAPS IN THE LINE, BUT, YES, I CAN GET THE SOLDIERS THERE. ARE THE HALF-BREEDS REALLY HEADED FOR REBELLION ?
I'LL DO EVERYTHING I CAN TO MAKE SURE THEY ARE.
MACDONALD ARRIVES BACK IN OTTAWA IN DECEMBER 1884:
SIR, WE'VE RECEIVED A PETITION THAT RIEL APPARENTLY ORGANIZED.
AH, GOOD.
WE'VE ALSO RECEIVED A LETTER FROM DAVID MACDOWALL, WHO'S A MEMBER OF THE TERRITORIAL COUNCIL FOR THE DISTRICT THAT RIEL IS IN RIGHT NOW. HE'S MET WITH RIEL AND HE THINKS THAT RIEL WOULD BE WILLING TO LEAVE CANADA IF WE OFFERED HIM ENOUGH MONEY.
HOW MUCH ?
RIEL CLAIMS THAT THE GOVERNMENT OWES HIM ABOUT 100,000 DOLLARS FOR THE TIME HE SPENT GOVERNING THE RED RIVER SETTLEMENT IN 1869 AND 1870 AND "FOR ALL THE LOSSES HE SUFFERED FROM BEING OBLIGED TO ABANDON HIS COUNTRY FOR SO LONG."
100,000 ? OUT OF THE QUESTION.
WELL, HE SAYS HE'LL TAKE 35,000. BUT MACDOWALL WRITES: "I BELIEVE MYSELF THAT 3,000 TO 5,000 WOULD CART THE WHOLE RIEL FAMILY ACROSS THE BOUNDARY."
WE HAVE NO MONEY TO GIVE RIEL. HOW WOULD IT LOOK TO HAVE TO CONFESS THAT WE COULD NOT GOVERN THE COUNTRY AND WERE OBLIGED TO BRIBE A MAN TO GO AWAY ?

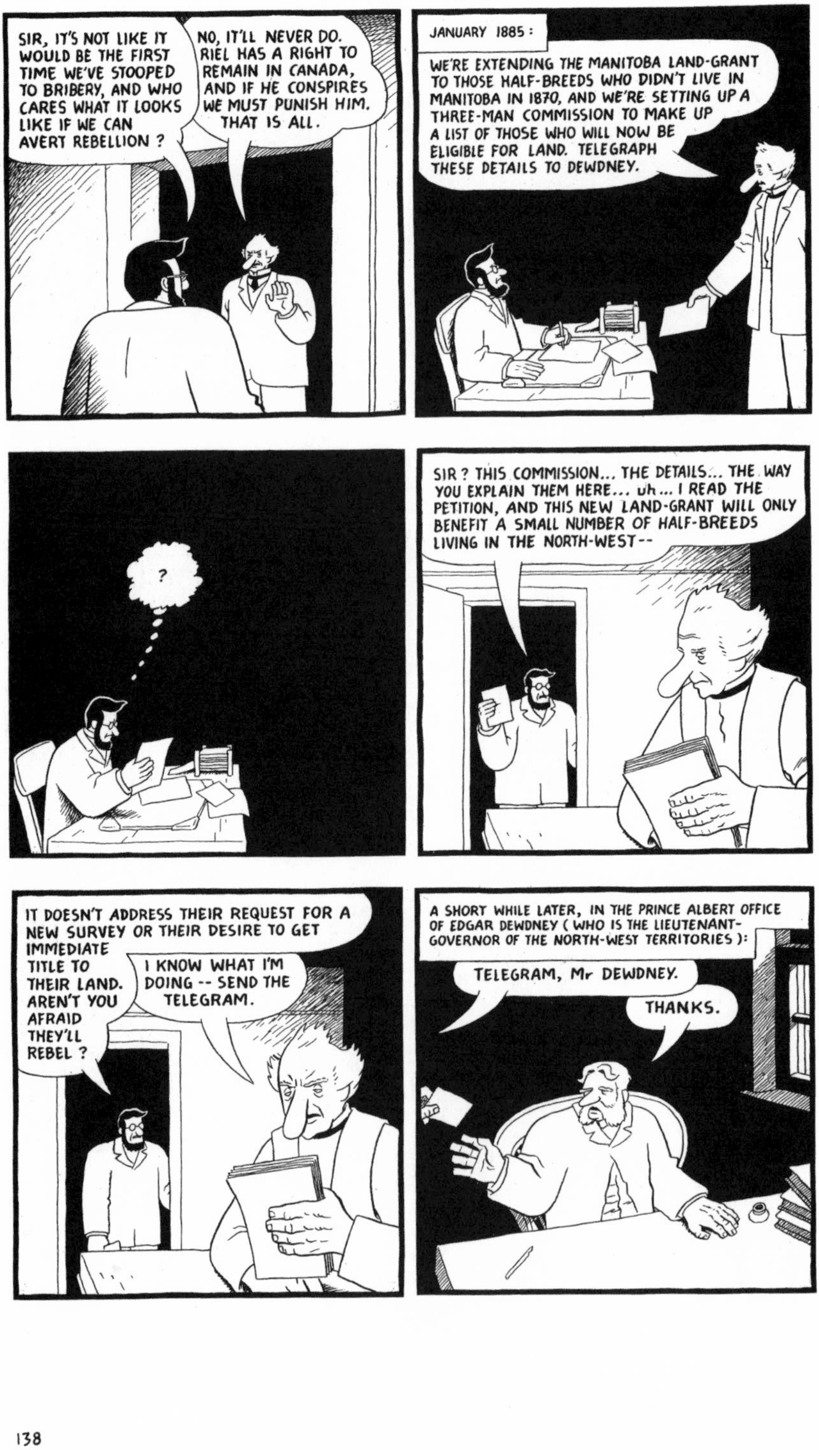

SIR, IT'S NOT LIKE IT WOULD BE THE FIRST TIME WE'VE STOOPED TO BRIBERY, AND WHO CARES WHAT IT LOOKS LIKE IF WE CAN AVERT REBELLION ?
NO, IT'LL NEVER DO. RIEL HAS A RIGHT TO REMAIN IN CANADA, AND IF HE CONSPIRES WE MUST PUNISH HIM. THAT IS ALL.
JANUARY 1885 :
WE'RE EXTENDING THE MANITOBA LAND-GRANT TO THOSE HALF-BREEDS WHO DIDN'T LIVE IN MANITOBA IN 1870, AND WE'RE SETTING UP A THREE-MAN COMMISSION TO MAKE UP A LIST OF THOSE WHO WILL NOW BE ELIGIBLE FOR LAND. TELEGRAPH THESE DETAILS TO DEWDNEY.
?
SIR ? THIS COMMISSION... THE DETAILS... THE WAY YOU EXPLAIN THEM HERE... uh... I READ THE PETITION, AND THIS NEW LAND-GRANT WILL ONLY BENEFIT A SMALL NUMBER OF HALF-BREEDS LIVING IN THE NORTH-WEST--
IT DOESN'T ADDRESS THEIR REQUEST FOR A NEW SURVEY OR THEIR DESIRE TO GET IMMEDIATE TITLE TO THEIR LAND. AREN'T YOU AFRAID THEY'LL REBEL ?
I KNOW WHAT I'M DOING -- SEND THE TELEGRAM.
A SHORT WHILE LATER, IN THE PRINCE ALBERT OFFICE OF EDGAR DEWDNEY (WHO IS THE LIEUTENANT-GOVERNOR OF THE NORTH-WEST TERRITORIES):
TELEGRAM, Mr DEWDNEY.
THANKS.

< LADIES AND GENTLEMEN, IT LOOKS LIKE MY WORK HERE IS DONE. I HELPED YOU DRAFT THE PETITION AND WE HAVE RECEIVED A FAVOURABLE REPLY. >

< GIVEN THE HOSTILITY THAT THE AUTHORITIES FEEL FOR ME, I WOULD ONLY BE A DISTRACTION IN YOUR NEGOTIATIONS WITH THE GOVERNMENT. SO I'VE DECIDED TO LEAVE AND RETURN TO MONTANA. >

< NO ! > < NO ! > < DON'T LEAVE ! > < WE NEED YOU ! >
< NO ! > < STAY ! > < NO ! >

< BUT WHAT ABOUT THE CONSEQUENCES ? >

< WE WILL SUFFER THE CONSEQUENCES ! > < YES ! > < PLEASE STAY ! >
< WE WILL ! >

THE PRIME-MINISTER'S OFFICE IN OTTAWA -- FEBRUARY 1885 :

YOU WANTED TO SEE ME, SIR JOHN ?

YES, CLARKE -- I HEARD THAT YOU WERE IN OTTAWA FOR A SHORT VISIT, AND I WANTED TO SEE YOU BEFORE YOU HEADED BACK OUT WEST. TO BE QUITE FRANK, I WANT THE HALF-BREEDS TO REBEL.

LAWRENCE CLARKE -- THE HUDSON'S BAY COMPANY'S CHIEF FACTOR FOR FORT CARLTON (WHICH IS NEAR BATOCHE)

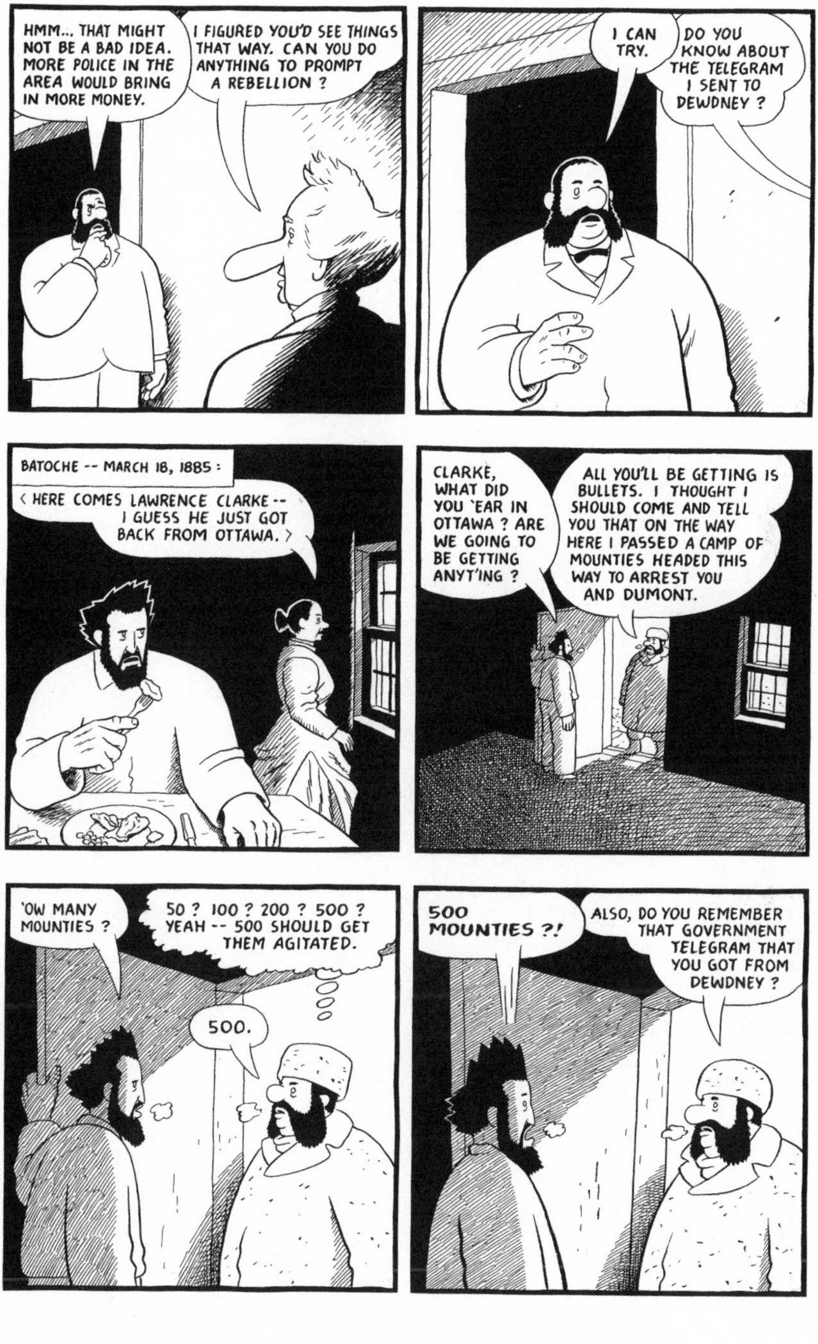
HMM... THAT MIGHT NOT BE A BAD IDEA. MORE POLICE IN THE AREA WOULD BRING IN MORE MONEY.
I FIGURED YOU'D SEE THINGS THAT WAY. CAN YOU DO ANYTHING TO PROMPT A REBELLION ?
I CAN TRY.
DO YOU KNOW ABOUT THE TELEGRAM I SENT TO DEWDNEY ?
BATOCHE -- MARCH 18, 1885 :
< HERE COMES LAWRENCE CLARKE -- I GUESS HE JUST GOT BACK FROM OTTAWA. >
CLARKE, WHAT DID YOU `EAR IN OTTAWA ? ARE WE GOING TO BE GETTING ANYT'ING ?
ALL YOU'LL BE GETTING IS BULLETS. I THOUGHT I SHOULD COME AND TELL YOU THAT ON THE WAY HERE I PASSED A CAMP OF MOUNTIES HEADED THIS WAY TO ARREST YOU AND DUMONT.
'OW MANY MOUNTIES ?
50 ? 100 ? 200 ? 500 ? YEAH -- 500 SHOULD GET THEM AGITATED.
500.
500 MOUNTIES ?!
ALSO, DO YOU REMEMBER THAT GOVERNMENT TELEGRAM THAT YOU GOT FROM DEWDNEY ?

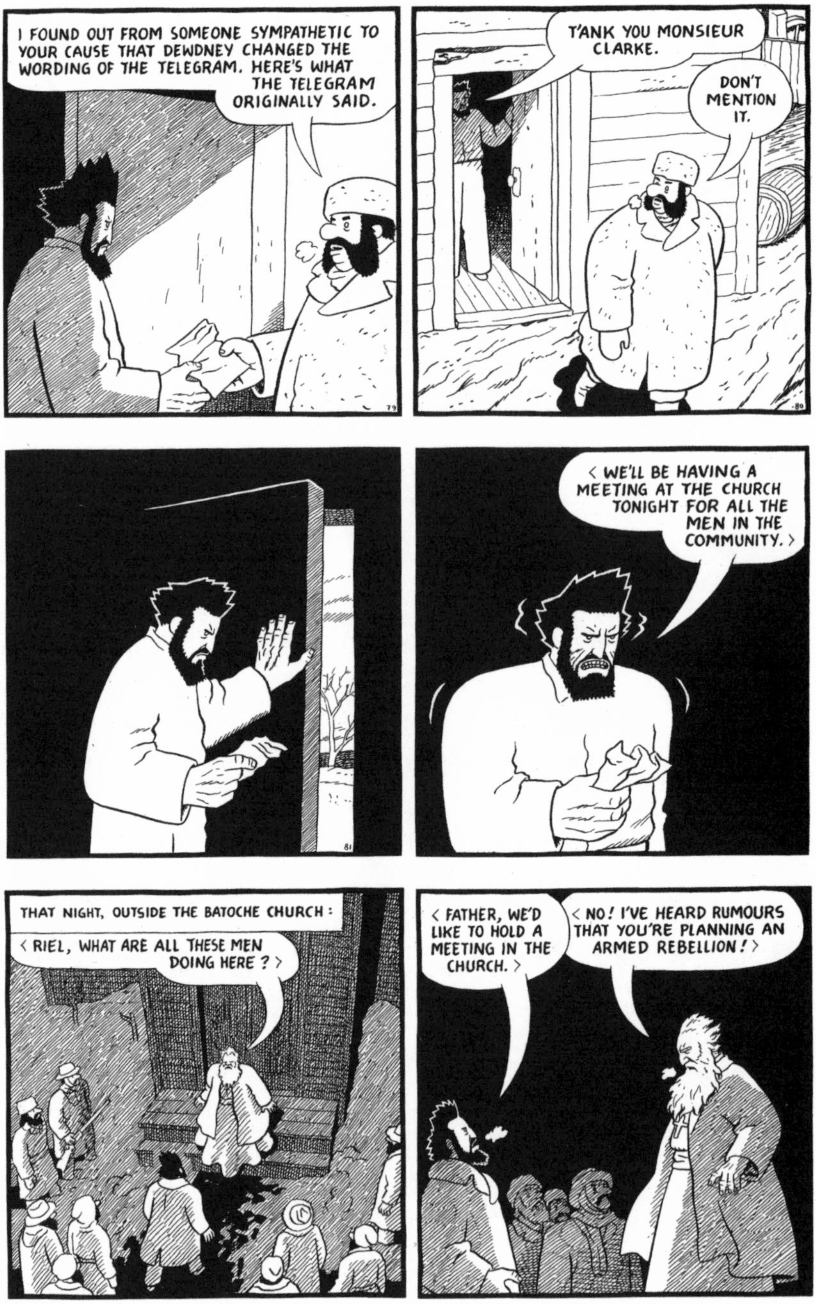
I FOUND OUT FROM SOMEONE SYMPATHETIC TO YOUR CAUSE THAT DEWDNEY CHANGED THE WORDING OF THE TELEGRAM. HERE'S WHAT THE TELEGRAM ORIGINALLY SAID.
T'ANK YOU MONSIEUR CLARKE.
DON'T MENTION IT.
< WE'LL BE HAVING A MEETING AT THE CHURCH TONIGHT FOR ALL THE MEN IN THE COMMUNITY. >
THAT NIGHT, OUTSIDE THE BATOCHE CHURCH :
< RIEL, WHAT ARE ALL THESE MEN DOING HERE ? >
< FATHER, WE'D LIKE TO HOLD A MEETING IN THE CHURCH. >
< NO! I'VE HEARD RUMOURS THAT YOU'RE PLANNING AN ARMED REBELLION! >

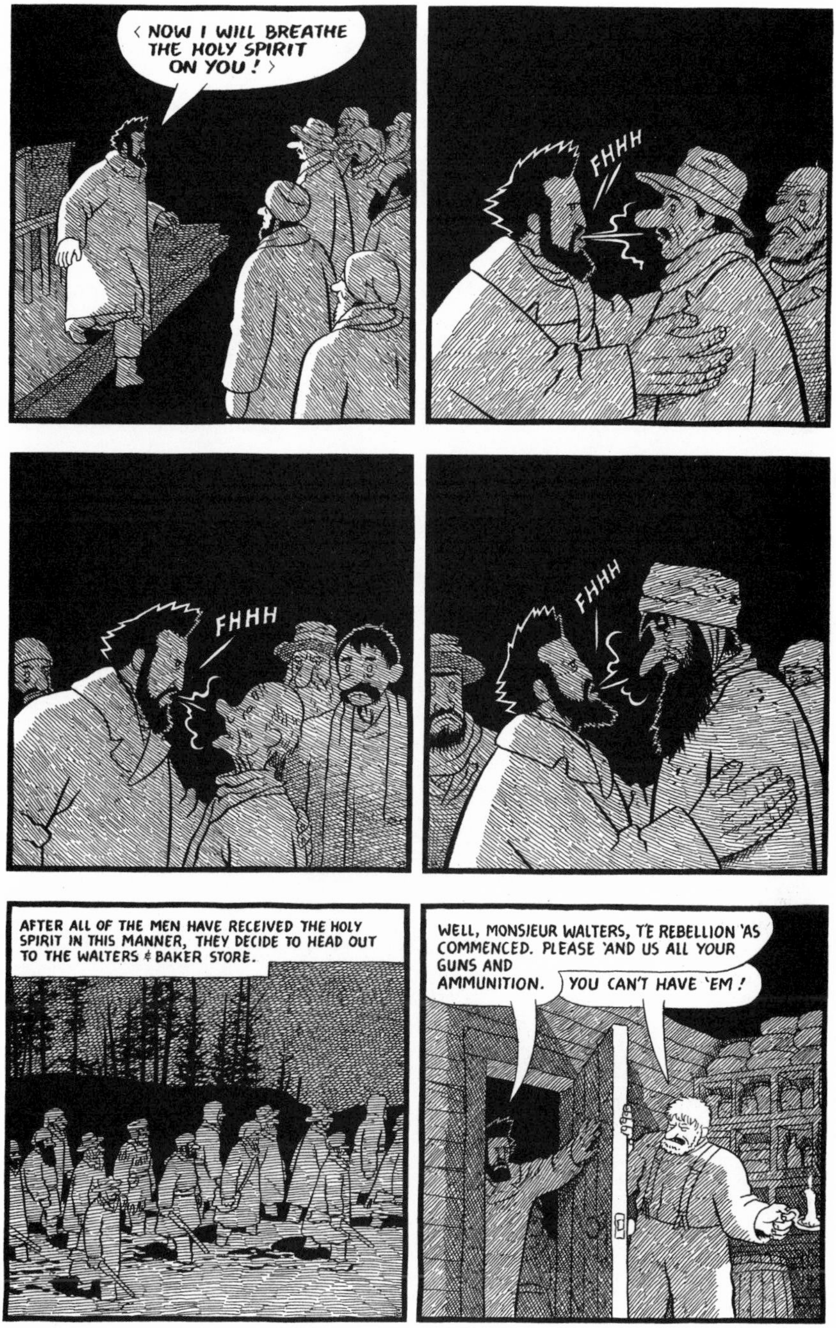
< NOW I WILL BREATHE THE HOLY SPIRIT ON YOU! >
FHHH
FHHH
FHHH
AFTER ALL OF THE MEN HAVE RECEIVED THE HOLY SPIRIT IN THIS MANNER, THEY DECIDE TO HEAD OUT TO THE WALTERS & BAKER STORE.
WELL, MONSIEUR WALTERS, T'E REBELLION 'AS COMMENCED. PLEASE 'AND US ALL YOUR GUNS AND AMMUNITION.
YOU CAN'T HAVE 'EM!

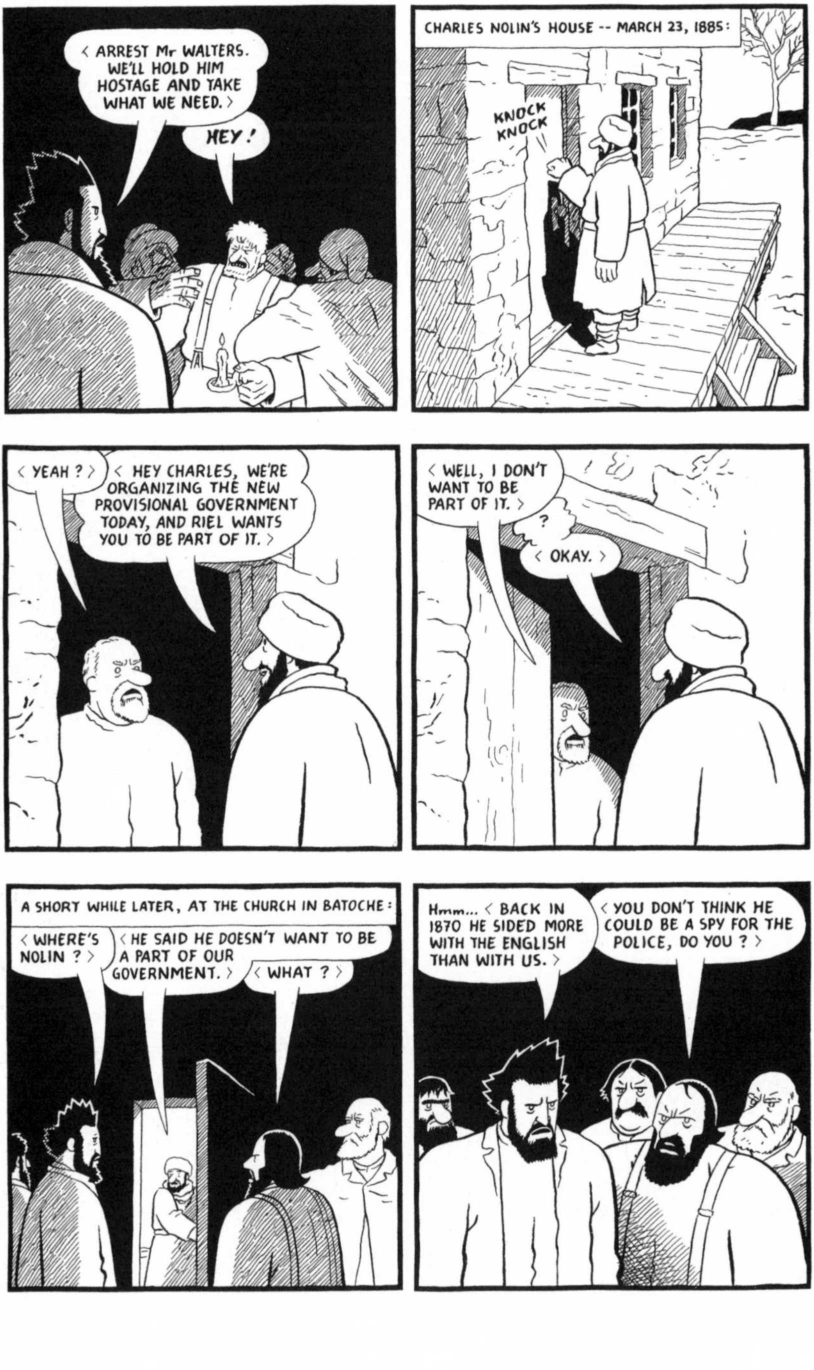
< ARREST Mr WALTERS. WE'LL HOLD HIM HOSTAGE AND TAKE WHAT WE NEED. >
HEY !
CHARLES NOLIN'S HOUSE -- MARCH 23, 1885:
KNOCK KNOCK
< YEAH ? >
< HEY CHARLES, WE'RE ORGANIZING THE NEW PROVISIONAL GOVERNMENT TODAY, AND RIEL WANTS YOU TO BE PART OF IT. >
< WELL, I DON'T WANT TO BE PART OF IT. >
?
< OKAY. >
A SHORT WHILE LATER, AT THE CHURCH IN BATOCHE:
< WHERE'S NOLIN ? >
< HE SAID HE DOESN'T WANT TO BE A PART OF OUR GOVERNMENT. >
< WHAT ? >
Hmm... < BACK IN 1870 HE SIDED MORE WITH THE ENGLISH THAN WITH US. >
< YOU DON'T THINK HE COULD BE A SPY FOR THE POLICE, DO YOU ? >

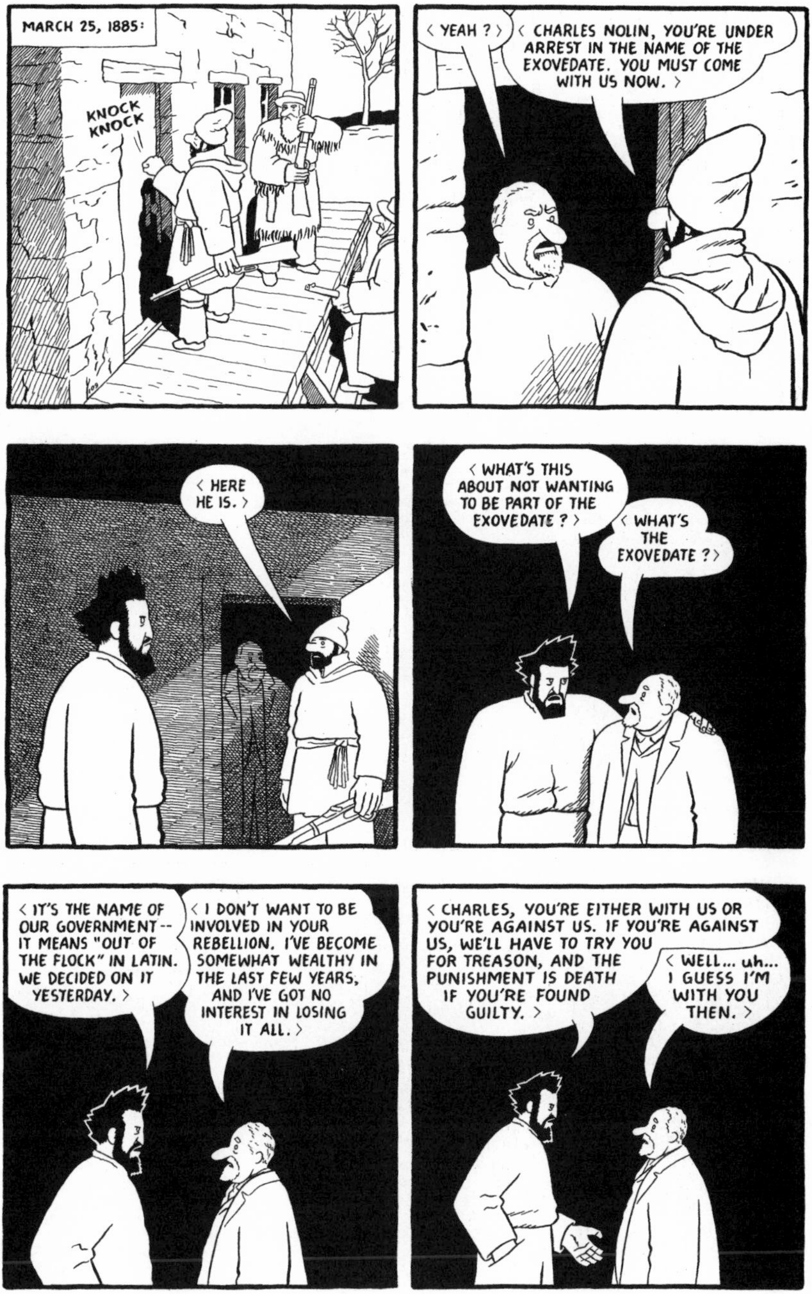
MARCH 25, 1885:
KNOCK KNOCK
< YEAH ? >
< CHARLES NOLIN, YOU'RE UNDER ARREST IN THE NAME OF THE EXOVEDATE. YOU MUST COME WITH US NOW. >
< HERE HE IS. >
< WHAT'S THIS ABOUT NOT WANTING TO BE PART OF THE EXOVEDATE ? >
< WHAT'S THE EXOVEDATE ? >
< IT'S THE NAME OF OUR GOVERNMENT -- IT MEANS "OUT OF THE FLOCK" IN LATIN. WE DECIDED ON IT YESTERDAY. >
< I DON'T WANT TO BE INVOLVED IN YOUR REBELLION. I'VE BECOME SOMEWHAT WEALTHY IN THE LAST FEW YEARS, AND I'VE GOT NO INTEREST IN LOSING IT ALL. >
< CHARLES, YOU'RE EITHER WITH US OR YOU'RE AGAINST US. IF YOU'RE AGAINST US, WE'LL HAVE TO TRY YOU FOR TREASON, AND THE PUNISHMENT IS DEATH IF YOU'RE FOUND GUILTY. >
< WELL... uh... I GUESS I'M WITH YOU THEN. >

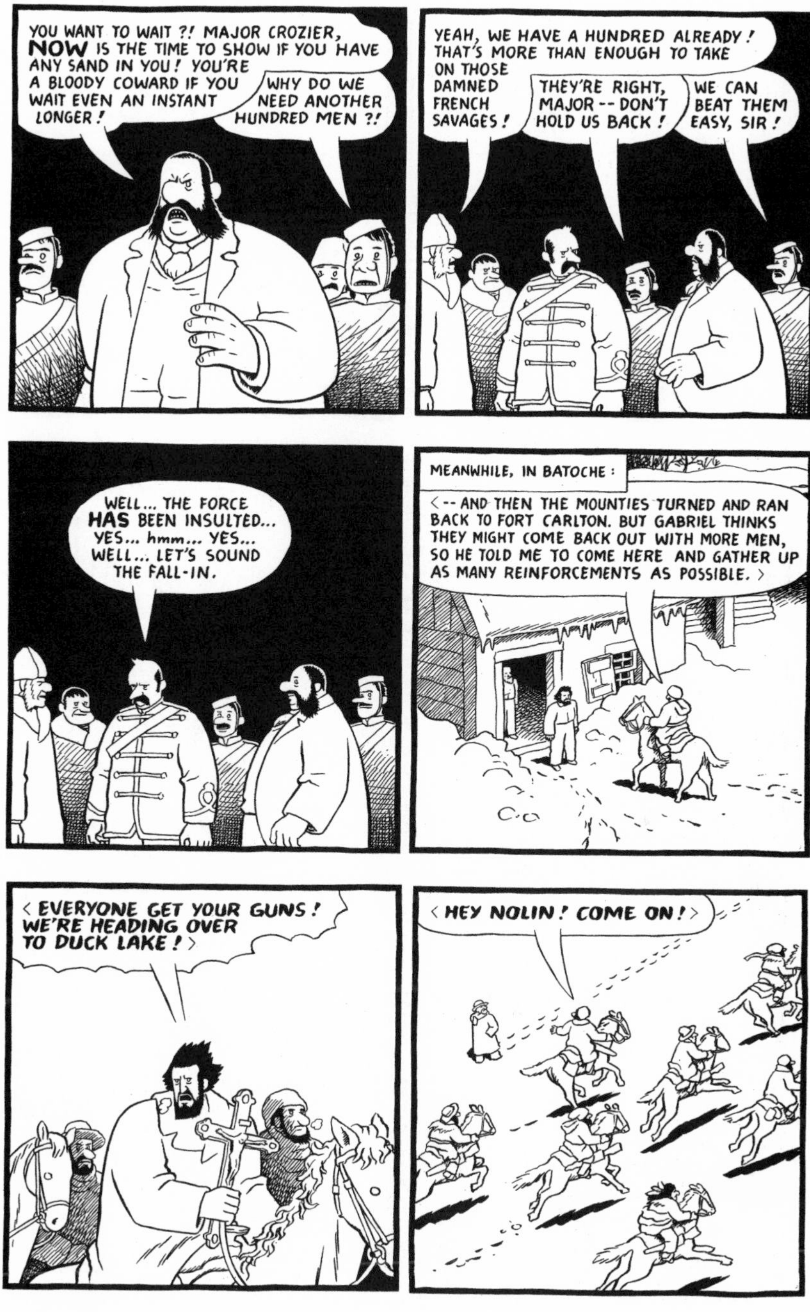
YOU WANT TO WAIT ?! MAJOR CROZIER, NOW IS THE TIME TO SHOW IF YOU HAVE ANY SAND IN YOU! YOU'RE A BLOODY COWARD IF YOU WAIT EVEN AN INSTANT LONGER!
WHY DO WE NEED ANOTHER HUNDRED MEN ?!
YEAH, WE HAVE A HUNDRED ALREADY! THAT'S MORE THAN ENOUGH TO TAKE ON THOSE DAMNED FRENCH SAVAGES!
THEY'RE RIGHT, MAJOR -- DON'T HOLD US BACK!
WE CAN BEAT THEM EASY, SIR!
WELL... THE FORCE HAS BEEN INSULTED... YES... hmm... YES... WELL... LET'S SOUND THE FALL-IN.
MEANWHILE, IN BATOCHE:
< -- AND THEN THE MOUNTIES TURNED AND RAN BACK TO FORT CARLTON. BUT GABRIEL THINKS THEY MIGHT COME BACK OUT WITH MORE MEN, SO HE TOLD ME TO COME HERE AND GATHER UP AS MANY REINFORCEMENTS AS POSSIBLE. >
< EVERYONE GET YOUR GUNS! WE'RE HEADING OVER TO DUCK LAKE! >
< HEY NOLIN! COME ON! >

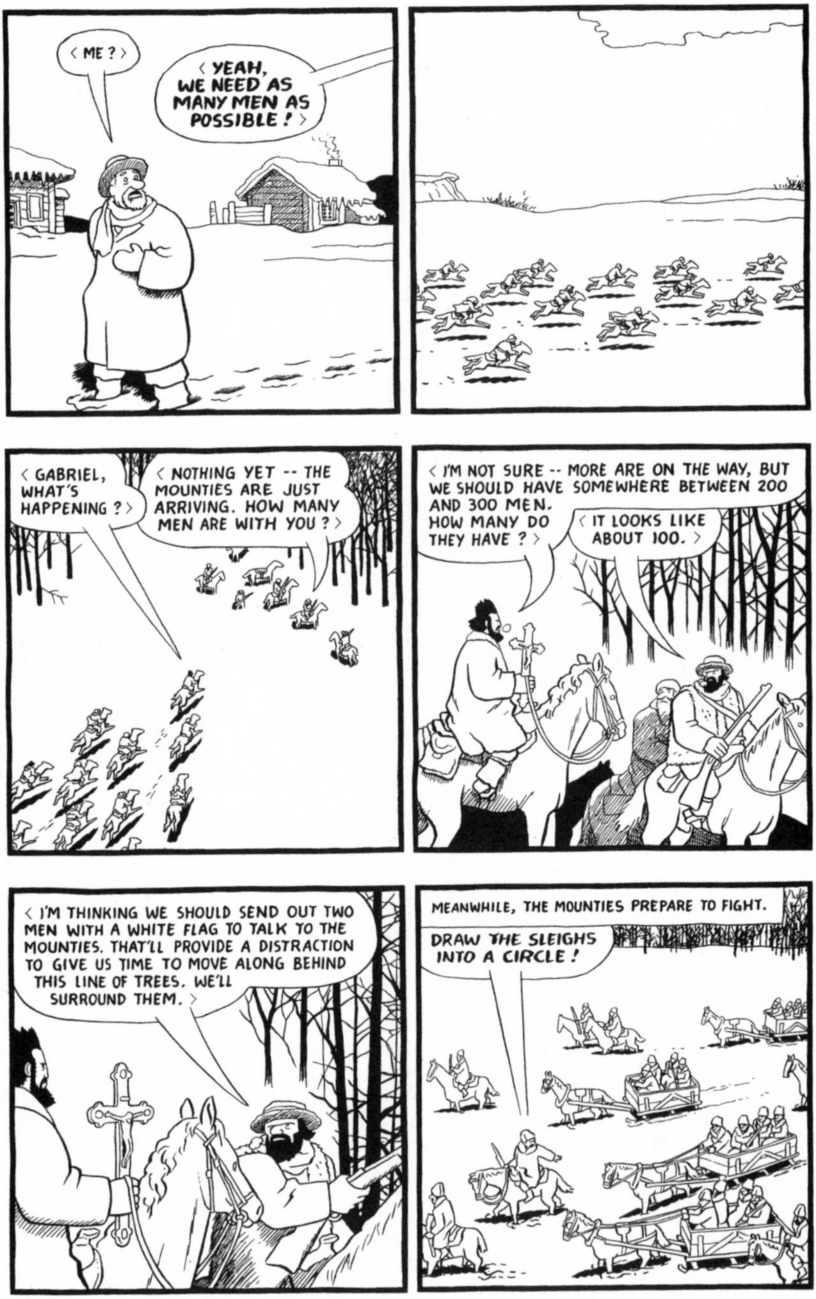

< ME ? >
< YEAH, WE NEED AS MANY MEN AS POSSIBLE ! >
< GABRIEL, WHAT'S HAPPENING ? >
< NOTHING YET -- THE MOUNTIES ARE JUST ARRIVING. HOW MANY MEN ARE WITH YOU ? >
< I'M NOT SURE -- MORE ARE ON THE WAY, BUT WE SHOULD HAVE SOMEWHERE BETWEEN 200 AND 300 MEN. HOW MANY DO THEY HAVE ? >
< IT LOOKS LIKE ABOUT 100. >
< I'M THINKING WE SHOULD SEND OUT TWO MEN WITH A WHITE FLAG TO TALK TO THE MOUNTIES. THAT'LL PROVIDE A DISTRACTION TO GIVE US TIME TO MOVE ALONG BEHIND THIS LINE OF TREES. WE'LL SURROUND THEM. >
MEANWHILE, THE MOUNTIES PREPARE TO FIGHT.
DRAW THE SLEIGHS INTO A CIRCLE !

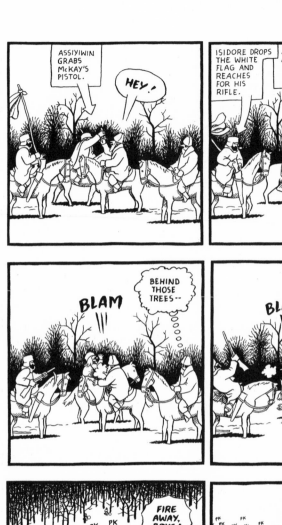

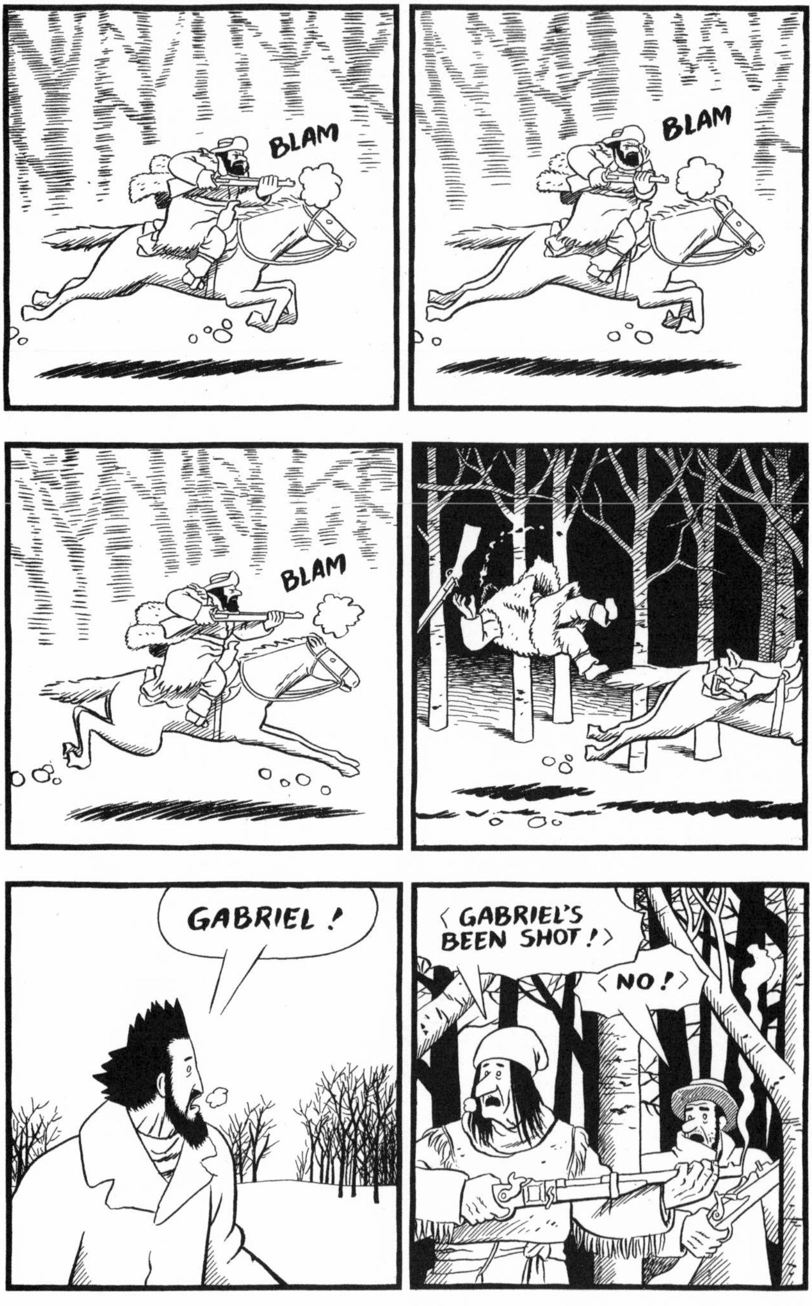
BLAM
BLAM
BLAM
GABRIEL !
⟨ GABRIEL'S BEEN SHOT ! ⟩
⟨ NO ! ⟩

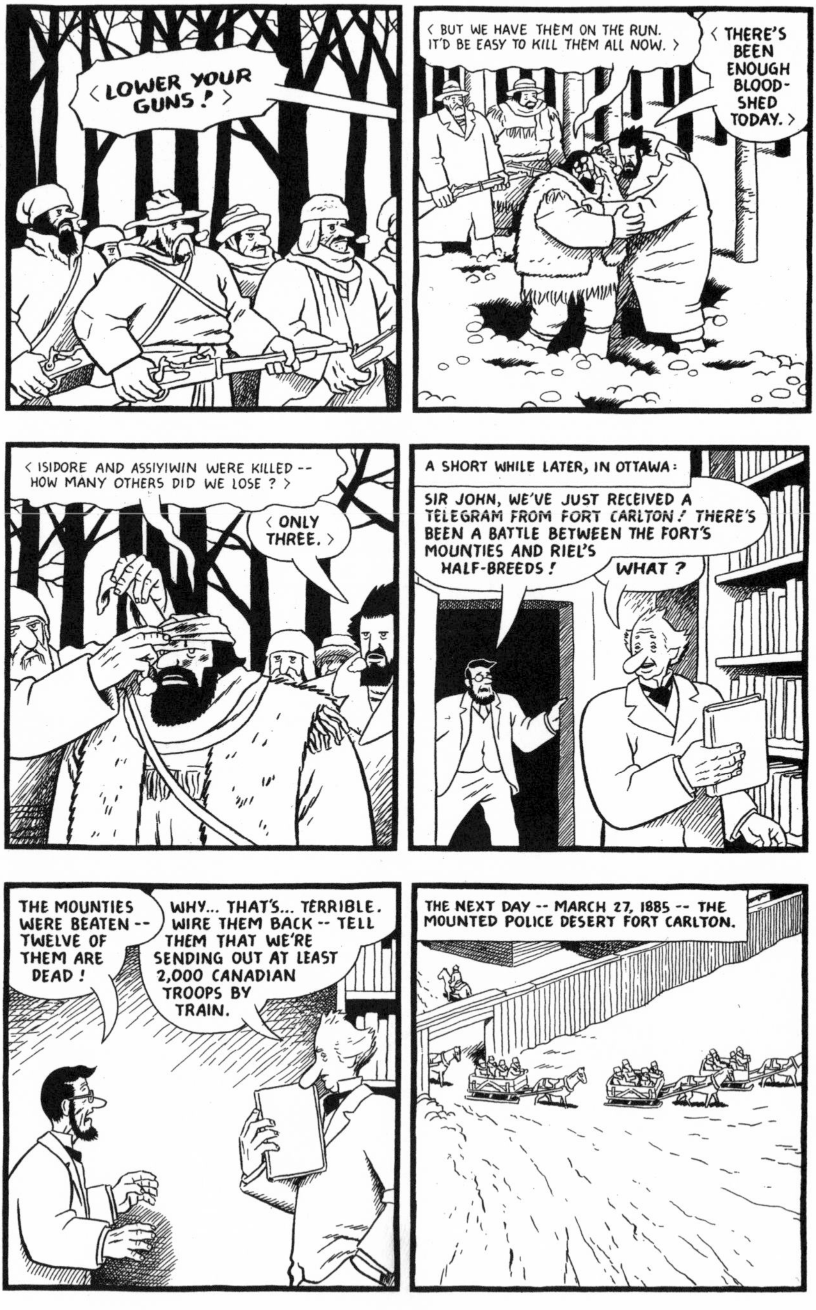
< LOWER YOUR GUNS ! >
< BUT WE HAVE THEM ON THE RUN. IT'D BE EASY TO KILL THEM ALL NOW. >
< THERE'S BEEN ENOUGH BLOOD-SHED TODAY. >
< ISIDORE AND ASSIYIWIN WERE KILLED -- HOW MANY OTHERS DID WE LOSE ? >
< ONLY THREE. >
A SHORT WHILE LATER, IN OTTAWA:
SIR JOHN, WE'VE JUST RECEIVED A TELEGRAM FROM FORT CARLTON! THERE'S BEEN A BATTLE BETWEEN THE FORT'S MOUNTIES AND RIEL'S HALF-BREEDS !
WHAT ?
THE MOUNTIES WERE BEATEN -- TWELVE OF THEM ARE DEAD !
WHY... THAT'S... TERRIBLE. WIRE THEM BACK -- TELL THEM THAT WE'RE SENDING OUT AT LEAST 2,000 CANADIAN TROOPS BY TRAIN.
THE NEXT DAY -- MARCH 27, 1885 -- THE MOUNTED POLICE DESERT FORT CARLTON.

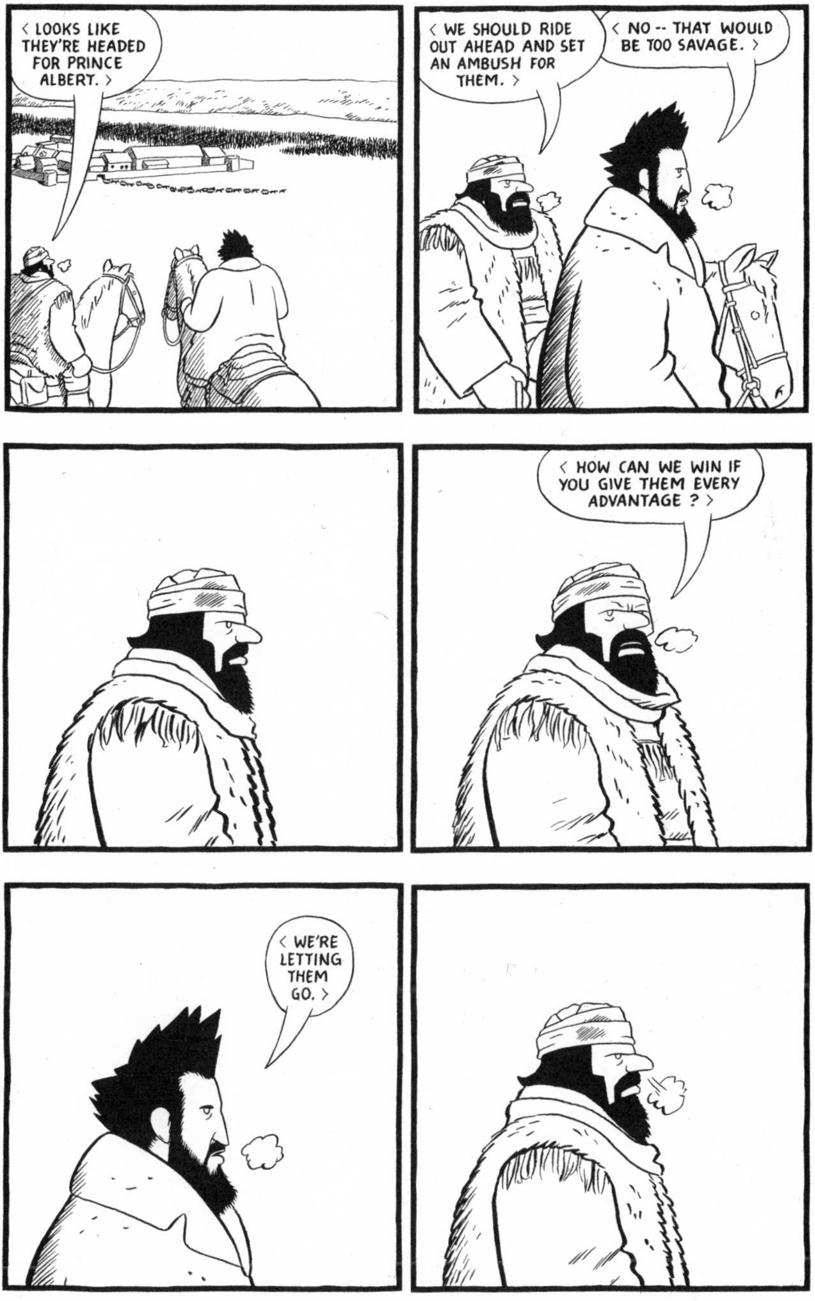
< LOOKS LIKE THEY'RE HEADED FOR PRINCE ALBERT. >
< WE SHOULD RIDE OUT AHEAD AND SET AN AMBUSH FOR THEM. >
< NO -- THAT WOULD BE TOO SAVAGE. >
< HOW CAN WE WIN IF YOU GIVE THEM EVERY ADVANTAGE ? >
< WE'RE LETTING THEM GO. >

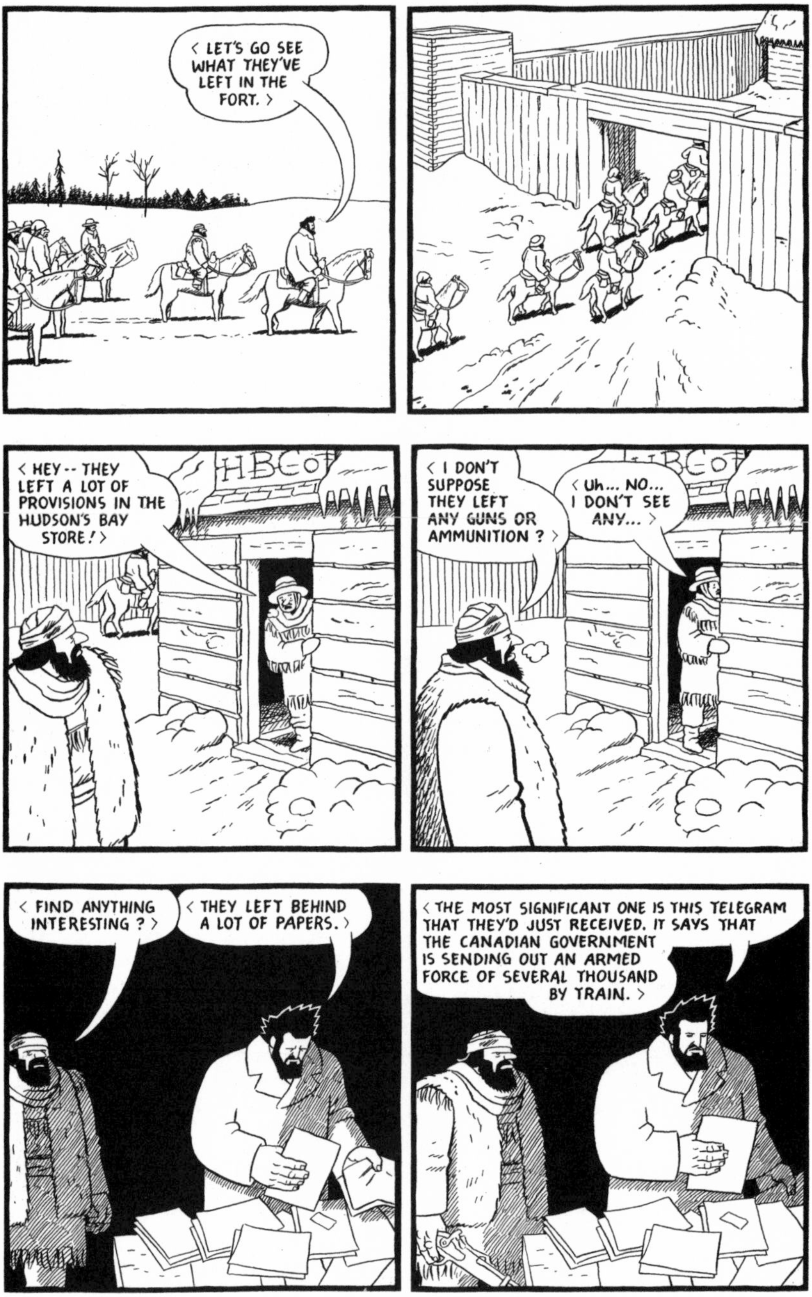

< LET'S GO SEE WHAT THEY'VE LEFT IN THE FORT. >
< HEY -- THEY LEFT A LOT OF PROVISIONS IN THE HUDSON'S BAY STORE! >
HBCo
< I DON'T SUPPOSE THEY LEFT ANY GUNS OR AMMUNITION ? >
< Uh... NO... I DON'T SEE ANY... >
< FIND ANYTHING INTERESTING ? >
< THEY LEFT BEHIND A LOT OF PAPERS. >
< THE MOST SIGNIFICANT ONE IS THIS TELEGRAM THAT THEY'D JUST RECEIVED. IT SAYS THAT THE CANADIAN GOVERNMENT IS SENDING OUT AN ARMED FORCE OF SEVERAL THOUSAND BY TRAIN. >

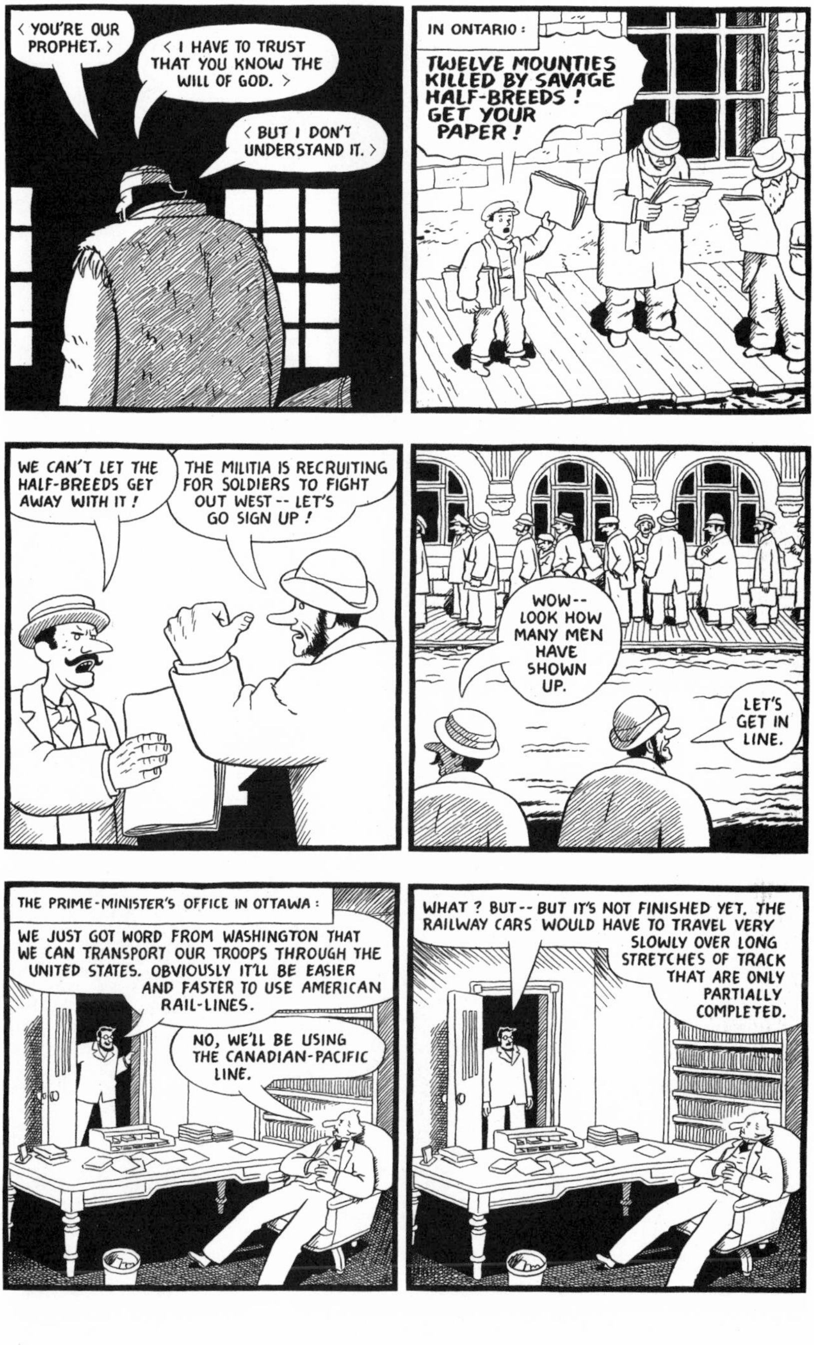
< YOU'RE OUR PROPHET. >
< I HAVE TO TRUST THAT YOU KNOW THE WILL OF GOD. >
< BUT I DON'T UNDERSTAND IT. >
IN ONTARIO :
TWELVE MOUNTIES KILLED BY SAVAGE HALF-BREEDS ! GET YOUR PAPER !
WE CAN'T LET THE HALF-BREEDS GET AWAY WITH IT !
THE MILITIA IS RECRUITING FOR SOLDIERS TO FIGHT OUT WEST -- LET'S GO SIGN UP !
WOW-- LOOK HOW MANY MEN HAVE SHOWN UP.
LET'S GET IN LINE.
THE PRIME-MINISTER'S OFFICE IN OTTAWA :
WE JUST GOT WORD FROM WASHINGTON THAT WE CAN TRANSPORT OUR TROOPS THROUGH THE UNITED STATES. OBVIOUSLY IT'LL BE EASIER AND FASTER TO USE AMERICAN RAIL-LINES.
NO, WE'LL BE USING THE CANADIAN-PACIFIC LINE.
WHAT ? BUT -- BUT IT'S NOT FINISHED YET. THE RAILWAY CARS WOULD HAVE TO TRAVEL VERY SLOWLY OVER LONG STRETCHES OF TRACK THAT ARE ONLY PARTIALLY COMPLETED.

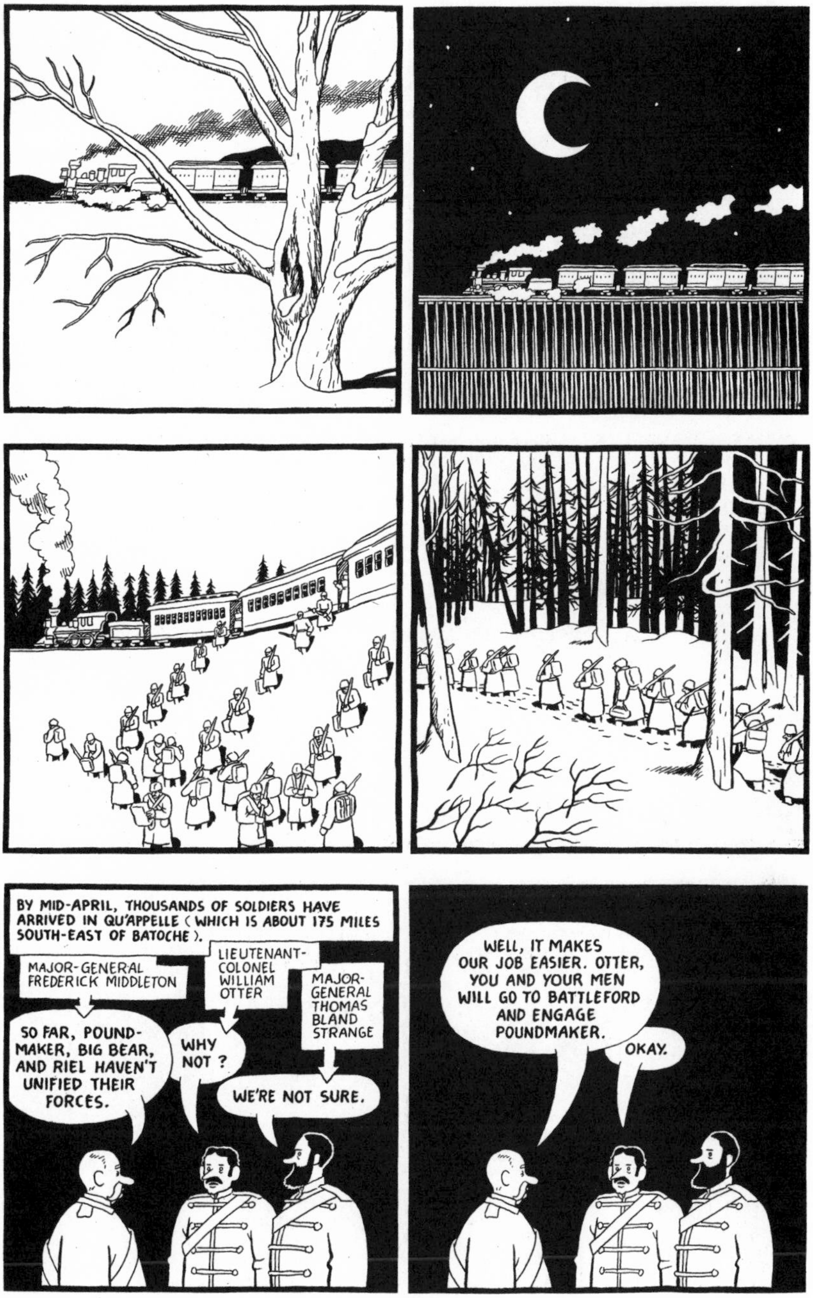

BY MID-APRIL, THOUSANDS OF SOLDIERS HAVE ARRIVED IN QU'APPELLE (WHICH IS ABOUT 175 MILES SOUTH-EAST OF BATOCHE).
MAJOR-GENERAL FREDERICK MIDDLETON
LIEUTENANT-COLONEL WILLIAM OTTER
MAJOR-GENERAL THOMAS BLAND STRANGE
SO FAR, POUND-MAKER, BIG BEAR, AND RIEL HAVEN'T UNIFIED THEIR FORCES.
WHY NOT ?
WE'RE NOT SURE.
WELL, IT MAKES OUR JOB EASIER. OTTER, YOU AND YOUR MEN WILL GO TO BATTLEFORD AND ENGAGE POUNDMAKER.
OKAY.

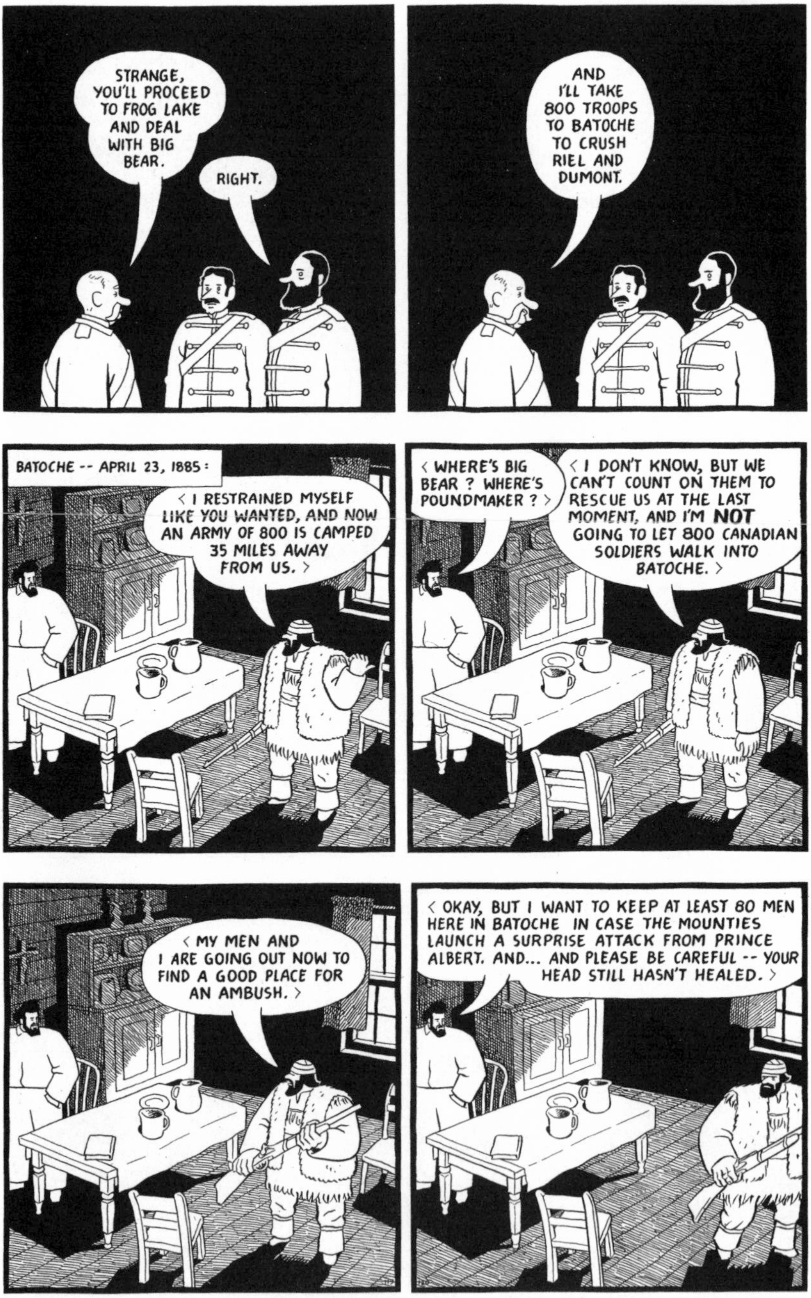
STRANGE, YOU'LL PROCEED TO FROG LAKE AND DEAL WITH BIG BEAR.
RIGHT.
AND I'LL TAKE 800 TROOPS TO BATOCHE TO CRUSH RIEL AND DUMONT.
BATOCHE -- APRIL 23, 1885:
< I RESTRAINED MYSELF LIKE YOU WANTED, AND NOW AN ARMY OF 800 IS CAMPED 35 MILES AWAY FROM US. >
< WHERE'S BIG BEAR ? WHERE'S POUNDMAKER ? >
< I DON'T KNOW, BUT WE CAN'T COUNT ON THEM TO RESCUE US AT THE LAST MOMENT, AND I'M **NOT** GOING TO LET 800 CANADIAN SOLDIERS WALK INTO BATOCHE. >
< MY MEN AND I ARE GOING OUT NOW TO FIND A GOOD PLACE FOR AN AMBUSH. >
< OKAY, BUT I WANT TO KEEP AT LEAST 80 MEN HERE IN BATOCHE IN CASE THE MOUNTIES LAUNCH A SURPRISE ATTACK FROM PRINCE ALBERT. AND... AND PLEASE BE CAREFUL -- YOUR HEAD STILL HASN'T HEALED. >

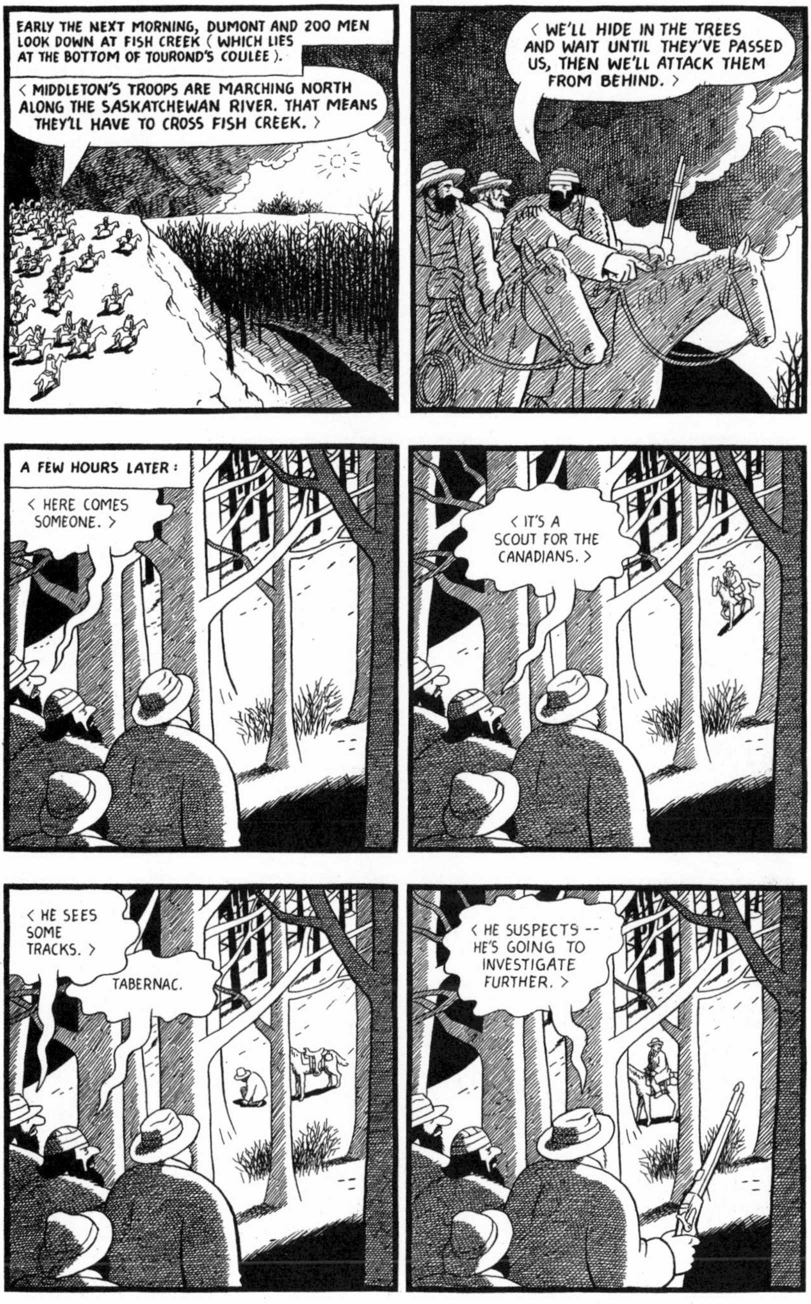
EARLY THE NEXT MORNING, DUMONT AND 200 MEN LOOK DOWN AT FISH CREEK (WHICH LIES AT THE BOTTOM OF TOUROND'S COULEE).
< MIDDLETON'S TROOPS ARE MARCHING NORTH ALONG THE SASKATCHEWAN RIVER. THAT MEANS THEY'LL HAVE TO CROSS FISH CREEK. >
< WE'LL HIDE IN THE TREES AND WAIT UNTIL THEY'VE PASSED US, THEN WE'LL ATTACK THEM FROM BEHIND. >
A FEW HOURS LATER :
< HERE COMES SOMEONE. >
< IT'S A SCOUT FOR THE CANADIANS. >
< HE SEES SOME TRACKS. >
TABERNAC.
< HE SUSPECTS -- HE'S GOING TO INVESTIGATE FURTHER. >

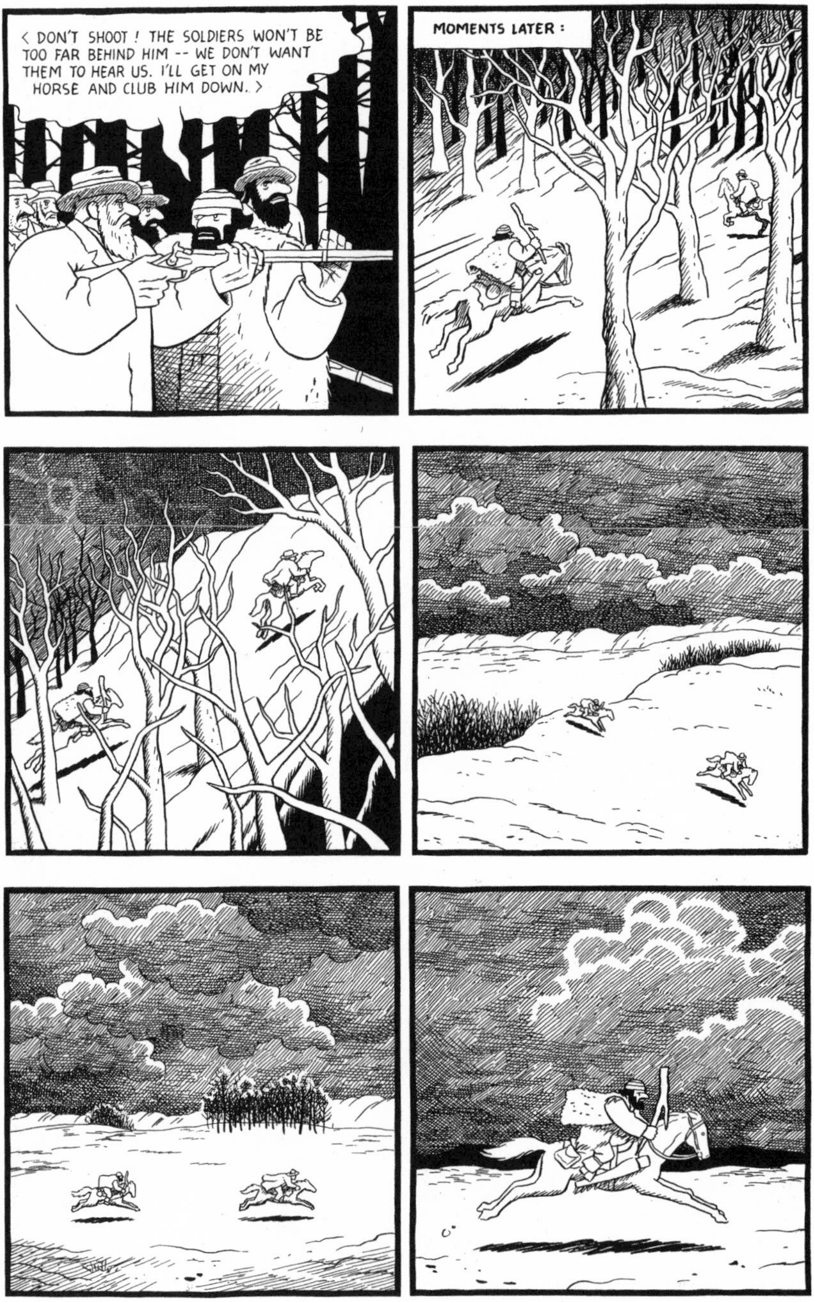
< DON'T SHOOT ! THE SOLDIERS WON'T BE TOO FAR BEHIND HIM -- WE DON'T WANT THEM TO HEAR US. I'LL GET ON MY HORSE AND CLUB HIM DOWN. >
MOMENTS LATER :

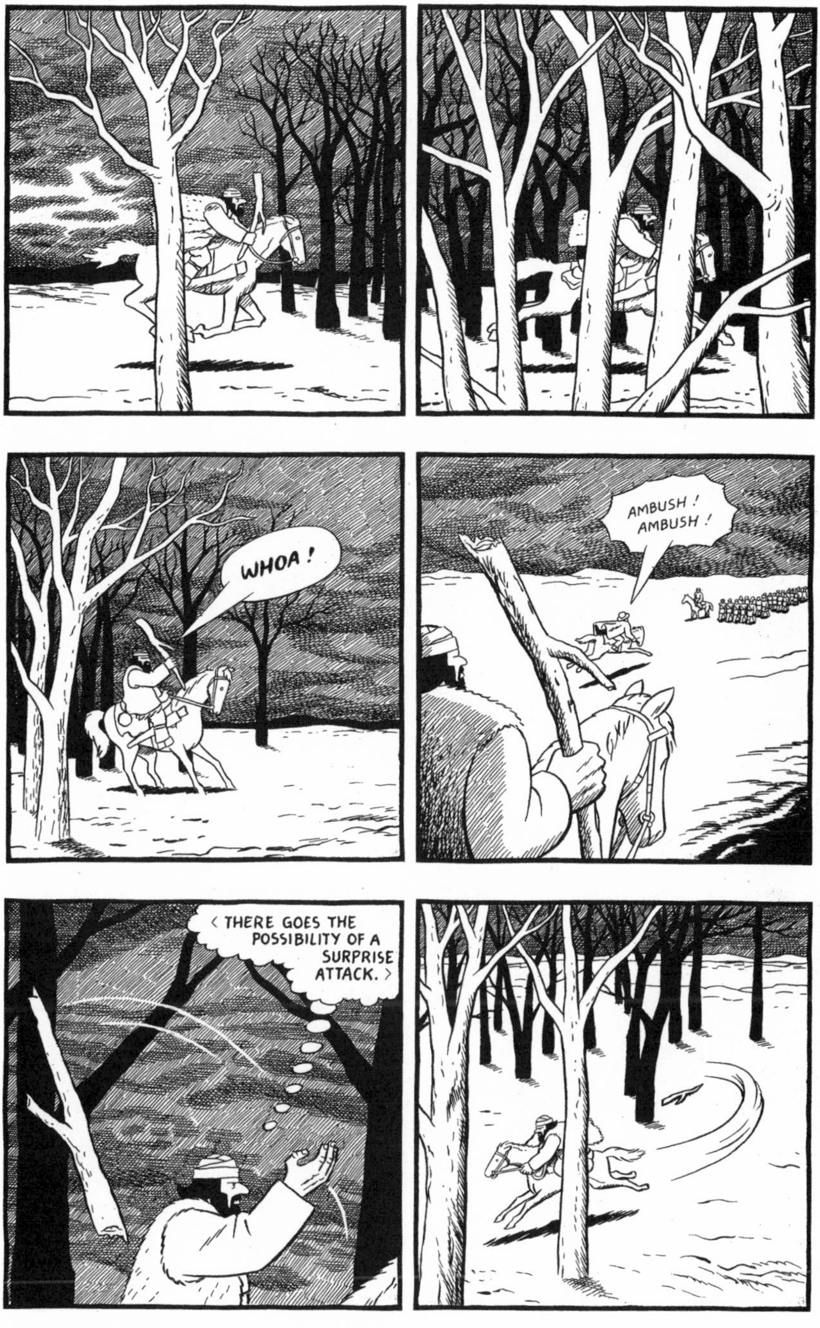
WHOA!
AMBUSH! AMBUSH!
< THERE GOES THE POSSIBILITY OF A SURPRISE ATTACK. >

BLAM BLAM

≶ AK ≶ ≶ UGH ≶

PK PK PK PK PK PK PK

‹ THAT CANNON IS WORTHLESS IN THIS SITUATION. ›

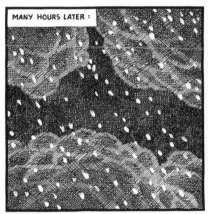

MANY HOURS LATER :

PK PK PK PK PK PK PK

PK PK KRK PK KRK PK PK KRK

‹ WE'RE VERY LOW ON BULLETS, BUT, EVEN IF WE WANTED TO RETREAT, IT WOULD BE DIFFICULT WITH SO MANY OF OUR HORSES DEAD. ›

BLAM

KRK PK PK PK KRK PK KRK PK KRK

‹ WE NEED REINFORCEMENTS. ›

BLAM

‹ I'LL RIDE TO BATOCHE AND GET MORE MEN. ›

178

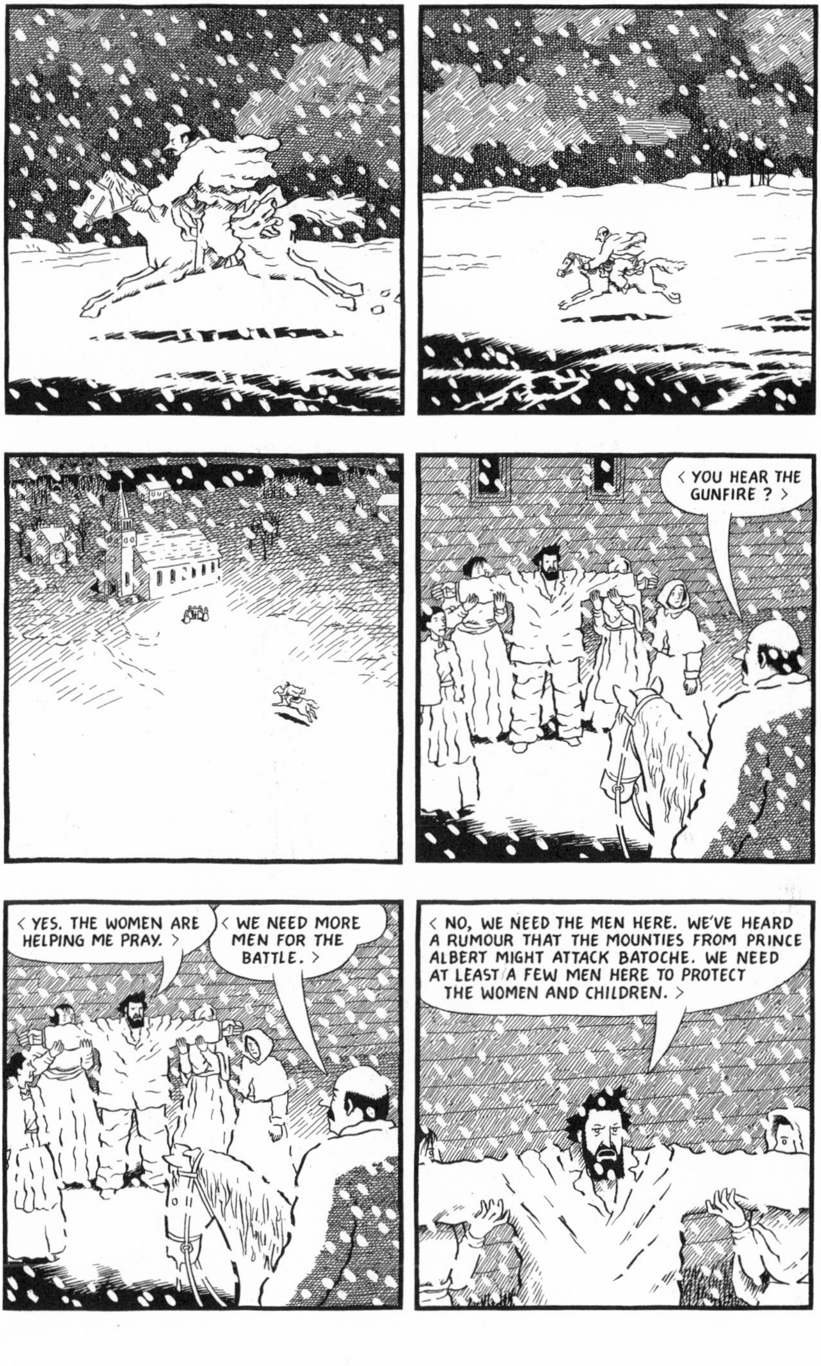
< YOU HEAR THE GUNFIRE ? >
< YES. THE WOMEN ARE HELPING ME PRAY. >
< WE NEED MORE MEN FOR THE BATTLE. >
< NO, WE NEED THE MEN HERE. WE'VE HEARD A RUMOUR THAT THE MOUNTIES FROM PRINCE ALBERT MIGHT ATTACK BATOCHE. WE NEED AT LEAST A FEW MEN HERE TO PROTECT THE WOMEN AND CHILDREN. >

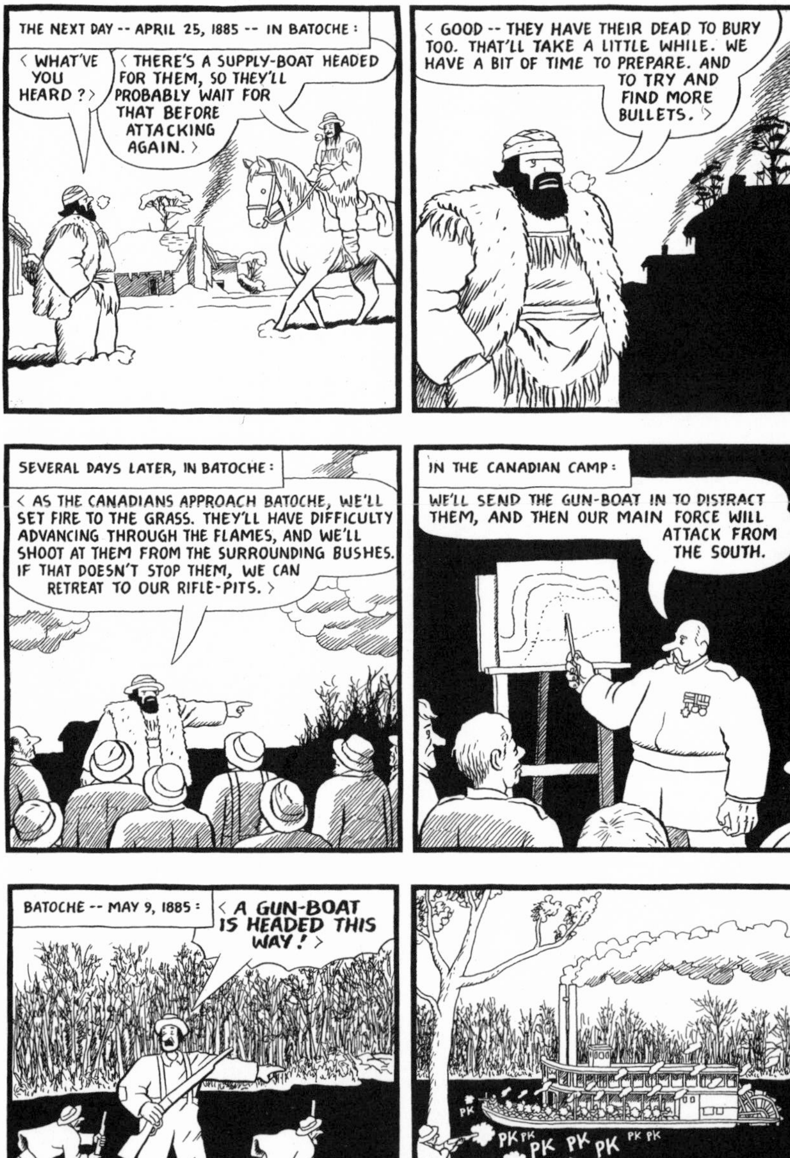
THE NEXT DAY -- APRIL 25, 1885 -- IN BATOCHE :
< WHAT'VE YOU HEARD ? >
< THERE'S A SUPPLY-BOAT HEADED FOR THEM, SO THEY'LL PROBABLY WAIT FOR THAT BEFORE ATTACKING AGAIN. >
< GOOD -- THEY HAVE THEIR DEAD TO BURY TOO. THAT'LL TAKE A LITTLE WHILE. WE HAVE A BIT OF TIME TO PREPARE. AND TO TRY AND FIND MORE BULLETS. >
SEVERAL DAYS LATER, IN BATOCHE :
< AS THE CANADIANS APPROACH BATOCHE, WE'LL SET FIRE TO THE GRASS. THEY'LL HAVE DIFFICULTY ADVANCING THROUGH THE FLAMES, AND WE'LL SHOOT AT THEM FROM THE SURROUNDING BUSHES. IF THAT DOESN'T STOP THEM, WE CAN RETREAT TO OUR RIFLE-PITS. >
IN THE CANADIAN CAMP :
WE'LL SEND THE GUN-BOAT IN TO DISTRACT THEM, AND THEN OUR MAIN FORCE WILL ATTACK FROM THE SOUTH.
BATOCHE -- MAY 9, 1885 :
< A GUN-BOAT IS HEADED THIS WAY ! >
PK
PK PK PK PK PK PK PK

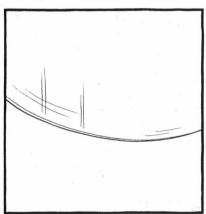

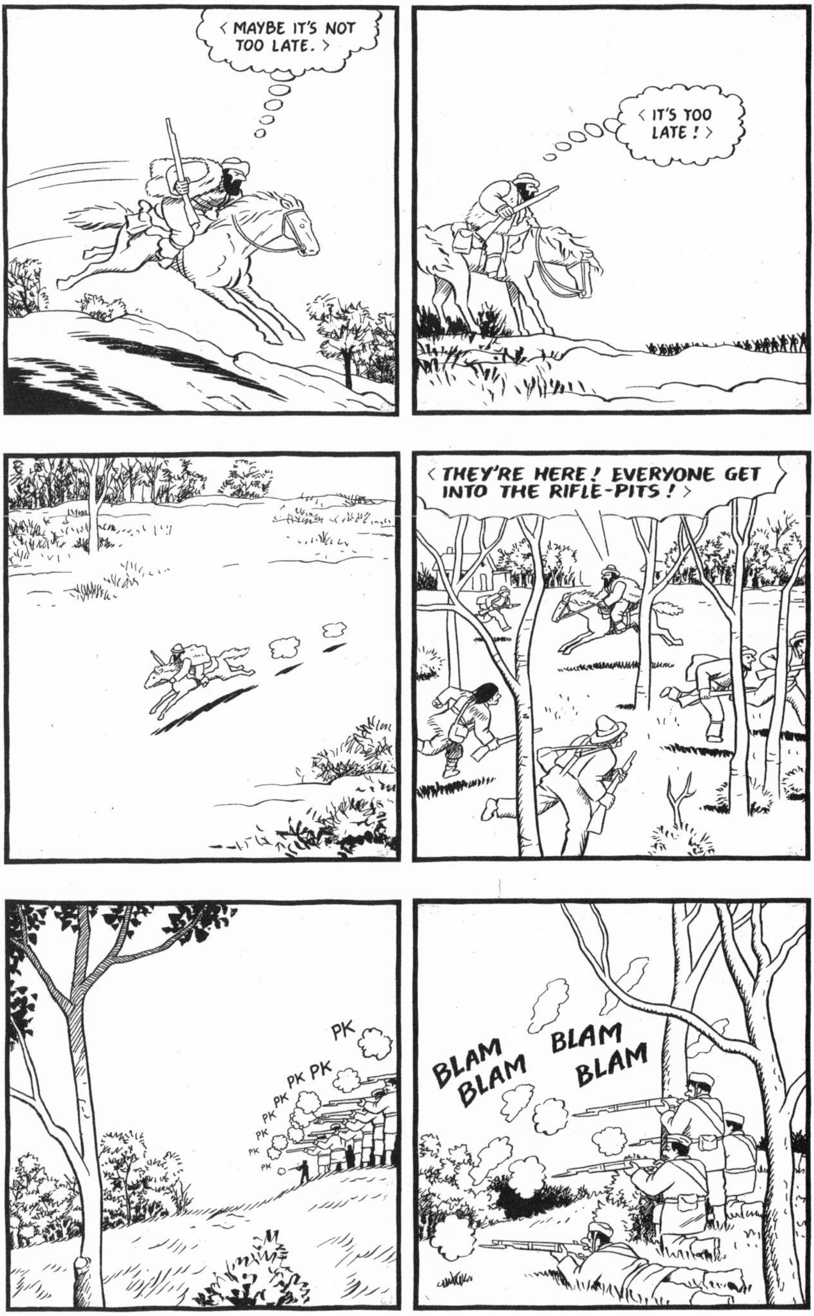
< MAYBE IT'S NOT TOO LATE. >
< IT'S TOO LATE ! >
< THEY'RE HERE! EVERYONE GET INTO THE RIFLE-PITS ! >
PK
PK PK
PK
PK
PK
PK
PK
PK
BLAM
BLAM
BLAM
BLAM

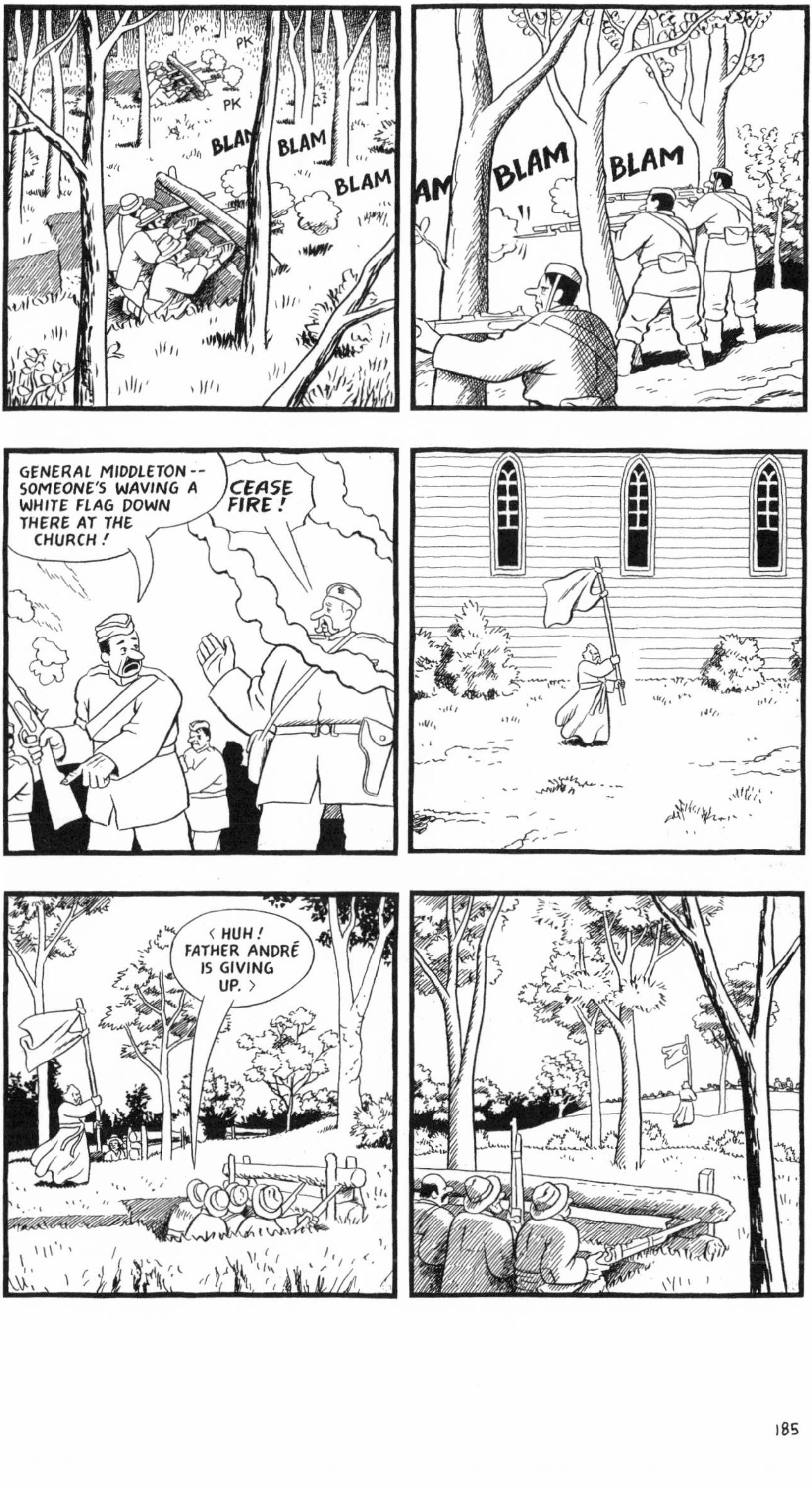
PK
PK
PK
BLA
BLAM
BLAM
AM
BLAM
BLAM
GENERAL MIDDLETON -- SOMEONE'S WAVING A WHITE FLAG DOWN THERE AT THE CHURCH!
CEASE FIRE!
< HUH! FATHER ANDRÉ IS GIVING UP. >

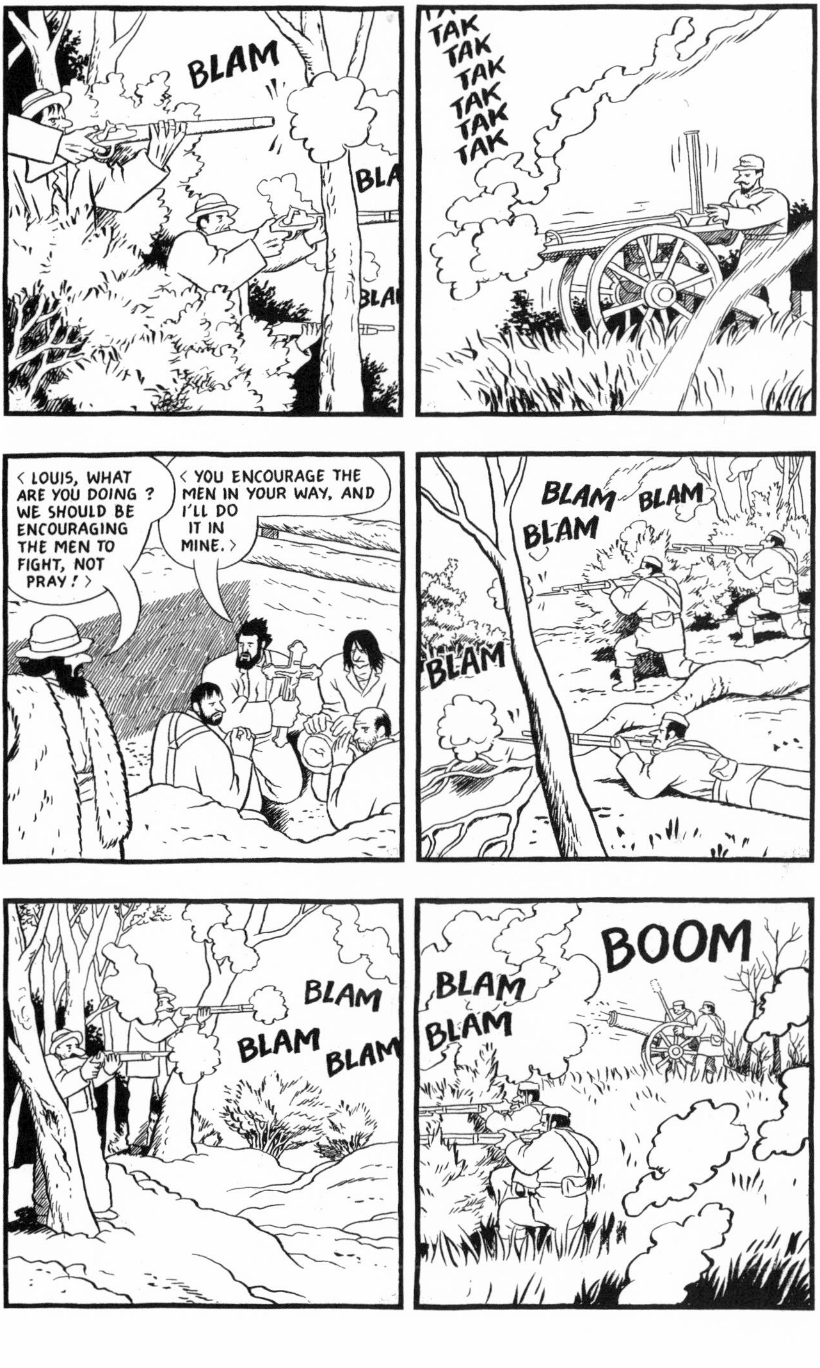
BLAM
BLA
BLA
TAK
TAK
TAK
TAK
TAK
TAK
< LOUIS, WHAT ARE YOU DOING ? WE SHOULD BE ENCOURAGING THE MEN TO FIGHT, NOT PRAY ! >
< YOU ENCOURAGE THE MEN IN YOUR WAY, AND I'LL DO IT IN MINE. >
BLAM
BLAM
BLAM
BLAM
BLAM
BLAM
BLAM
BOOM
BLAM
BLAM

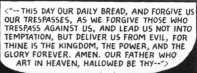

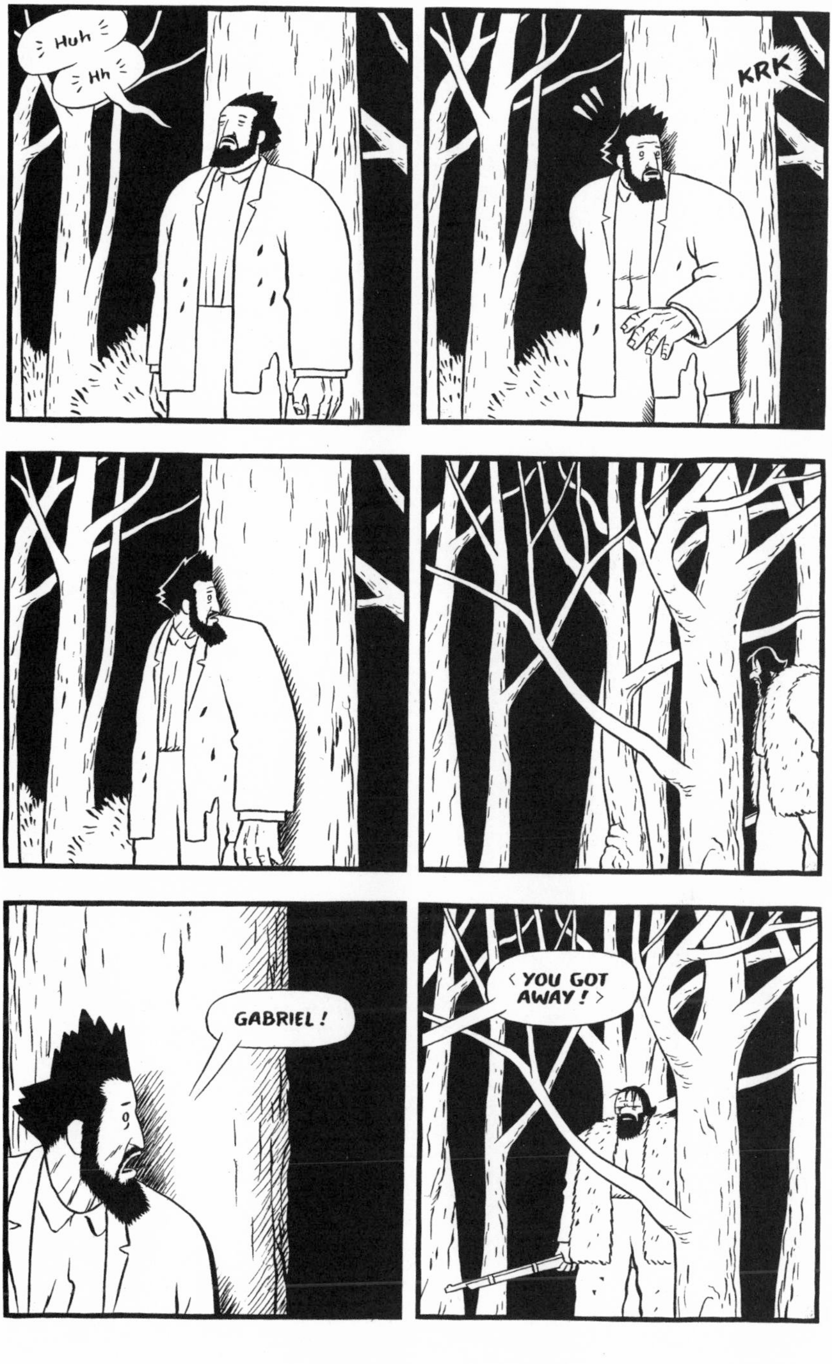
Huh
Hh
KRK
GABRIEL!
< YOU GOT AWAY! >

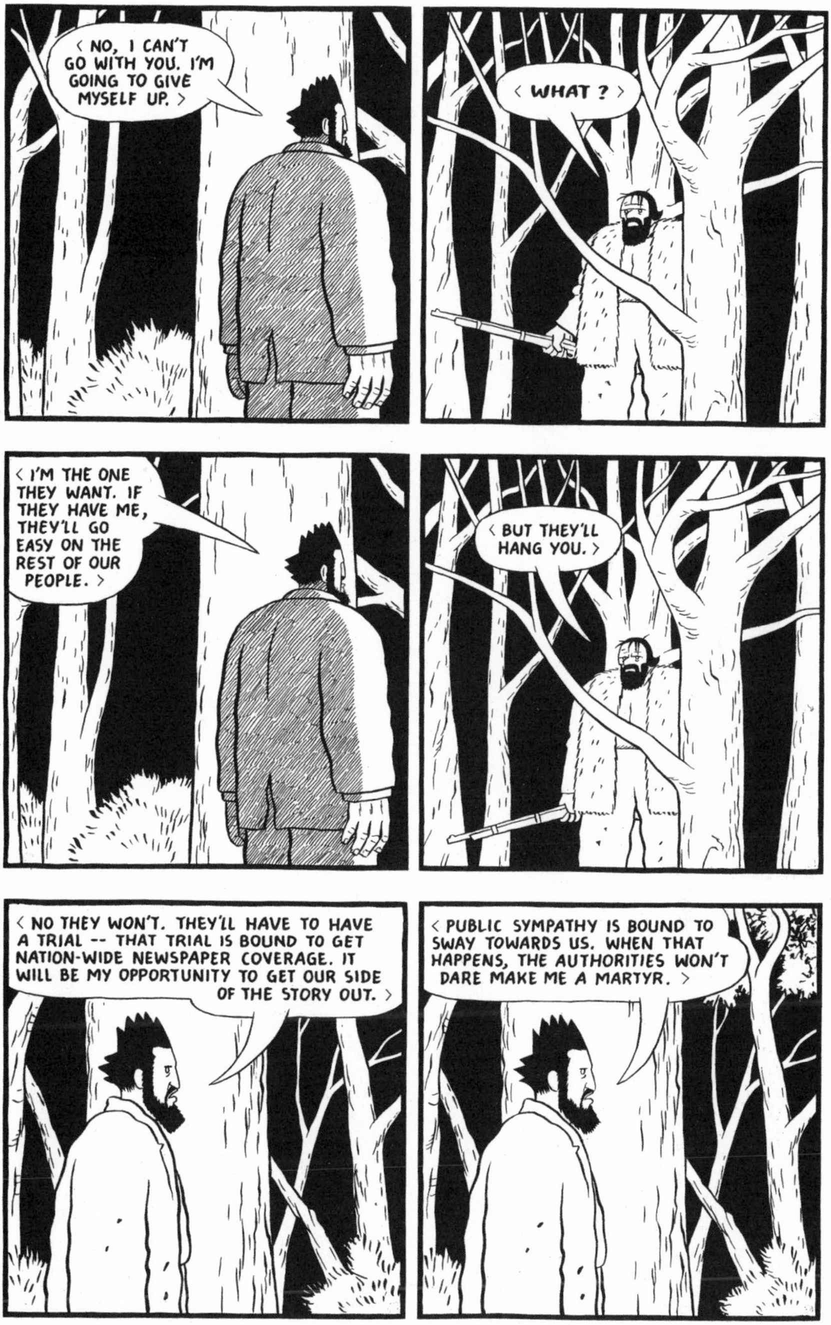
< NO, I CAN'T GO WITH YOU. I'M GOING TO GIVE MYSELF UP. >
< WHAT ? >
< I'M THE ONE THEY WANT. IF THEY HAVE ME, THEY'LL GO EASY ON THE REST OF OUR PEOPLE. >
< BUT THEY'LL HANG YOU. >
< NO THEY WON'T. THEY'LL HAVE TO HAVE A TRIAL -- THAT TRIAL IS BOUND TO GET NATION-WIDE NEWSPAPER COVERAGE. IT WILL BE MY OPPORTUNITY TO GET OUR SIDE OF THE STORY OUT. >
< PUBLIC SYMPATHY IS BOUND TO SWAY TOWARDS US. WHEN THAT HAPPENS, THE AUTHORITIES WON'T DARE MAKE ME A MARTYR. >

PART FOUR

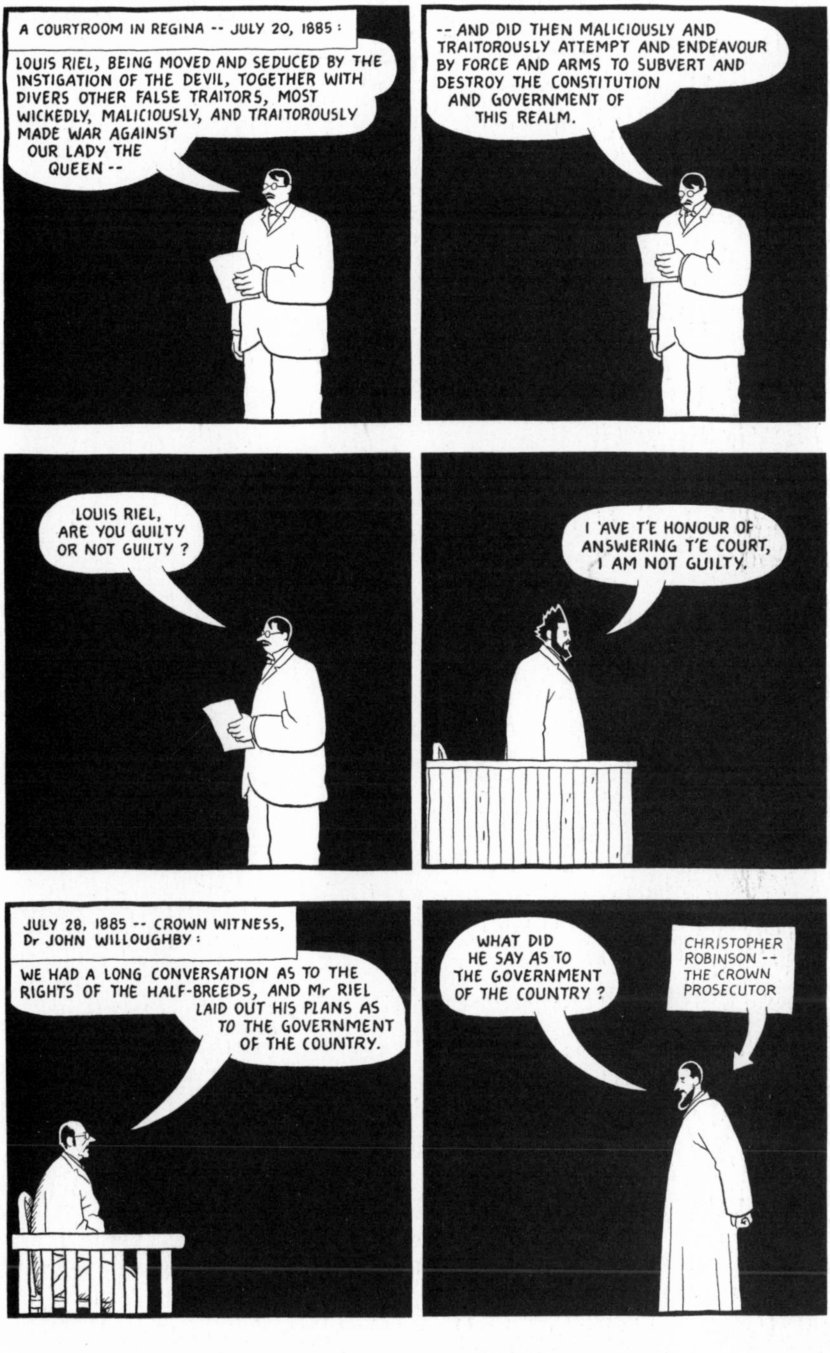
A COURTROOM IN REGINA -- JULY 20, 1885 :
LOUIS RIEL, BEING MOVED AND SEDUCED BY THE INSTIGATION OF THE DEVIL, TOGETHER WITH DIVERS OTHER FALSE TRAITORS, MOST WICKEDLY, MALICIOUSLY, AND TRAITOROUSLY MADE WAR AGAINST OUR LADY THE QUEEN --
-- AND DID THEN MALICIOUSLY AND TRAITOROUSLY ATTEMPT AND ENDEAVOUR BY FORCE AND ARMS TO SUBVERT AND DESTROY THE CONSTITUTION AND GOVERNMENT OF THIS REALM.
LOUIS RIEL, ARE YOU GUILTY OR NOT GUILTY ?
I 'AVE T'E HONOUR OF ANSWERING T'E COURT, I AM NOT GUILTY.
JULY 28, 1885 -- CROWN WITNESS, Dr JOHN WILLOUGHBY :
WE HAD A LONG CONVERSATION AS TO THE RIGHTS OF THE HALF-BREEDS, AND Mr RIEL LAID OUT HIS PLANS AS TO THE GOVERNMENT OF THE COUNTRY.
WHAT DID HE SAY AS TO THE GOVERNMENT OF THE COUNTRY ?
CHRISTOPHER ROBINSON -- THE CROWN PROSECUTOR

THEY WERE TO HAVE A NEW GOVERNMENT IN THE NORTH-WEST. IT WAS TO BE COMPOSED OF GOD-FEARING MEN -- THEY WOULD HAVE NO SUCH PARLIAMENT AS THE HOUSE AT OTTAWA.

DID RIEL'S PLAN FOR THE CONQUEST OF THE NORTH-WEST STRIKE YOU AS BEING A VERY RATIONAL PROPOSITION?

FRANÇOIS-XAVIER LEMIEUX -- RIEL'S LAWYER

NO, IT DID NOT.

CROWN WITNESS, THOMAS McKAY:

RIEL BECAME VERY EXCITED AND GOT UP AND SAID, "YOU DON'T KNOW WHAT WE'RE AFTER -- IT IS BLOOD, BLOOD -- WE WANT BLOOD!"

"THIS IS A WAR OF EXTERMINATION -- EVERY-BODY THAT IS AGAINST US IS TO BE DRIVEN OUT OF THE COUNTRY! THERE ARE TWO CURSES IN THE COUNTRY -- THE GOVERNMENT AND THE HUDSON'S BAY COMPANY!"

WAS HE IN A VERY EXCITED STATE OF MIND WHEN HE TALKED OF BLOOD?

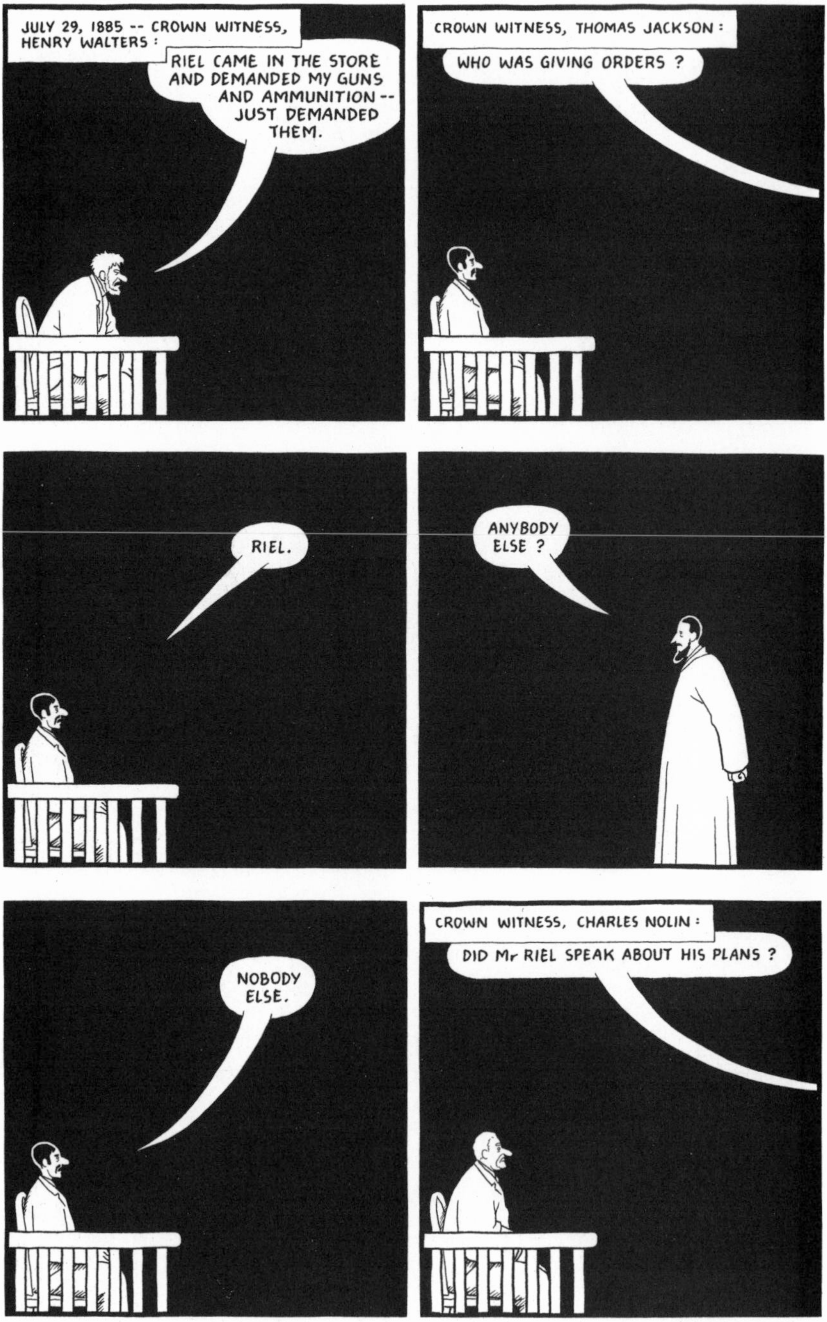
JULY 29, 1885 -- CROWN WITNESS, HENRY WALTERS :
RIEL CAME IN THE STORE AND DEMANDED MY GUNS AND AMMUNITION -- JUST DEMANDED THEM.
CROWN WITNESS, THOMAS JACKSON :
WHO WAS GIVING ORDERS ?
RIEL.
ANYBODY ELSE ?
NOBODY ELSE.
CROWN WITNESS, CHARLES NOLIN :
DID Mr RIEL SPEAK ABOUT HIS PLANS ?

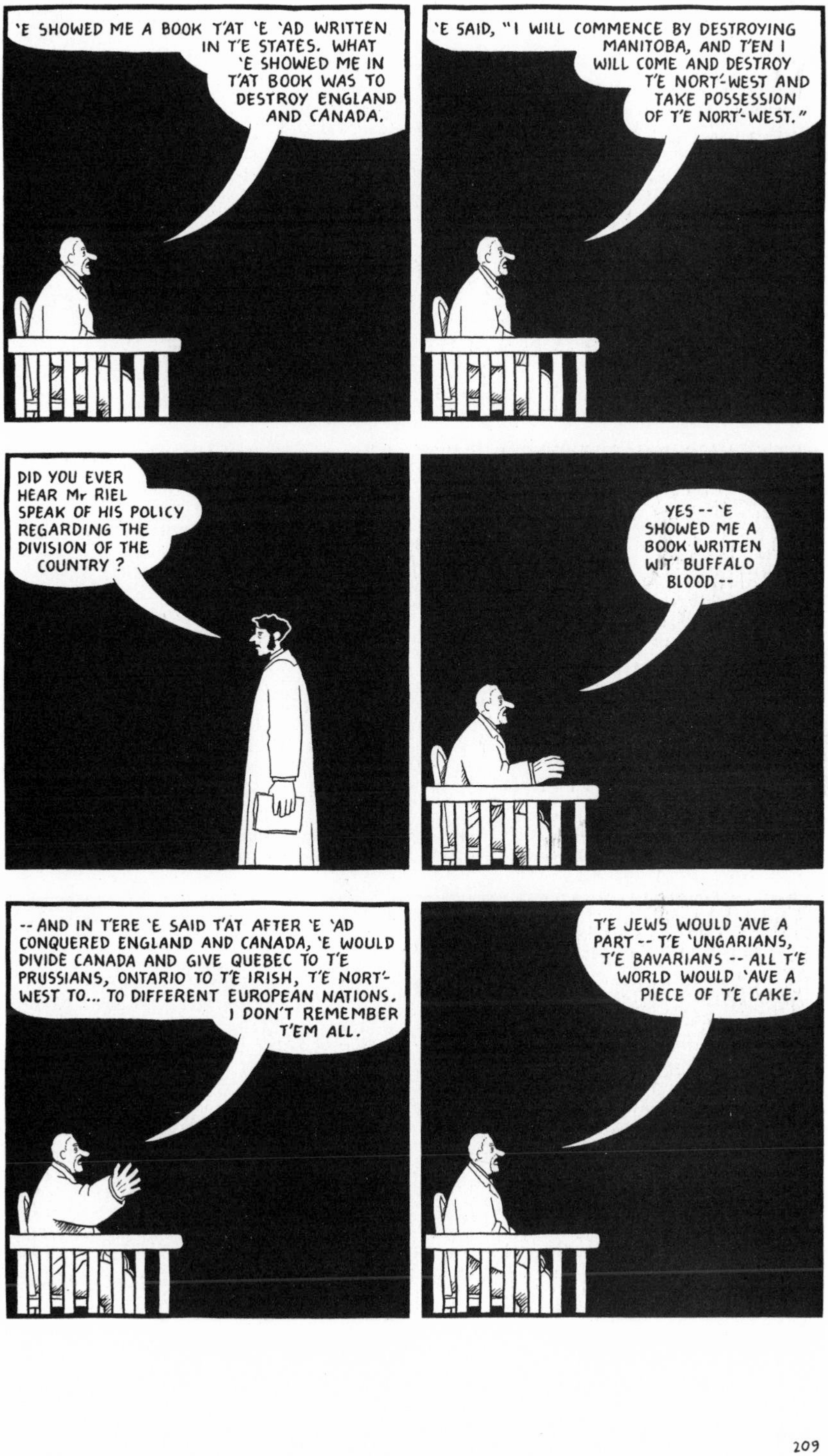
'E SHOWED ME A BOOK T'AT 'E 'AD WRITTEN IN T'E STATES. WHAT 'E SHOWED ME IN T'AT BOOK WAS TO DESTROY ENGLAND AND CANADA.
'E SAID, "I WILL COMMENCE BY DESTROYING MANITOBA, AND T'EN I WILL COME AND DESTROY T'E NORT'-WEST AND TAKE POSSESSION OF T'E NORT'-WEST."
DID YOU EVER HEAR Mr RIEL SPEAK OF HIS POLICY REGARDING THE DIVISION OF THE COUNTRY ?
YES -- 'E SHOWED ME A BOOK WRITTEN WIT' BUFFALO BLOOD --
-- AND IN T'ERE 'E SAID T'AT AFTER 'E 'AD CONQUERED ENGLAND AND CANADA, 'E WOULD DIVIDE CANADA AND GIVE QUEBEC TO T'E PRUSSIANS, ONTARIO TO T'E IRISH, T'E NORT'-WEST TO... TO DIFFERENT EUROPEAN NATIONS. I DON'T REMEMBER T'EM ALL.
T'E JEWS WOULD 'AVE A PART -- T'E 'UNGARIANS, T'E BAVARIANS -- ALL T'E WORLD WOULD 'AVE A PIECE OF T'E CAKE.

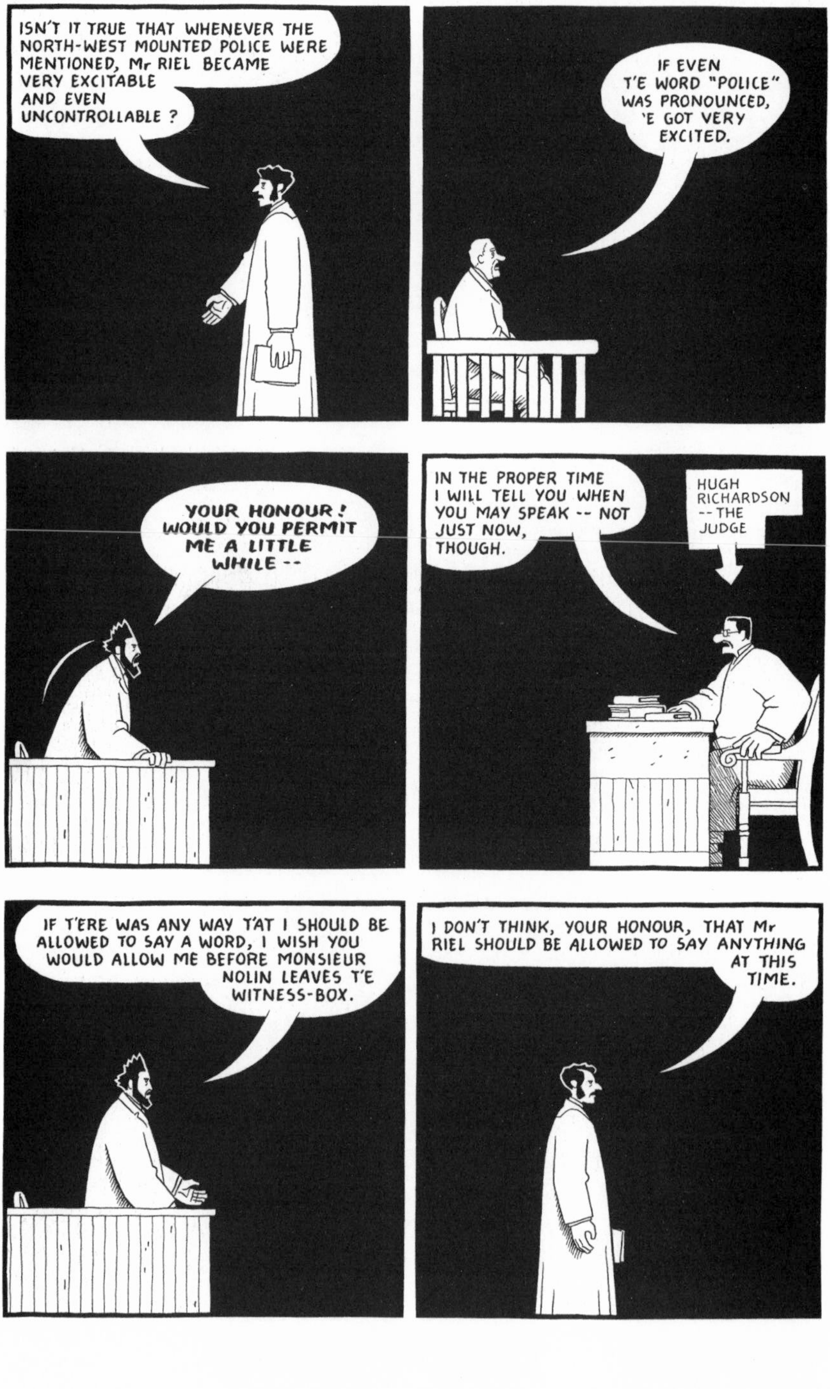
ISN'T IT TRUE THAT WHENEVER THE NORTH-WEST MOUNTED POLICE WERE MENTIONED, Mr RIEL BECAME VERY EXCITABLE AND EVEN UNCONTROLLABLE ?
IF EVEN T'E WORD "POLICE" WAS PRONOUNCED, 'E GOT VERY EXCITED.
YOUR HONOUR! WOULD YOU PERMIT ME A LITTLE WHILE --
IN THE PROPER TIME I WILL TELL YOU WHEN YOU MAY SPEAK -- NOT JUST NOW, THOUGH.
HUGH RICHARDSON -- THE JUDGE
IF T'ERE WAS ANY WAY T'AT I SHOULD BE ALLOWED TO SAY A WORD, I WISH YOU WOULD ALLOW ME BEFORE MONSIEUR NOLIN LEAVES T'E WITNESS-BOX.
I DON'T THINK, YOUR HONOUR, THAT Mr RIEL SHOULD BE ALLOWED TO SAY ANYTHING AT THIS TIME.

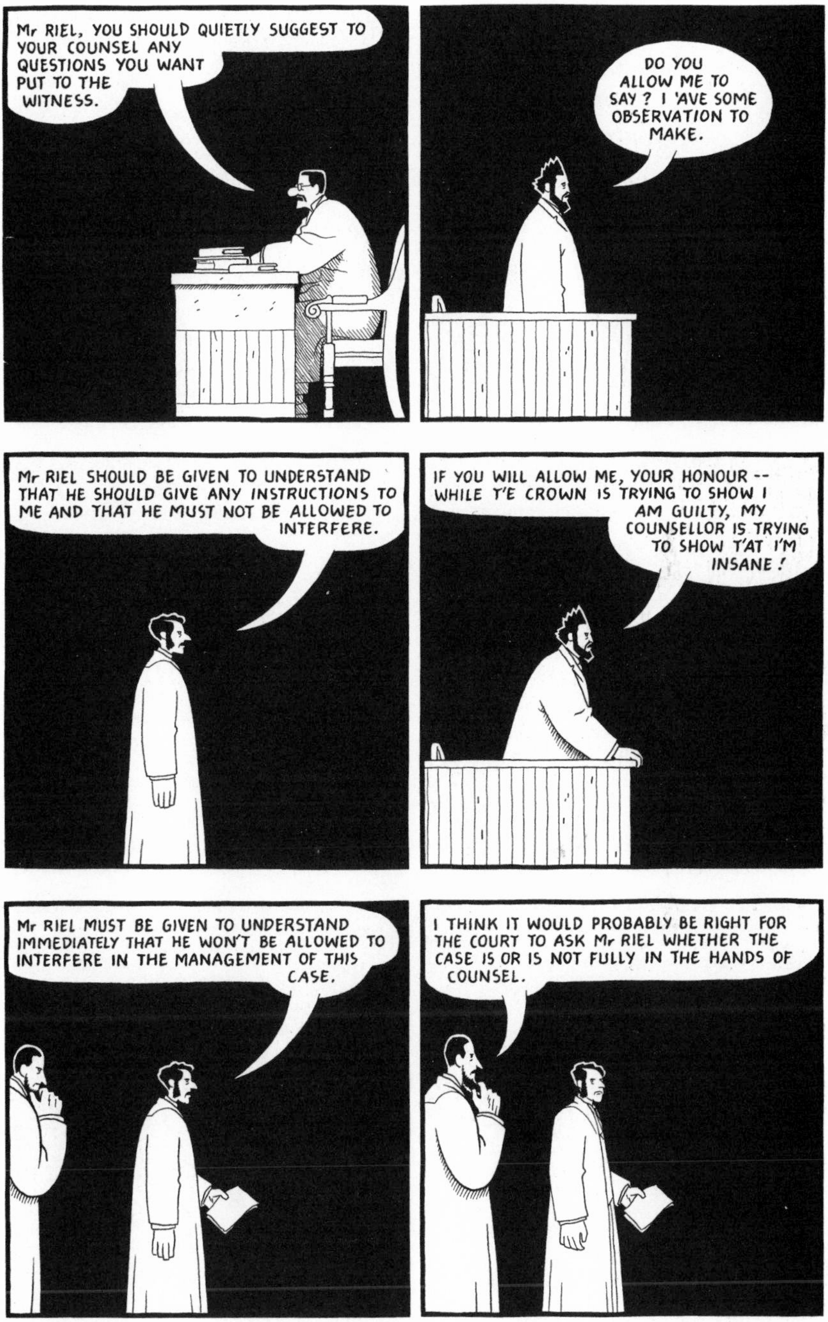
Mr RIEL, YOU SHOULD QUIETLY SUGGEST TO YOUR COUNSEL ANY QUESTIONS YOU WANT PUT TO THE WITNESS.
DO YOU ALLOW ME TO SAY ? I 'AVE SOME OBSERVATION TO MAKE.
Mr RIEL SHOULD BE GIVEN TO UNDERSTAND THAT HE SHOULD GIVE ANY INSTRUCTIONS TO ME AND THAT HE MUST NOT BE ALLOWED TO INTERFERE.
IF YOU WILL ALLOW ME, YOUR HONOUR -- WHILE T'E CROWN IS TRYING TO SHOW I AM GUILTY, MY COUNSELLOR IS TRYING TO SHOW T'AT I'M INSANE !
Mr RIEL MUST BE GIVEN TO UNDERSTAND IMMEDIATELY THAT HE WON'T BE ALLOWED TO INTERFERE IN THE MANAGEMENT OF THIS CASE.
I THINK IT WOULD PROBABLY BE RIGHT FOR THE COURT TO ASK Mr RIEL WHETHER THE CASE IS OR IS NOT FULLY IN THE HANDS OF COUNSEL.

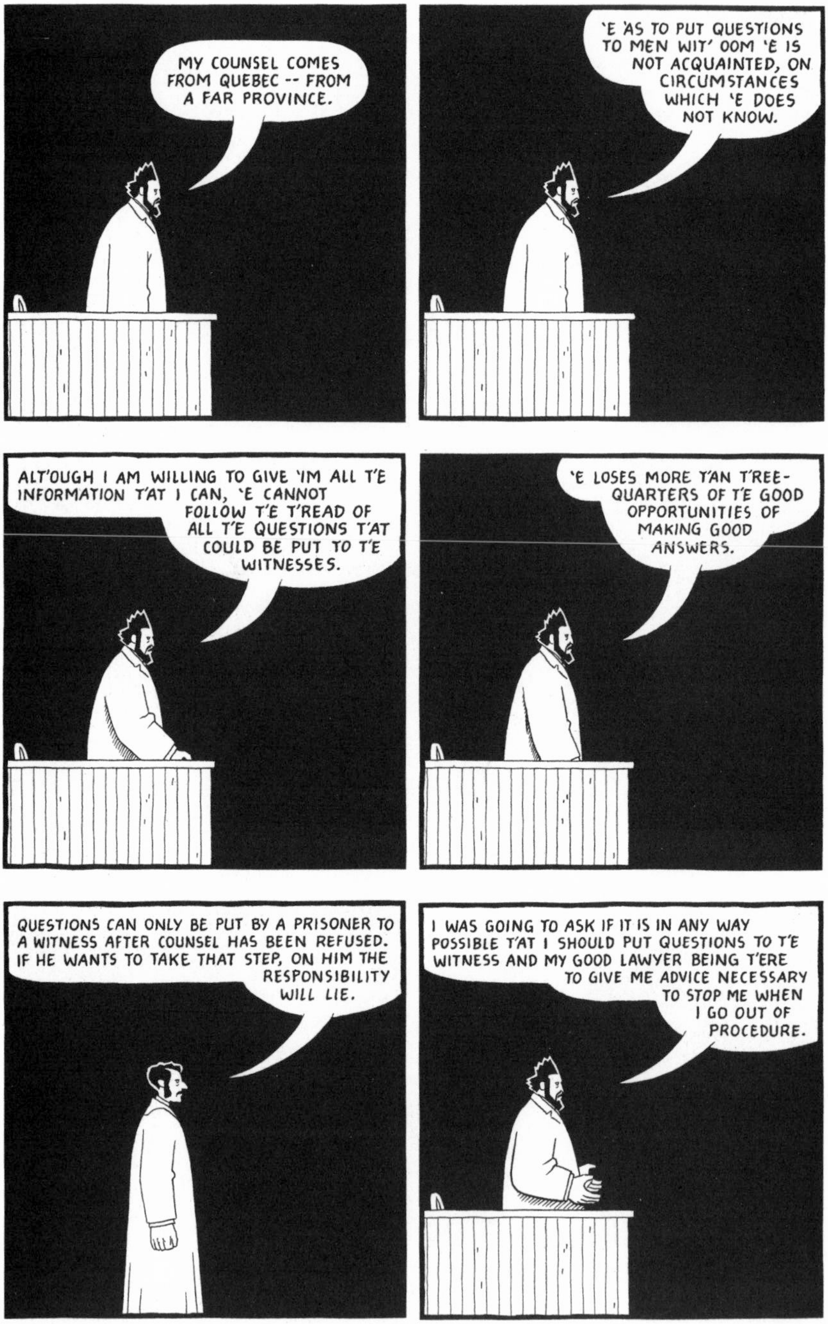
MY COUNSEL COMES FROM QUEBEC -- FROM A FAR PROVINCE.
'E 'AS TO PUT QUESTIONS TO MEN WIT' OOM 'E IS NOT ACQUAINTED, ON CIRCUMSTANCES WHICH 'E DOES NOT KNOW.
ALT'OUGH I AM WILLING TO GIVE 'IM ALL T'E INFORMATION T'AT I CAN, 'E CANNOT FOLLOW T'E T'READ OF ALL T'E QUESTIONS T'AT COULD BE PUT TO T'E WITNESSES.
'E LOSES MORE T'AN T'REE-QUARTERS OF T'E GOOD OPPORTUNITIES OF MAKING GOOD ANSWERS.
QUESTIONS CAN ONLY BE PUT BY A PRISONER TO A WITNESS AFTER COUNSEL HAS BEEN REFUSED. IF HE WANTS TO TAKE THAT STEP, ON HIM THE RESPONSIBILITY WILL LIE.
I WAS GOING TO ASK IF IT IS IN ANY WAY POSSIBLE T'AT I SHOULD PUT QUESTIONS TO T'E WITNESS AND MY GOOD LAWYER BEING T'ERE TO GIVE ME ADVICE NECESSARY TO STOP ME WHEN I GO OUT OF PROCEDURE.

215

T'EY 'AVE NOT RECEIVED T'E PATENTS FOR T'EIR LAND ON T'E--

I MUST OBJECT TO THIS CLASS OF QUESTIONS BEING INTRODUCED!

MY LEARNED FRIEND HAS OPENED A CASE OF TREASON JUSTIFIED BY INSANITY -- HE IS NOW SEEKING TO JUSTIFY ARMED REBELLION!

THESE TWO DEFENCES ARE INCONSISTENT. ALSO, HE IS DESCRIBING DOCUMENTS WHICH HE HAS NOT PRODUCED.

SUPPOSING HE IS GOING TO PRODUCE THESE WRITINGS?

THEY COULD NOT BE EVIDENCE. IF THEY WERE GIVEN IN EVIDENCE, THEN THERE WOULD BE THE QUESTION OF JUSTIFYING THE POLICY OF THE GOVERNMENT.

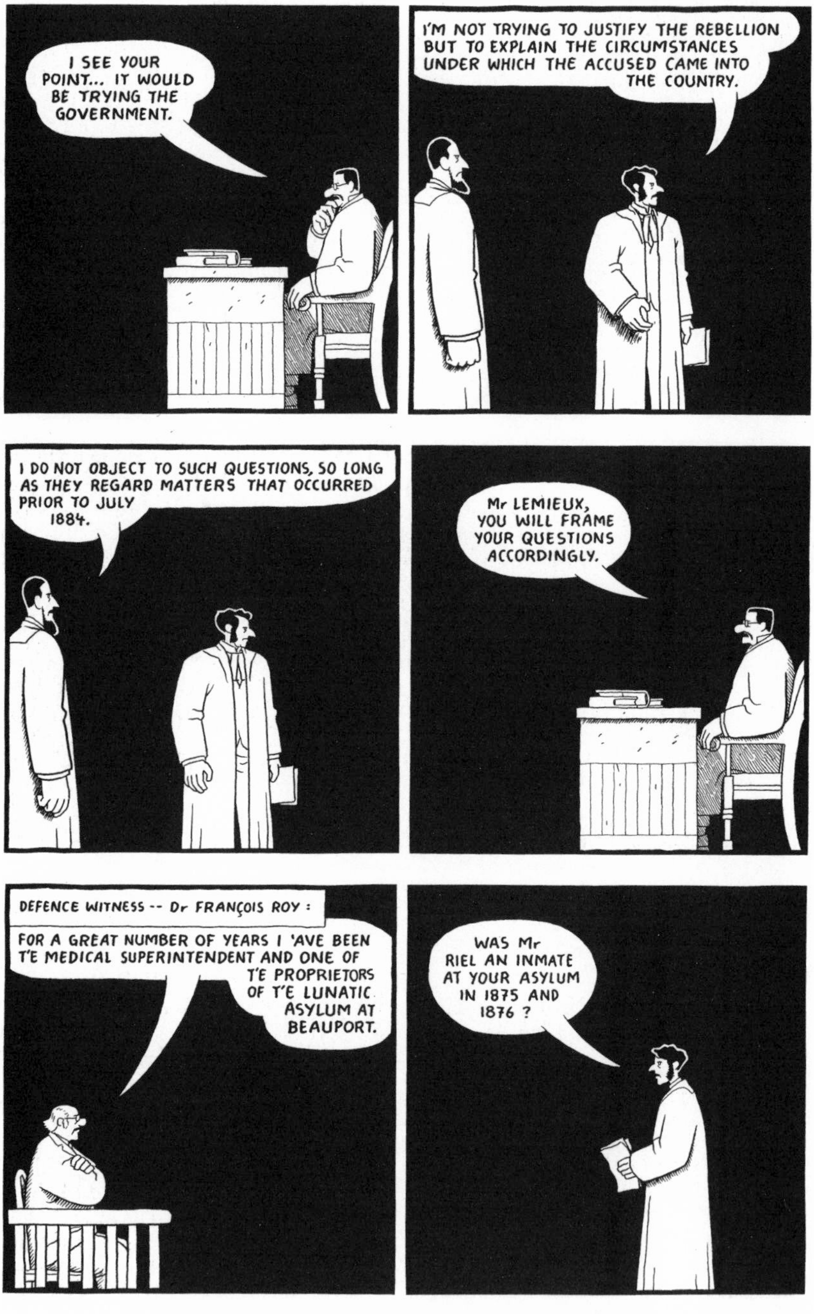
I SEE YOUR POINT... IT WOULD BE TRYING THE GOVERNMENT.
I'M NOT TRYING TO JUSTIFY THE REBELLION BUT TO EXPLAIN THE CIRCUMSTANCES UNDER WHICH THE ACCUSED CAME INTO THE COUNTRY.
I DO NOT OBJECT TO SUCH QUESTIONS, SO LONG AS THEY REGARD MATTERS THAT OCCURRED PRIOR TO JULY 1884.
Mr LEMIEUX, YOU WILL FRAME YOUR QUESTIONS ACCORDINGLY.
DEFENCE WITNESS -- Dr FRANÇOIS ROY :
FOR A GREAT NUMBER OF YEARS I 'AVE BEEN T'E MEDICAL SUPERINTENDENT AND ONE OF T'E PROPRIETORS OF T'E LUNATIC ASYLUM AT BEAUPORT.
WAS Mr RIEL AN INMATE AT YOUR ASYLUM IN 1875 AND 1876 ?

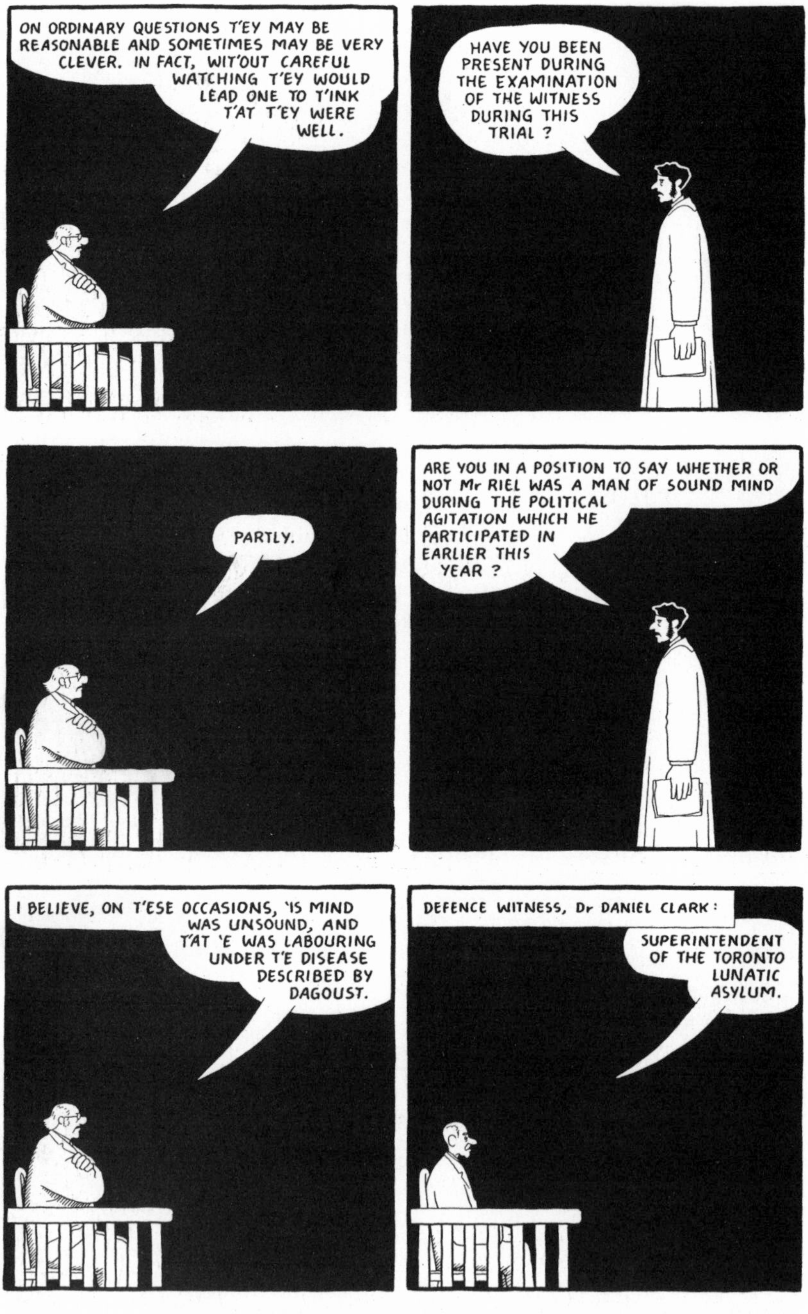
ON ORDINARY QUESTIONS T'EY MAY BE REASONABLE AND SOMETIMES MAY BE VERY CLEVER. IN FACT, WIT'OUT CAREFUL WATCHING T'EY WOULD LEAD ONE TO T'INK T'AT T'EY WERE WELL.
HAVE YOU BEEN PRESENT DURING THE EXAMINATION OF THE WITNESS DURING THIS TRIAL ?
PARTLY.
ARE YOU IN A POSITION TO SAY WHETHER OR NOT Mr RIEL WAS A MAN OF SOUND MIND DURING THE POLITICAL AGITATION WHICH HE PARTICIPATED IN EARLIER THIS YEAR ?
I BELIEVE, ON T'ESE OCCASIONS, 'IS MIND WAS UNSOUND, AND T'AT 'E WAS LABOURING UNDER T'E DISEASE DESCRIBED BY DAGOUST.
DEFENCE WITNESS, Dr DANIEL CLARK:
SUPERINTENDENT OF THE TORONTO LUNATIC ASYLUM.

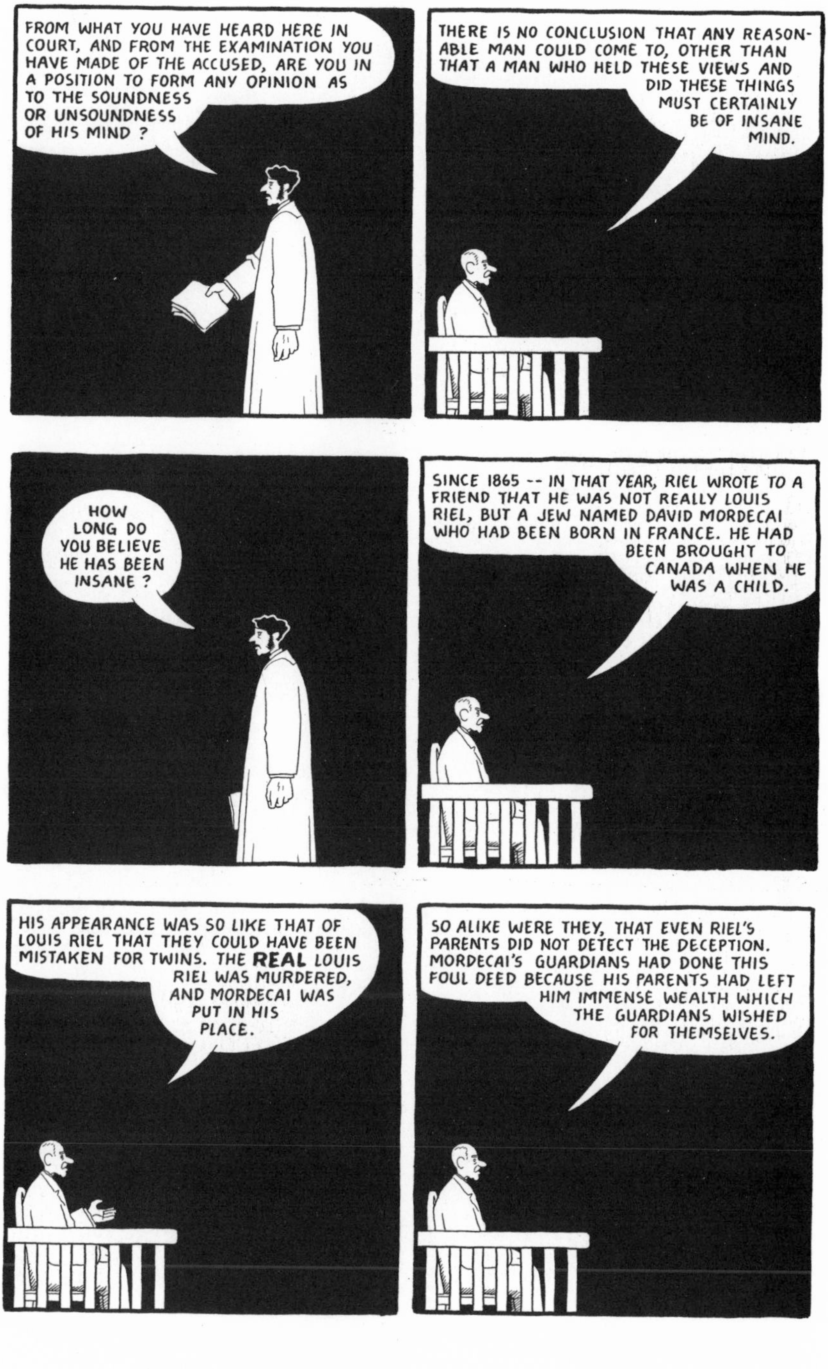
FROM WHAT YOU HAVE HEARD HERE IN COURT, AND FROM THE EXAMINATION YOU HAVE MADE OF THE ACCUSED, ARE YOU IN A POSITION TO FORM ANY OPINION AS TO THE SOUNDNESS OR UNSOUNDNESS OF HIS MIND ?
THERE IS NO CONCLUSION THAT ANY REASONABLE MAN COULD COME TO, OTHER THAN THAT A MAN WHO HELD THESE VIEWS AND DID THESE THINGS MUST CERTAINLY BE OF INSANE MIND.
HOW LONG DO YOU BELIEVE HE HAS BEEN INSANE ?
SINCE 1865 -- IN THAT YEAR, RIEL WROTE TO A FRIEND THAT HE WAS NOT REALLY LOUIS RIEL, BUT A JEW NAMED DAVID MORDECAI WHO HAD BEEN BORN IN FRANCE. HE HAD BEEN BROUGHT TO CANADA WHEN HE WAS A CHILD.
HIS APPEARANCE WAS SO LIKE THAT OF LOUIS RIEL THAT THEY COULD HAVE BEEN MISTAKEN FOR TWINS. THE **REAL** LOUIS RIEL WAS MURDERED, AND MORDECAI WAS PUT IN HIS PLACE.
SO ALIKE WERE THEY, THAT EVEN RIEL'S PARENTS DID NOT DETECT THE DECEPTION. MORDECAI'S GUARDIANS HAD DONE THIS FOUL DEED BECAUSE HIS PARENTS HAD LEFT HIM IMMENSE WEALTH WHICH THE GUARDIANS WISHED FOR THEMSELVES.

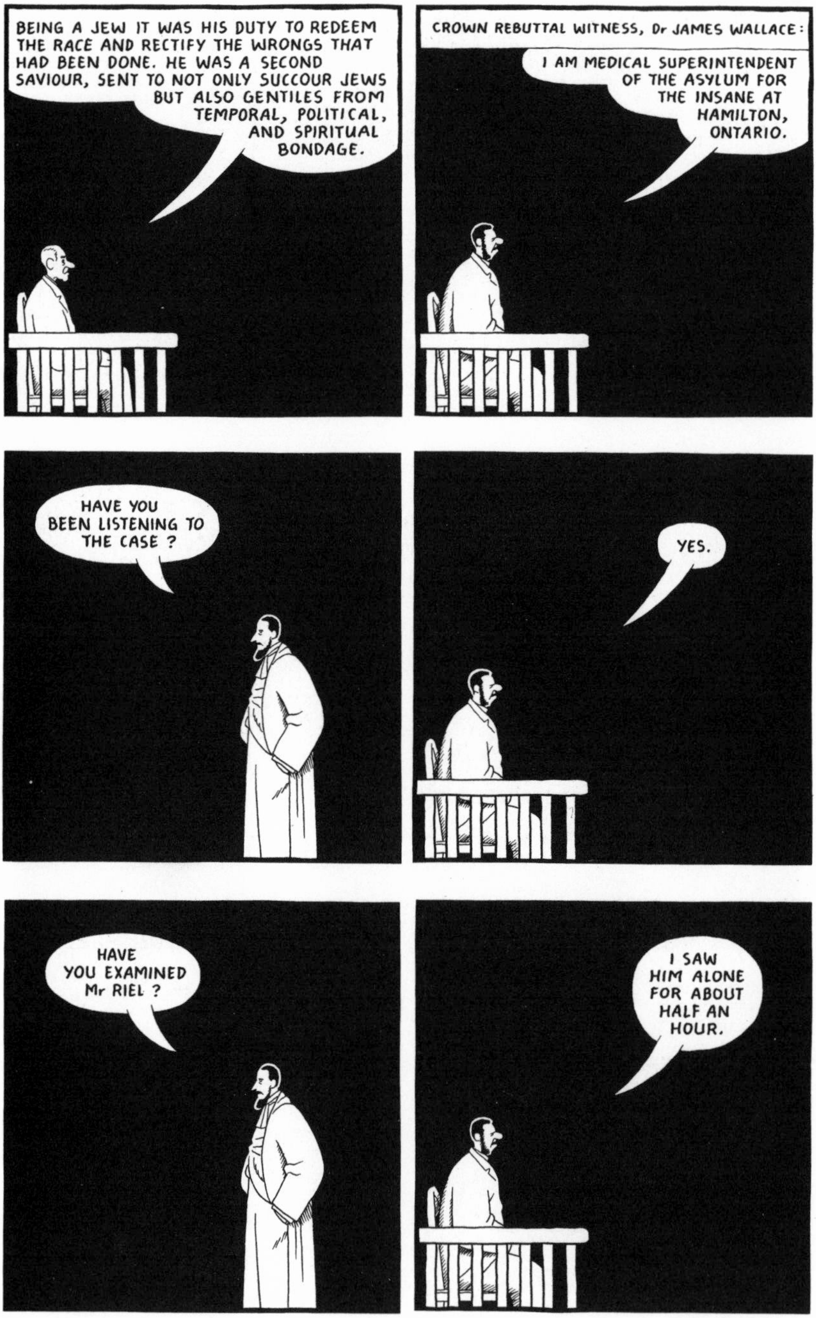
BEING A JEW IT WAS HIS DUTY TO REDEEM THE RACE AND RECTIFY THE WRONGS THAT HAD BEEN DONE. HE WAS A SECOND SAVIOUR, SENT TO NOT ONLY SUCCOUR JEWS BUT ALSO GENTILES FROM TEMPORAL, POLITICAL, AND SPIRITUAL BONDAGE.
CROWN REBUTTAL WITNESS, Dr JAMES WALLACE:
I AM MEDICAL SUPERINTENDENT OF THE ASYLUM FOR THE INSANE AT HAMILTON, ONTARIO.
HAVE YOU BEEN LISTENING TO THE CASE?
YES.
HAVE YOU EXAMINED Mr RIEL?
I SAW HIM ALONE FOR ABOUT HALF AN HOUR.

JULY 31, 1885 -- CROWN REBUTTAL WITNESS, CAPTAIN GEORGE YOUNG :

224

226

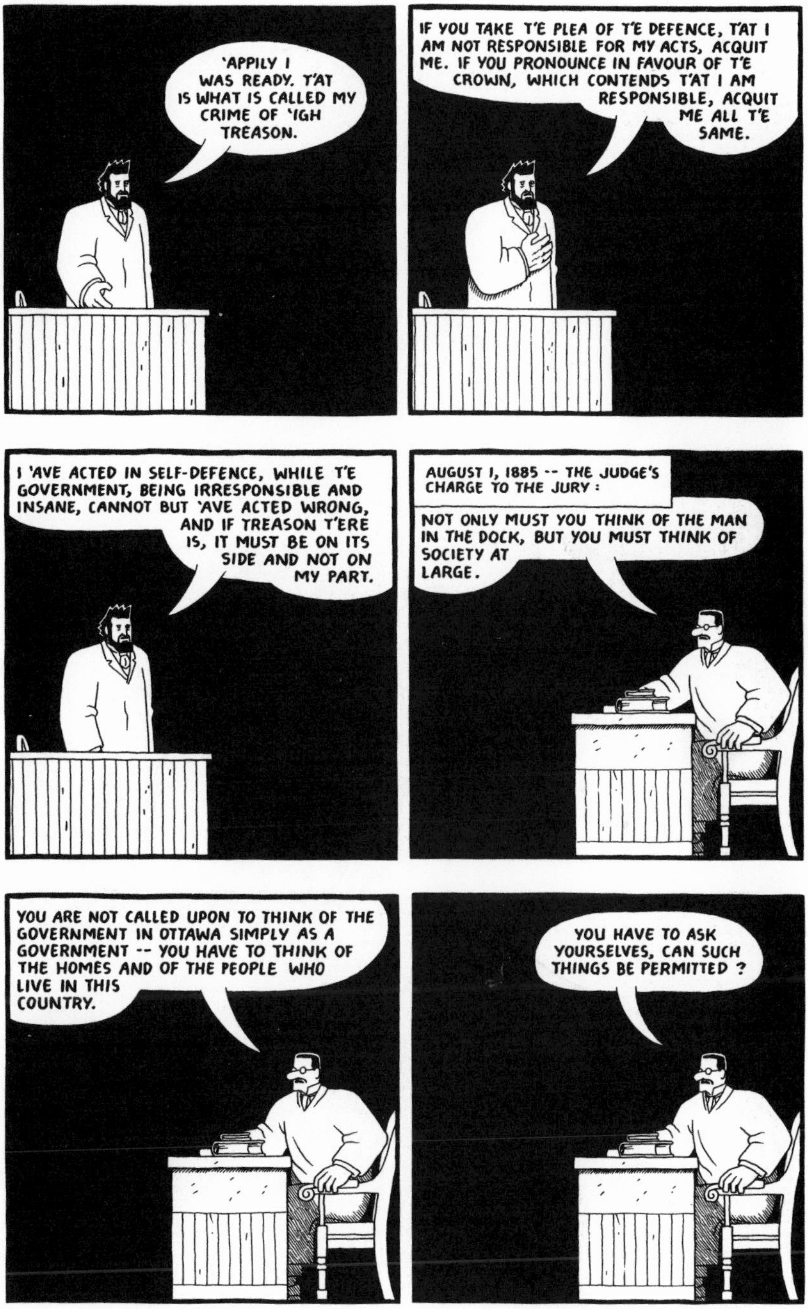
'APPILY I WAS READY. T'AT IS WHAT IS CALLED MY CRIME OF 'IGH TREASON.
IF YOU TAKE T'E PLEA OF T'E DEFENCE, T'AT I AM NOT RESPONSIBLE FOR MY ACTS, ACQUIT ME. IF YOU PRONOUNCE IN FAVOUR OF T'E CROWN, WHICH CONTENDS T'AT I AM RESPONSIBLE, ACQUIT ME ALL T'E SAME.
I 'AVE ACTED IN SELF-DEFENCE, WHILE T'E GOVERNMENT, BEING IRRESPONSIBLE AND INSANE, CANNOT BUT 'AVE ACTED WRONG, AND IF TREASON T'ERE IS, IT MUST BE ON ITS SIDE AND NOT ON MY PART.
AUGUST 1, 1885 -- THE JUDGE'S CHARGE TO THE JURY :
NOT ONLY MUST YOU THINK OF THE MAN IN THE DOCK, BUT YOU MUST THINK OF SOCIETY AT LARGE.
YOU ARE NOT CALLED UPON TO THINK OF THE GOVERNMENT IN OTTAWA SIMPLY AS A GOVERNMENT -- YOU HAVE TO THINK OF THE HOMES AND OF THE PEOPLE WHO LIVE IN THIS COUNTRY.
YOU HAVE TO ASK YOURSELVES, CAN SUCH THINGS BE PERMITTED ?

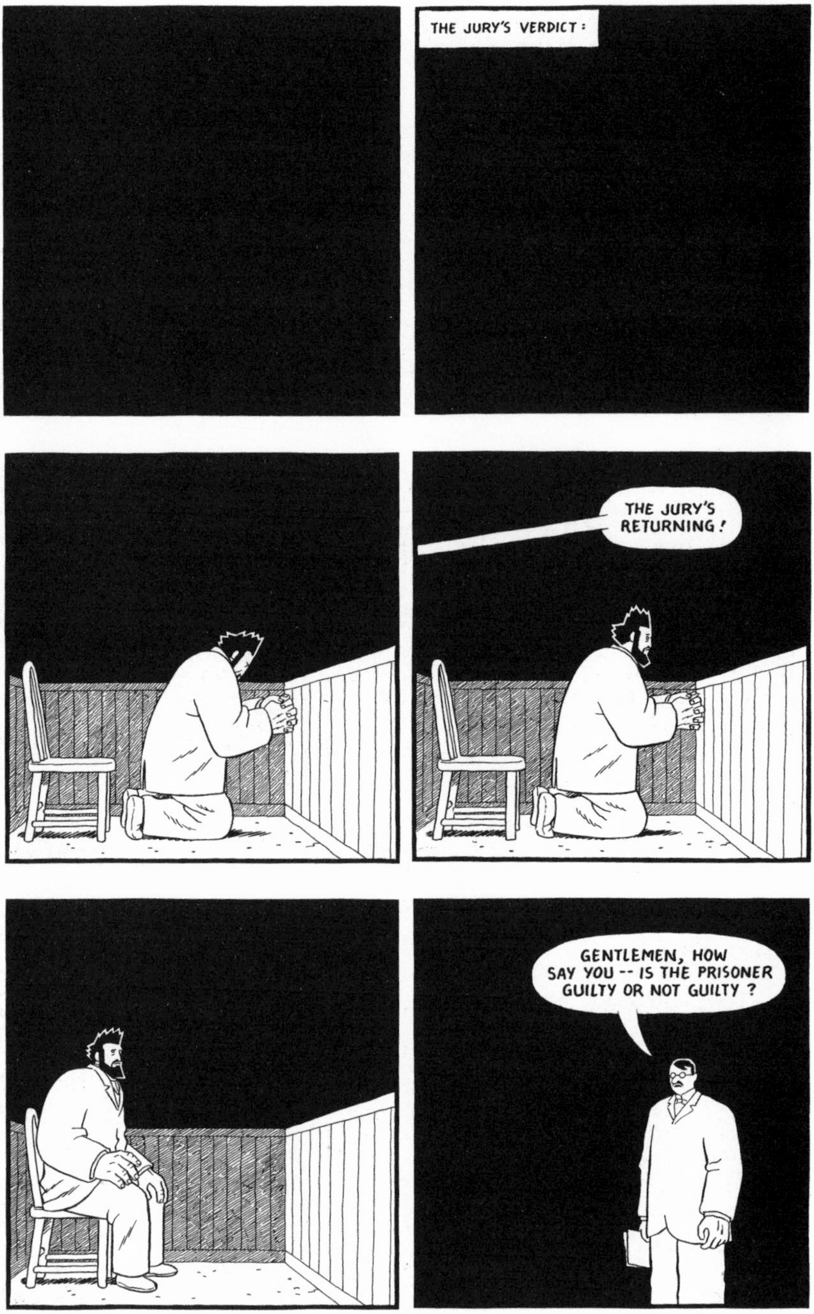
THE JURY'S VERDICT:
THE JURY'S RETURNING!
GENTLEMEN, HOW SAY YOU -- IS THE PRISONER GUILTY OR NOT GUILTY ?

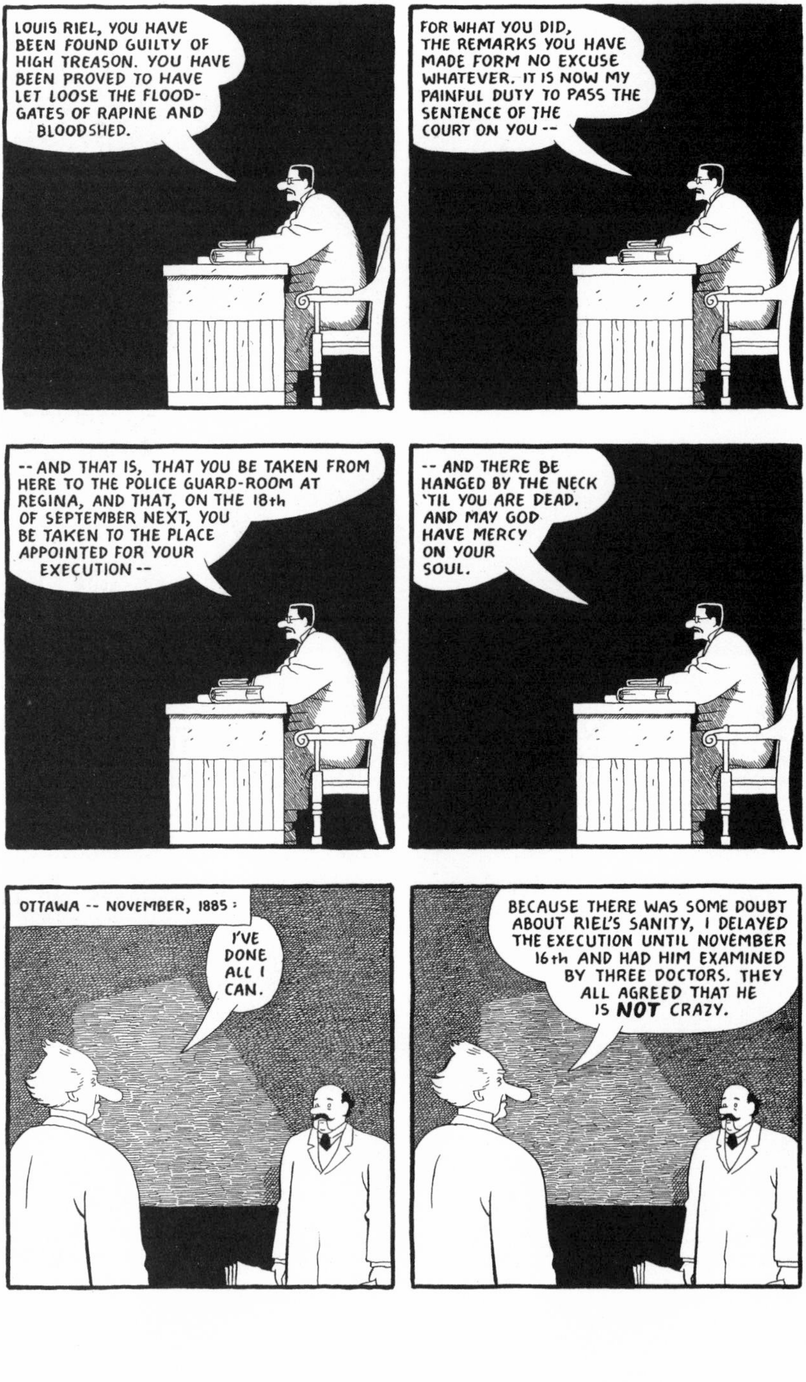
LOUIS RIEL, YOU HAVE BEEN FOUND GUILTY OF HIGH TREASON. YOU HAVE BEEN PROVED TO HAVE LET LOOSE THE FLOOD-GATES OF RAPINE AND BLOODSHED.
FOR WHAT YOU DID, THE REMARKS YOU HAVE MADE FORM NO EXCUSE WHATEVER. IT IS NOW MY PAINFUL DUTY TO PASS THE SENTENCE OF THE COURT ON YOU --
-- AND THAT IS, THAT YOU BE TAKEN FROM HERE TO THE POLICE GUARD-ROOM AT REGINA, AND THAT, ON THE 18th OF SEPTEMBER NEXT, YOU BE TAKEN TO THE PLACE APPOINTED FOR YOUR EXECUTION --
-- AND THERE BE HANGED BY THE NECK 'TIL YOU ARE DEAD. AND MAY GOD HAVE MERCY ON YOUR SOUL.
OTTAWA -- NOVEMBER, 1885 :
I'VE DONE ALL I CAN.
BECAUSE THERE WAS SOME DOUBT ABOUT RIEL'S SANITY, I DELAYED THE EXECUTION UNTIL NOVEMBER 16th AND HAD HIM EXAMINED BY THREE DOCTORS. THEY ALL AGREED THAT HE IS NOT CRAZY.

234

235

236

EPILOGUE

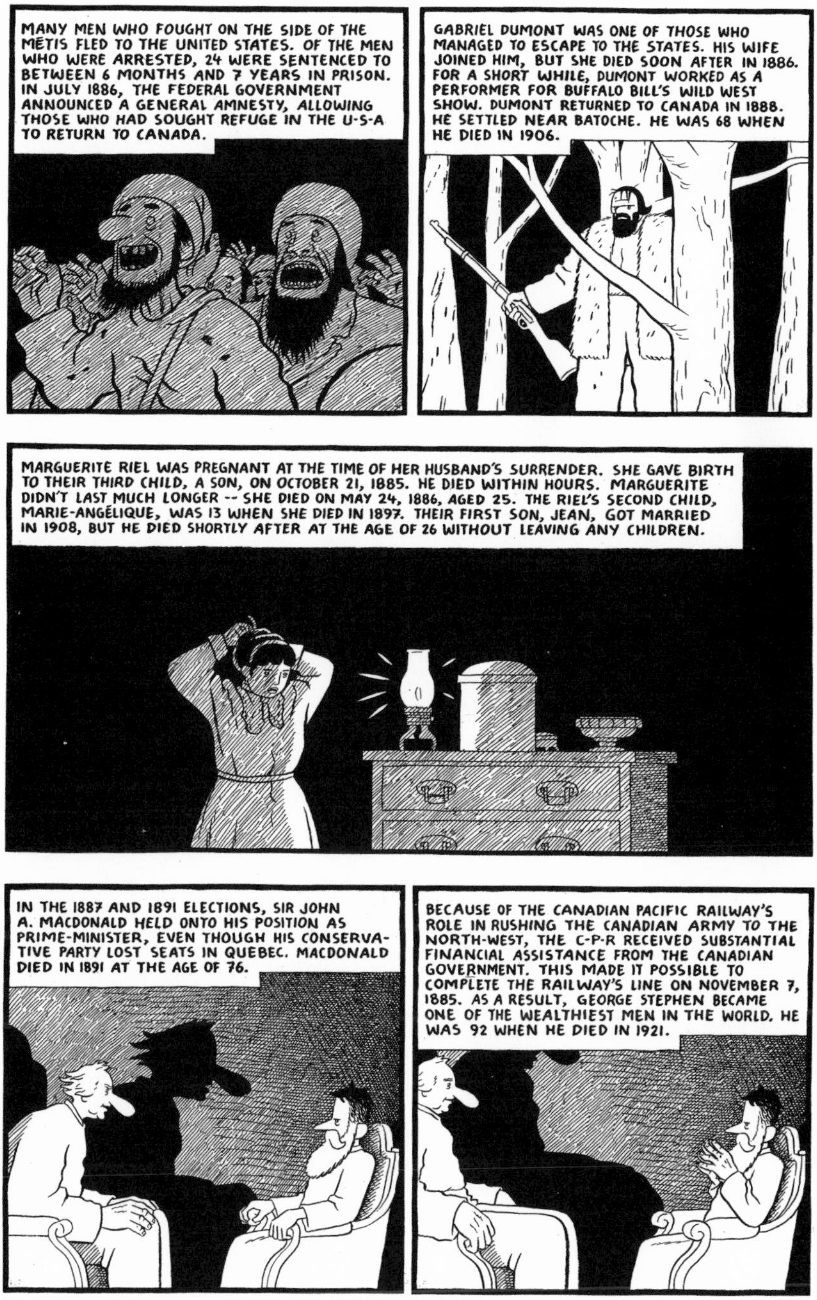
MANY MEN WHO FOUGHT ON THE SIDE OF THE MÉTIS FLED TO THE UNITED STATES. OF THE MEN WHO WERE ARRESTED, 24 WERE SENTENCED TO BETWEEN 6 MONTHS AND 7 YEARS IN PRISON. IN JULY 1886, THE FEDERAL GOVERNMENT ANNOUNCED A GENERAL AMNESTY, ALLOWING THOSE WHO HAD SOUGHT REFUGE IN THE U-S-A TO RETURN TO CANADA.
GABRIEL DUMONT WAS ONE OF THOSE WHO MANAGED TO ESCAPE TO THE STATES. HIS WIFE JOINED HIM, BUT SHE DIED SOON AFTER IN 1886. FOR A SHORT WHILE, DUMONT WORKED AS A PERFORMER FOR BUFFALO BILL'S WILD WEST SHOW. DUMONT RETURNED TO CANADA IN 1888. HE SETTLED NEAR BATOCHE. HE WAS 68 WHEN HE DIED IN 1906.
MARGUERITE RIEL WAS PREGNANT AT THE TIME OF HER HUSBAND'S SURRENDER. SHE GAVE BIRTH TO THEIR THIRD CHILD, A SON, ON OCTOBER 21, 1885. HE DIED WITHIN HOURS. MARGUERITE DIDN'T LAST MUCH LONGER -- SHE DIED ON MAY 24, 1886, AGED 25. THE RIEL'S SECOND CHILD, MARIE-ANGÉLIQUE, WAS 13 WHEN SHE DIED IN 1897. THEIR FIRST SON, JEAN, GOT MARRIED IN 1908, BUT HE DIED SHORTLY AFTER AT THE AGE OF 26 WITHOUT LEAVING ANY CHILDREN.
IN THE 1887 AND 1891 ELECTIONS, SIR JOHN A. MACDONALD HELD ONTO HIS POSITION AS PRIME-MINISTER, EVEN THOUGH HIS CONSERVATIVE PARTY LOST SEATS IN QUEBEC. MACDONALD DIED IN 1891 AT THE AGE OF 76.
BECAUSE OF THE CANADIAN PACIFIC RAILWAY'S ROLE IN RUSHING THE CANADIAN ARMY TO THE NORTH-WEST, THE C-P-R RECEIVED SUBSTANTIAL FINANCIAL ASSISTANCE FROM THE CANADIAN GOVERNMENT. THIS MADE IT POSSIBLE TO COMPLETE THE RAILWAY'S LINE ON NOVEMBER 7, 1885. AS A RESULT, GEORGE STEPHEN BECAME ONE OF THE WEALTHIEST MEN IN THE WORLD. HE WAS 92 WHEN HE DIED IN 1921.

NOTES

PAGE 3

Historian Stanley Ryerson observes that the Hudson's Bay Company charter that was signed by Charles II ignored "the rights of the native peoples dwelling there". (Ryerson, 1960, p. 138.)

PAGE 4

The 1869 population figures that I give on this page are actually from a census conducted in 1870.

PAGE 7 : PANEL 1

Macdonald was not in London in March 1869 and did not participate directly in the negotiations with the Hudson's Bay Company. The Canadian negotiators were William McDougall and George-Étienne Cartier. McDougall was then the Canadian government's Minister of Public Works, and Cartier was the deputy prime-minister. They left for London in either June 1868 (Bumsted, p. 40) or in the autumn of that year. (Sprague, p. 28.) Either way, the deal was concluded in March 1869.

7:3

The 7,000,000 acre figure was not mentioned in the March 1869 deal.

What was specified was that "the HBC would receive one-twentieth of all township land opened for settlement " (Siggins, p. 90) which "eventually amounted to 7,000,000 acres scattered through the West ". (Bumsted, p. 40.)

8:2

The Orange Order was founded in 1795 in Ireland and grew out of that island's religious and political struggles with England.

The lodges adopted a Masonic-type ritual and organization, providing for mutual aid and organizing social events. Orangemen who migrated to Britain and the colonies found the lodges useful in their adjustment to new environments.
The Grand Lodge of British North America was founded 1 January 1830 in Brockville, UC [ie. Upper Canada, now known as Ontario][.][...] By 1844 the power of the Orange vote induced John A. Macdonald to become an Orangeman. [Senior.]

8:3, 8:4

Macdonald took it for granted that representative institutions were admissible for a British majority only ; and until a satisfactory ethnic composition was obtained, the majority must be "kept down." [Ryerson, 1968, p. 389.]

9:2 - 9:4

The opinions that I have some of the inhabitants of the Red River Settlement expressing here were also expressed by at least one person outside of that community. In 1868 the Canadian government asked A.J. Russel (who was the Crown Lands Inspector) to look into the legal title of Rupert's Land. He wrote :

> [A]re we to be compelled to recognize the rights of the Hudson's Bay Company to lands which it has never bought or paid for ? And is it in conformity with justice to the Indians, so loudly proclaimed in Britain, that in taking possession of their lands, instead of paying them full value for it, we should make a gift of the greater part of this sum to the H.B.Co., which never acquired from the true proprietors the slightest right to these territories ? [Ryerson, 1960, p. 382.]

9:6

André Nault was the name of the Métis who spotted the Canadian surveyors on Edouard Marion's land. Nault was tending his cattle at the time -- a detail that I, for some reason, neglected to draw.

10:6

This is probably an exageration of the linguistic divide. In a group this large (sixteen or seventeen horsemen) there almost certainly would have been at least a few individuals with the ability to speak English.

11:5

During the confrontation, the Métis, or at least some of them, dismounted and stepped on the Surveyor's chain.

12:5

I based my drawings of McDougall on an 1867 photograph of him (Sprague, p. 32) and an 1869 sketch. (Charlebois, p. 40.) After I'd drawn most of the scenes that feature him, I came across a passage in Charlebois's book which describes McDougall as "portly". (Ibid, p. 36.) I turned to Siggins' RIEL for confirmation, and read there that McDougall was a "tall, heavily built man". (Siggins, p. 99.) As you can see, he doesn't come across as a large man in my strip. I considered redrawing all of the panels that feature him, but then decided that I could live with that level of inaccuracy.

13:5

McDougall arrived in Pembina by

ox-cart, not stage-coach. I'm not sure why I drew stage-coaches -- there is a note in my script specifying ox-cart.

14:2

This letter was actually signed : "By order of the President, John Bruce. Louis Riel, Secretary". I didn't draw Bruce into the story.

> [The Métis] elected as their president an ill-educated, weak man, named John Bruce, and as their secretary, Louis Riel. [...] Everyone knew that Bruce would be only a figurehead and that it was Riel who possessed the necessary education, sense of mission and power to direct that Bruce lacked. Riel [...] probably felt that, in view of the short time he had been back in the Settlement, it would be better for him to [take] a subordinate role, at least for the time being. [Stanley, p. 61.]

Bruce officially stepped down as president in mid-December 1869.

14:6

McDougall did spend the night in Pembina on October 30th. However, the next day he and his entourage ventured a mile and a half north beyond the U-S border, stopping at a Hudson's Bay Company post. McDougall hoped to stay there until being allowed into the Red River Settlement, but Métis horsemen forced him back to Pembina within days.

15:4 - 16:4

The way I've drawn this scene makes the conversation seem more casual than it probably was.

> [Provencher] was stopped at the Métis barricades at St. Norbert by some thirty to forty armed guards. Nearby a virtual army camp for two hundred men had sprung up [...]. Provencher was escorted into Ritchot's residence. It was only a few moments before services for All Saints' Day were to begin, and Provencher was invited to attend mass. He told his friends later that he had never prayed with such fervor as he did that morning. Later he met with Riel, John Bruce and other Métis [.] [Siggins, p. 107.]

15:5

Father Noel-Joseph Ritchot (1825-1905) was born in Lower Canada (now known as Quebec) and moved to the Red River in 1862.

20:6

Riel "confined the Company men to their quarters and posted guards." (Howard, p. 108.) I'm guessing that they weren't held as prisoners for very long, because their confinement never became an issue the way it did for the men who the

Métis imprisoned on December 7, 1869, (panels 31:3 and 31:4) and February 17, 1870, (panels 60:1 to 61:1).

21:2, 21:3

I should add a few more details to this brief sketch of Riel's early years.

He was born on October 22 or 23, 1844, and was his parent's first child.

> Two babies died in infancy, but eight more survived. It was a close family, and Louis seems to have been deeply attatched to his brothers and sisters. [Flanagan, 1996, p.4.]

In 1858 he was sent east to the Collège de Montréal, which was run by the Sulpician priests. His father died in early 1864. Shortly after, Riel became romantically involved with a young woman -- Marie-Julie Guernon. He began to skip classes and, in early 1865, he either quit the college (Siggins, p.62) or was dismissed. (Flanagan, 1996, p. 20.) Riel ended up working in the law-office of Rodolphe Laflamme, but by June 1886 it became clear that Marie-Julie's parents were going to keep their daughter from marrying the young Métis.

> We know almost nothing of Riel's life between his departure from Montreal on 19 June 1866 and his return to Red River on 26 July 1868. [...] Riel's own description of these years is anything but informative: "Left Montreal 19th June 1866. Came to St Paul, lived in Minneapolis, St Anthony and Saint Paul 2 years. Left St Anthony in July 68 and came to St Joe, Dakota." Nothing further is known for certain. [Ibid, p.27.]

Riel returned to the Red River Settlement to help run the family farm.

22:5-22:6, 25:4, 25:5

I've followed the sequence of events that Siggins gives, with the NOR'WESTER's press being used to print up copies of the "royal" proclamation and Riel putting a stop to the publication of the newspaper on December 2nd. (Siggins, pp. 121, 122.) But Bumsted claims that Riel took control of the NOR'WESTER's press in early November and that McDougall's proclamation then had to be copied out by hand for distribution in the settlement. (Bumsted, pp. 71, 91.)
Riel also shut down the Settlement's other newspaper, the RED RIVER PIONEER.

23:6

Dr John Schultz (1840-1896) was born in Amherstburg, Upper Canada (Ontario). He moved to the Red River Settlement to set up his medical practice in 1861. "[T]here is no record of his having received a medical degree." (Bumsted, p. 322.)

25:6, 26:1

Despite what I have Dennis saying in these panels, he was able to enlist about 380 men to fight the Métis, but "almost all the long-time English-speaking settlers refused point blank to have anything to do with their 'inglorious schemes'." (Siggins, p. 122.) A large number of Dennis's men were Salteaux and Sioux, and Dennis was heavily criticized at the time for arming Indians. Arming his recruits was another problem: "He had only two hundred guns, many of them old and dysfunctional". (Ibid.)

28:5

While I don't know what was on this list of demands, it's probably a safe guess that the primary one was that McDougall be allowed into the settlement.

33:1

According to Siggins, Riel asked for £1,000 and found £1,090 in the safe. (Siggins, p. 129.) Bumsted claims that the requested amount was £10,000 and that the Métis left with "all the cash in the coffers of the HBC." (Bumsted, pp. 105, 106.)

33:5 - 35:3

In late 1869, Prime-Minister Macdonald sent Donald Smith as a "special commissioner" to the Red River settlement. Smith was at that time the Hudson's Bay Company's chief factor for the Montreal district. He arrived in the settlement in December, claiming that his mission was to make "the people both French and English fully acquainted with the liberal views of the Canadian Government so that a peaceful transfer of the Territory might be affected." (Bumsted, p. 121.) Another (not publicly stated) part of his role as "special commissioner" was handing out bribes.
Suspicious of the man, Riel tried to have Smith's papers seized in the hope that they would contain incriminating information or at least state exactly how much power Macdonald had given him. Riel failed to get ahold of the papers, but Smith said that he would publicly read them if the Métis

leader called a general meeting for the whole settlement. This was the outdoor January 19th meeting. My statement in panel 33:5 that this meeting was "particularly [for] the English" is untrue -- Smith wanted to win over the French as much as the English. He spoke for five hours, and then it was agreed that the meeting would reconvene on the next day. Smith again spoke for several hours on the 20th. Both days he mostly read from boring letters written by Canadian politicians who proposed nothing concrete. Sensing that Smith was failing to win over the audience, Riel got up during the second meeting and made his suggestion for the Convention of Forty. As the strip indicates, this was met with cheers of approval. Unlike Smith, Riel was apparently a charismatic speaker.

36:6

The vote on this issue was actually 23 to 16. The chair -- who was English -- didn't vote, which means that four French Métis voted against Riel's proposal.

37:5 - 39:2

Riel sent out twelve men to arrest Nolin but two got to the Nolin residence ahead of the other ten. Charles Nolin had four brothers, and most or all of them were guarding him that night.

39:4 – 43:3

Schultz was not the only December 7th prisoner who escaped from the Métis. After spending several weeks in Fort Garry, most of the prisoners were moved from the fort "to a common jail outside the walls, where six cells held forty prisoners." (Siggins, p. 135.) Only Schultz was kept in the fort, because he was considered to be the most dangerous. On January 9th, eight men escaped from the common jail, though five of them were re-captured the next day.

I have Mrs Schultz smuggling in the pocket-knife to her husband on January 23rd and show him escaping that night. While Schultz did escape on the 23rd, the apple-brown-betty-with-the-knife was probably delivered to him several days before, since Siggins implies that it took Schultz that amount of time to cut up the buffalo-robe. (Ibid. pp. 150, 151.)

42:5

Schultz did not break his leg, but it was twisted so badly that he walked with a limp for the rest of his life.

46:3

Sutherland was a member of the Convention of Forty.

46:4

Crediting Schultz alone with raising the 300 men is a bit of an oversimplification. Charles Mair and Thomas Scott were two of the men who escaped from the Métis on January 9th. (See the note for panels 39:4 to 43:3.) They fled to Portage-la-Prairie and managed to convince Major Charles Boulton (who'd had ten years of service in the British Army) to help them. "Of all of Riel's opponents, Boulton was the one who wore a sheen of respectability -- so much so that he began to win converts among the English-speaking settlers." (Siggins, p. 149.) Boulton was able to gather together about 100 fighting men. Meanwhile, Schultz was in St Andrew rounding up about 200 men. (A lot of the men Schultz mobilized were the Salteaux and Sioux who'd been ready to fight for Colonel Dennis -- see the note for panels 25:6 and 26:1.) The Boulton and Schultz forces met in Kildonan.

48:4

Hugh didn't volunteer to ride to Kildonan -- his father had to ask him to.

54:5 - 55:5

Scott was born in 1842 and was a native of Northern Ireland who emigrated to Canada West [Ontario] in the early 1860s. Of Scots-Irish descent, he was a member of [...] the Orange Order. He was also, contemporaries who knew him for the most part agreed, a "violent and boisterous man" who made his opinions known in a loud voice and a rude manner. [Bumsted, p. 163.]

During the beating of Parisien, "Thomas Scott was particularly vicious; he struck Parisien on the head with an axe" (Siggins, p. 154). Still, my depiction probably exaggerates Scott's viciousness. I don't know whether his axe hit Parisien once or many times. The way I've written the scene virtually implies that Scott alone killed Parisien, and in reality it's likely that the murder was more of a group effort.

Neither Sutherland nor Parisien died immediately. Sutherland passed on the next morning (February 17th), while Parisien lingered for "a few days" (Howard, p. 159), "several weeks" (Bumsted, p. 153), or a "month and a half" (Siggins, p. 154) before expiring. (Stanley (p. 106) agrees with Howard, while Siggins is corroborated by Charlebois (p.64), who gives Parisien's date of death as April 4th.)

53:4

Before dying, Sutherland "begged that Norbert Parisien not be punished." (Siggins, p. 154.)

58:2

I show the men on foot. William Sanderson (who was one of this group) said that they were all walking as they approached Fort Garry (Spry, p. 129), but Stanley seems to think that they were all in sleighs. (Stanley, pp. 106, 107.) "Alexander Begg, who claimed to be able to see events from the village, insisted that there were carrioles, as well as men on foot." (Bumsted, p. 155.)

58:5

Were the men armed? Sanderson stated that "Each of us was given [...] a muzzle loader [...] and only three bullets". (Spry, p. 128.) But Boulton remembered that "We were not armed". (Bumsted, p. 156.) When the men were led into the fort, they were described as having "empty holsters, looking as if they had thrown away their weapons. A Métis party was detailed to find the weapons. It failed to discover any". (Ibid.)

59:2

In panel 6:6 I said that there were 50 men, and I here show one walking away, which would leave 49. Actually, 48 men ended up at Fort Garry.

59:4

And the day they ended up at Fort Garry was either February 17, 1870 (Bumsted, p. 154, and Howard, p. 160), or February 18th. (Charlebois, p. 64, Siggins, p. 155, and Stanley, p. 107.)

60:3 - 60:6

My depiction of a peaceful surrender is based on Sanderson's account. Of the question asked in panel 9:1, Sanderson wrote, "we wouldn't dream of refusing such an invitation as we had not had too much to eat since we left home." (Spry, p. 129.) According to Bumsted, as the horsemen drew near to Boulton's men, a fight started between a Métis and one of the English. Boulton quickly put a stop to it and then surrendered. (Bumsted, p. 156.)

62:1

I show Schultz fleeing alone, but he was accompanied by a friend and a guide.

After it was determined that Schultz was not among the prisoners, five of them -- including Boulton and Scott -- were judged to be the leaders of the group. A Métis tribunal sentenced these five to be killed. Hearing about the proposed execution, the mother of Hugh Sutherland rushed to the fort and pleaded for the lives of the condemned men. Riel agreed to spare four of them but insisted that Boulton must die. Donald Smith showed up and begged that mercy be shown to Boulton. The elections for Riel's provisional government were coming up, and many in the English community were starting to re-think whether they wanted to participate. Riel said that he would forego executing Boulton if Smith convinced the English parishes to elect representatives. Over the next few days, Smith did, and Boulton was allowed to live.

62:5

William Sanderson on Thomas Scott:

We were all put into a large room [...]. We would have been quite comfortable had it not been for that man Scott making such a racket [...]. This Scott was so obnoxious and made so much trouble that some of our men asked the guard to have him removed. He was put into a room next to the one we occupied [.] [Spry, pp. 129, 130.]

William Sanderson on his imprisonment:

Some years ago I picked up and began to read a history of the Manitoba Rebellion, the story told of great hardships we endured as prisoners and how we were starved.

It must have been written by someone who knew nothing about it for it was nothing but a lot of damn lies, we were well treated. [Ibid, p.130.]

64:3, 64:4

Racette has been able to find references to nine Métis flags from the 1869-70 period. (Racette, pp. 13-17.) Most of these included at least one fleur-de-lis and one shamrock in their design. In North America the fleur-de-lis is the primary symbol of French cultural identity, much as the shamrock is to the Irish. So what was an Irish symbol doing on Métis flags? A small but significant number of Riel's supporters were Fenians -- anti-British Irish-Catholics. Chief among these was William O'Donoghue, who was Riel's right-hand man for awhile. The Fenians wanted the settlement to join the United States and, as it became clear that the sympathies of the provisional government's president were with Britain, the relationship between the two men soured.

Why did Riel favour British political ties over American ones? Siggins speculates that he was concerned that "the French language and culture would be diluted in the American melting-pot." (Siggins, p.95.)

65:1 - 66:2

On March 1, Scott and Murdoch McLeod forced the door of their cell and jumped two guards, shouting that the other prisoners should do the same. This outrage by Scott was the last straw. The guards dragged the big man, cursing and screaming, into the courtyard, and were just starting to beat him when a member of the provisional government heard the noise and intervened. [Siggins, p.161.]

65:1

A "tête-carrée" (square-head) is an English person. This French expression is used in Quebec today-- I don't know if it would have been used in the 19th century.

69:2

I didn't address this in the strip (and no one I've read on the subject has either) but I couldn't help but wonder if revenge wasn't a possible motive for Scott's execution. It would depend on whether the Métis knew of Scott's role in the beating of Parisien. While several men had participated in the beating, it seems possible that

THE GUY WHO USED THE AXE might have been singled out for pay-back. Perhaps Parisien could have given enough of a physical description (young, tall, Irish accent, side-whiskers) that when Scott called attention to himself in Fort Garry, he was either recognized or suspected.

69:5 - 73:3

Reports varied as to whether [Scott] emerged blindfolded, or was blindfolded later. Scott apparently prayed continually while in the open air. [...] Reverend Young's much later report was that Scott said, "This is horrible! This is cold-blooded murder. Be sure to make a true statement." Scott then asked Reverend Young whether he should stand or kneel. He then knelt in the snow and said, "Farewell." [Bumsted, p.165.]

Donald Smith and others asked Riel not to go through with the execution, but the Métis leader was adamant. James Taylor, the American consul in the Red River Settlement, wrote:

Riel firmly believed the execution necessary not only to prevent bloodshed within the walls of the prison itself but to check further attempts at insurrection with the possible contingency of an Indian war. "I take a life to save lives," was his reply to an appeal for mercy. [Siggins, p.163.]

71:2

"He stays standing or we put him on his knees?"

72:2

"Fire when the handkerchief falls from my hand."

73:4 - 74:2

Why did Macdonald have to ask the British government for soldiers? Why not just send in Canadian militia-men? "[A]ny such expedition would have to be undertaken under British auspices, since Canada had 'no authority beyond her own limits.'" (Bumsted, p.146.)

Granville was not in Ottawa in March, 1870, and for all I know he may never have visited Canada. The conversation between the two men was conducted, not in person, but through telegrams and letters.

74:5

There were actually three men

chosen to represent the Red River Settlement in Ottawa : Ritchot, a saloon barkeeper named Alfred Scott (no relation to Thomas Scott), and Judge John Black. Scott and Black contributed almost nothing to the negotiations, so I've dropped them from the story.

75:4 - 76:2

Ritchot and Alfred Scott traveled together and had to avoid Toronto as I show here. With Schultz encouraging him to do so,

> Thomas Scott's brother, Hugh, [...] went to the police magistrate in Toronto and applied for a warrant charging Father Ritchot and Alfred Scott with aiding and abetting the murder of Thomas Scott. This was granted and then sent on to the Ottawa police department. [Siggins, p. 177.]

Ritchot and Alfred Scott arrived in Ottawa on April 11th. Alfred was arrested by Ottawa police on the 12th and Ritchot gave himself up to the authorities on the 13th. Although an Ottawa judge deemed the Toronto warrant to be invalid in Ottawa and freed the two men, Hugh Scott immediately filed a warrant in Ottawa and Ritchot and Alfred were re-arrested. "[T]hey remained under guard [at their lodgings] in a kind of house arrest." (Ibid.) On April 23rd the charges were dismissed for lack of evidence. The negotiations between the Red River delegates (Ritchot, Alfred Scott, and Black) and the Canadian government (represented by the prime-minister, Sir John A. Macdonald, and the deputy prime-minister, Sir George-Étienne Cartier) started on April 25th.

76:3 - 77:1

Ritchot could not speak English. (Bumsted, p. 318.)

77:4 - 78:2

Riel and Ritchot had been in contact by letter, and Riel would have known all the details of the agreement -- which was called the Manitoba Act -- by the time that Ritchot arrived back in the settlement, so the two men would not have had this conversation. I have Riel and Ritchot talking as if the Act was a done deal, but it still had to be voted on by the Legislative Assembly of Riel's provisional government. This happened on June 24th, with the act passing unanimously.

77:5

1,400,000 acres was "about one-seventh of the total area of Manitoba as it then was. " (Flanagan, 1996, p. 138.) Manitoba in 1870 was "roughly 11,000 square miles". (Bumsted,

p. 179.) The province has been expanded on three occasions. (1881, 1884, and 1912.) Its present size is 250,934 square miles.

To clarify what the 1,400,000 acres were intended for : The Red River Métis in 1870 already had their river-front farms. Ritchot proposed that 1,400,000 acres be set aside for the Métis, not because they needed more land at that point, but because the next generation would need land to settle on -- the 1,400,000 acres were intended for the Métis who would have been children in 1870.

> Manitoba statutes were changed on a number of occasions in order to allow Metis children to sell their land -- this at a time when the law made it clear that non-Metis children had no right to sell land. [... i]n 1881 Manitoba legislation allowed Metis children of any age to sell their land without parental consent. [Purich, p. 69.]

77:6

Alert readers will note the crucial word "if " in this sentence. The act did not specify what land the Métis would get or how or when it would be distributed.

78:3 - 79:6

Dumont was born in 1837.

> Gabriel Dumont was a frontiersman's frontiersman, the stuff of legends. He was the best shot in the North-West, the best rider, the best gambler among a people who gambled for days on end, the best buffalo hunter, the greatest leader. He was a good canoeist and swimmer, unusual talents on the plains, and a better-than-average billiards player. He owned the fastest horses in a society that loved horse-racing. He was fluent in French and several Indian languages but never bothered to learn much English. He was a shrewd trader and businessman. To his friends he was the most gracious, most generous person in the North-West; to his enemies he was a dangerous foe. [Beal & Macleod, p. 37.]

> Some writers have cast doubt on Dumont's presence at the Red River, but the evidence suggests that he went at least once. Dumont himself said that he met Riel at Fort Garry on 17 June 1870 [.] [Woodcock, p. 81.]

79:1

> With marksmen placed in strategic spots, the Métis could destroy a force of Canadians and Brits who had no experience whatsoever of the wilderness. At first Riel was tempted, especially since the long-promised amnesty had not arrived, but Bishop Taché talked him out of it. [Siggins, p. 186.]

79:2 - 79:4

Wolseley's letter arrived in the settlement on July 22nd (not in early July).

80:3 - 80:6

[Riel] sent four boatloads of Métis to help guide the troops and clear the road to the Winnipeg River. The word these men sent back caused the entire Red River Valley to shudder. Around the campfires at night, the Canadian soldiers talked of little but revenge. [Siggins, p. 186]

81:1 - 81:3

Bishop Alexandre-Antonin Taché was a Red River settlement priest with political connections in Ottawa. In February 1870 he traveled to that city and received from Macdonald, Cartier, and Secretary of State Joseph Howe a verbal promise of an amnesty for everyone involved in the settlement's political turmoil. It doesn't seem to have occurred to him to get this in writing. Father Ritchot, on the other hand, definitely tried -- without success -- to get the amnesty promise in writing while he negotiated the Manitoba Act. (Macdonald's deviousness in this matter is probably best recounted by Sprague. The prime-minister not only lied to the priests but also to Cartier, who was able to convincingly assure the priests that an amnesty was coming because he actually believed it himself. See Sprague pp. 56, 57, 69-74.)

The exchange in these panels would seem to imply that hostile feelings had developed between Ritchot and Riel, but that wasn't the case -- it was between Taché and Riel that antagonism grew. I've combined the two priests into one character.

81:4 - 85:6

On the evening of August 23rd, Riel did tell all of his followers in the Fort to get their personal belongings to safety, but not themselves. There were still many Métis in the fort as dawn broke on the 24th. It wasn't until the English settler James G. Stewart rode into the fort with his warning, that

[m]embers of the old Métis council began to lose courage and drift away [...]. Riel went down to the courtyard and dismissed the guards. He and O'Donoghue were alone in Fort Garry. [Howard, p. 181.]

For awhile the two men watched the British-Canadian force moving toward them. When the soldiers drew close, Riel and O'Donoghue walked out of the fort, down to the Assiniboine River, "and crossed on a raft they fashioned of fence posts lashed with their woven sashes." (Ibid., p.183.)

89:2

Two soldiers and a civilian chased [Elzéar] Goulet [a member of the court-martial that had tried Thomas Scott] to the Red River. Terrified, he leaped into the water to swim to the opposite shore and safety. The soldiers [...], and their companions, stoned him to death in the water. [...] François Guillemette, a member of the firing squad that had executed Scott, was murdered near Pembina. H.F. O'Lone, a friend of O'Donoghue's was murdered. An attempt was made on the life of Father Kavanaugh. [English Métis] James Tanner's horse was deliberately frightened in the dark causing it to rear and throw him to his death. Thomas Spence, editor of THE NEW NATION [a Red River Settlement newspaper], was horse-whipped by John Schultz's friends. André Nault was viciously beaten. [Charlebois, p. 89.]

Disorders in the first few weeks of Canadian administration claimed many times more casualties than had occurred in ten months of Métis rule, and the trouble continued for months. [Howard, p. 185.]

Regarding the reference to rape in this panel :

Standard histories seldom refer to this unsavoury crime against the civilian population because there is "little documentary evidence". But one of the few historians entirely sympathetic to the Métis cause, Auguste de Tremaudan, claims he was told by many "oldtimers" about such rapes. [Siggins, p.193.]

89:5, 89:6

The government's first delaying tactic was to say that no lands could be registered until after a thorough land survey and census of the Manitoba population had been completed. That might have seemed logical enough, except that an Order-in-Council dated May 26, 1871, allowed all newcomers to stake land wherever they found it. [...] The government officials ruled that the old settlers were not allowed this privilege because supposedly their lands were already protected under the Manitoba Act. [...] In disputes between Métis and newly arrived homesteaders over ownership of land, the new settlers almost always won. Many Métis families were thrown off land they had occupied for decades [.] [Siggins, pp. 281, 282.]

90:1

Riel returned to the settlement on May 3, 1871.

90:2

The military force of 1,200 had consisted of 400 British soldiers and 800 Canadians. The British were sent home in September, 1870. 720 of the Canadians were freed from service in the spring of 1871 (Sprague, p. 98), but

Many of the Ontario soldiers had decided to remain permanently in Red River, mainly because they had been rewarded for their "valiant service" with 160-acre land grants. [Siggins, p. 202.]

In the summer and fall of 1871, William O'Donoghue tried to round up men in Minnesota and Dakota for a Fenian invasion of Manitoba. Hearing of this, Adams G. Archibald (Manitoba's new lieutenant-governor) was concerned. He knew that the Métis were unhappy with how things were going and feared that they would again join forces with the Fenians. He turned to Riel for help. Riel (hoping that a show of loyalty to Canada would speed the arrival of his amnesty) complied and urged his fellow Métis to fight for Canada should the Fenians actually attack. O'Donoghue's plans came to nothing, but Archibald was still grateful to Riel for his support, and in a public ceremony on October 8, 1871, he shook Riel's hand -- as well as the hand of Ambroise Lépine (a member of Riel's provisional government who had also participated in Thomas Scott's court-martial).

> The results of this dramatic scene were not at all what Archibald or Riel had antici-pated. [...] A howl of rage issued forth from Orangemen across the land; how dare Her Majesty's representative actually grasp the "bloody hands" of Riel and Lépine ? The Ontario press lambasted the lieutenant-governor for his compliancy and Prime Minister Macdonald said he was "embarrassed" that Riel had been publicly recognized. Instead of receiving gratitude for their loyal devotion to the Canadian government, the Métis were accused of abetting the Fenian cause.[...] The long-promised amnesty receded even further into the background. [Siggins, p. 206.]

90:3 - 91:3

It was Bishop Taché, not Father Ritchot, who visited Ottawa in December, 1871.

91:3

> On 27 December, Macdonald provided Taché with a sight draft on the Bank of Montreal for $1,000 for "the individ-ual we have talked about." [...] After leaving Montreal in January of 1872, Taché received en route to Sarnia a letter from Cartier saying that Ambroise Lépine should also depart and that the money should be divided. [...Riel and Lépine] requested $1,000 each, plus eight to ten pounds sterling every month for their families. [...] Bishop Taché had to go to Lieutenant - Governor Archibald for financial assistance. Archibald him-self had no funds available, and so he called upon Donald A. Smith (as representative of the [Hudson's Bay Company] acting as bankers for the province) to furnish the money, on the understanding that it would eventually be reimbursed by Ottawa. Smith obliged, and the bishop gave Riel and Lépine $1,600 each, holding $1,000 back for their families. Although Sir John Macdonald and Sir George Cartier acknowledged Smith's advance, it was never repaid [.] [Bumsted, pp. 232, 233.]

Flanagan gives a different set of figures :

> In December 1871 Sir John A. Macdonald sent Archbishop Taché $5,000 for Riel and Ambroise Lépine to persuade them to leave the country for a year. Riel and Lépine took the money after Donald A. Smith, then MP for Selkirk, supplemented it with another $3,000.
> [Flanagan, 2000, pp. 117, 118.]

91:4

Taché and Riel had this conversa-tion in February 1871. Riel went into exile in the United States with Ambrois Lépine.

91:5

> On March 9, the Ontario government [...] officially announced the $5,000 award for [Riel's] capture -- an incredible amount of money when the average working man made less than $500 a year. " [Siggins, p. 210.]

92:2 - 93:1

Lépine was with Riel when this happened.

93:2 - 94:3

> Riel happened to glance out his window and spotted two suspicious-looking charac-ters standing at the door of the hotel. He and Lépine fled out the back. It was later discovered that the two men had been hired by Schultz to kill Riel as he came out of the hotel. [Siggins, p. 211.]

94:4

Father Ritchot and others contacted Riel in the summer of 1872 -- there was a federal election coming up, and they believed that he could win if he ran. Riel was persuaded to move back to the Red River. The settlement was divided into four electoral ridings : Marquette, Selkirk, Lisgar, and Provencher. The latter had the highest number of French-speaking constituents, so that's where he ran as a Conservative candi-date. (The two main parties in Cana-dian politics were the Conservatives and the Liberals. Prime-Minister Macdonald and Deputy Prime-Minister Cartier were Conservatives. "[T]he Liberals were considered friends of Schultz and his group". (Siggins, p. 212.)) For some reason Quebec electors voted several weeks ahead of their Manitoban counter-parts and, as it turned out, Sir George-Étienne Cartier lost his seat in Montreal. Not wanting to lose his deputy prime-minister, Macdonald "frantically sent a coded telegram to Archibald -- 'get Sir George elected in your province.'" (Siggins, p.214.) Knowing that Provencher was the safest bet for Cartier (who was French) as long as Cartier didn't run against a strong French candidate like Riel, Archibald asked Riel to withdraw from the election. Hoping that this sacrifice would at last win him his amnesty, Riel stepped aside for Cartier, who won the election by acclamation in September 1872. Of course, no amnesty was forthcoming. Far from being grateful, Macdonald was angry that Riel had campaigned to begin with, since the money he'd given Taché in December 1871 had been intended to ensure Riel's "invisibility" during the election. (See panel 91:2.)

On May 20, 1873, Cartier died of Bright's disease, freeing up Provencher for the by-election that I show Riel winning.

94:5

So Riel didn't return to the Red River settlement in June 1873 as I claim in this panel -- he was already there.

96:5

It wasn't much of a race. "Since there were no Liberals who dared run in Provencher, Riel was elected by acclamation "(Siggins, p. 223.)

98:2

Riel had many friends in the east thanks to his school-days in Montreal.

99:2 - 100:5

In 1874 Bishop Ignace Bourget (1799 - 1885) "was nearing the end of a long, illustrious, and controversial career in the church. [... H]e was deeply involved in politics, both ecclesiastical and civil." (Flanagan, 1996, p. 44.) Bourget was a vigorous promoter of French-Canadian interests.

100:5

Riel did fall to his knees in front of Bishop Bourget's bed on January 8, 1874, but the words I have Bourget saying in this panel come from a letter that he wrote to Riel on July 14, 1875. The relevant passage reads,

God who has up until the present directed you and assisted you will not abandon you in your most difficult of struggles, for He has given you a mission which you must accomplish step by step [and] with the Grace of God you must persevere on the path that has been laid out for you. [Siggins, p. 248.]

"Riel never parted with this letter. He carried it with him every day, next to his heart, and he placed it at the head of his bed every night."(Stanley, p. 222.)

101:6

In 1873, an incriminating telegram surfaced in which John A. [Macdonald] shamefully begged for more campaign money from [Canadian Pacific Railway] backers. The public was outraged, and the ensuing Pacific Scandal, as it was known, forced Macdonald to resign in

disgrace. [Ferguson, p. 241.]

Macdonald announced the resignation of his government in November, and the call for a new election came on January 7, 1874 (not "late January" as this panel implies).

102:6 - 103:3

On March 26, 1874, Riel did enter one of the parliament buildings without being recognized and walked into the chief clerk's office to register as a Member of Parliament. The clerk didn't realize who he was signing in until he saw the signature. He ran to inform the Minister of Justice, but Riel was already quickly retreating from the building.

104:1

It was Conservative Member of Parliament Mackenzie Bowell (who later became prime-minister in 1894) who made this proposal, not John Schultz -- Schultz, though, was quick to second the suggestion.

105:1, 105:2

Ambroise Lépine and William O'Donoghue were also banished from Canada at this time.

105:3 - 106:2

Riel spent most of 1875 planning and organizing an invasion of Manitoba. In October 1875 he met with American Senator Oliver P. Morton to discuss his proposed invasion. Morton was polite but uninterested. The senator's legs were paralysed, and after the meeting Riel tried unsuccessfully to cure, through prayer, at least one of his legs.

On December 8th, while in church, Riel had a mystical experience of intense joy followed by (what he called) "almost insupportable sadness [...]. Not long afterwards, only a few days, people began to treat me like a madman."(Flanagan, 1996, p.56.)

The meeting with Grant happened somewhere between the 10th and the 15th of December.

Riel stayed at the home of his friend Edmond Mallet while in Washington. "Mallet thought that Riel had lost his mind from repeated disappointments culminating in the failure of President Grant to respond to his proposals."(Flanagan, 1996, p.59.)

106:3 - 107:4

This is a combination of two mystical experiences that Riel claimed to have had. On December 14th "the spirit of God comes upon him, [...] transports him to the fourth heaven and instructed him about the nations of the earth"(Riel referring to himself in the third person -- Flanagan, 1996, p. 57.) At an unknown date,

> While standing alone on a mountain top near Washington, DC, the same spirit that appeared to Moses in the midst of clouds of flame appeared to me in the same manner. [ibid.]

My use of pointed brackets in these panels would seem to indicate that this spirit spoke French, but according to Riel it spoke Latin.

107:5, 107:6

I searched through the various Riel biographies for specific behaviours (as opposed to beliefs) that led to his imprisonment in an asylum.

> He slept neither day nor night, he paced incessantly up and down, up and down, and he cried and howled so horribly that the priest's mother was terrified of him and wouldn't go near him. [...]
> "He continued to cry in the train. I told the travellers that he was a poor lunatic and to please excuse him. When they talked or laughed, Louis said, 'Keep still. Do not laugh, I beg you. I am a prophet.'" [...]
> For the first six days of his stay, Louis refused to sleep or be quiet, and "had contortions like a man in a rage". [...T]hree times he locked himself in his room, stripped naked and tore all his clothes and bed coverings to shreds. [...] He had to be re-dressed like a little child. [...]
> As the [...] sermon ended, Louis stood up and in a loud and dramatic voice sang out three times: "Hear the voice of the priest!" [Siggins, pp. 257 & 258.]

All of these examples come from Siggins' book -- the other bios describe the same behaviours and incidents without mentioning any additional ones. (Which isn't to say that there weren't any additional incidents -- I'm sure that there were others that Riel's friends and family neglected to record for posterity.)

109:3 - 110:5

Riel was upset when a nun tore the inscription-page out of his prayer-book, but he was not placed in a strait-jacket on this occasion.

> Seven years after Riel had been confined [in St Jean de Dieu], Dr. Harold Tuke, a prominent British reformer advocating more humane treatment for the insane, made a tour of the asylums of North America. He said of [St Jean de Dieu], "In the course of seven and thirty years I have visited a large number of asylums in Europe, but I have rarely, if ever, seen anything more depressing...." It was horribly overcrowded, it stank, [...] and the food was disgusting. Each inmate was confined to a tiny, narrow room-- Tuke said it was more like an animal pen than a cell-- where there was hardly enough space for a bed. [Siggins, p. 259.]

111:1

Dr Henry Howard on Riel and murderers: "I believed him to be guilty of the murder he was accused of, and I believed every murderer to be either insane or a fool" (Flanagan, 1996, p. 65.)

I don't believe that the behaviours that people associate with "mental illnesses" are caused by biological abnormalities or malfunctions in the brain. To put it more simply: "mental illnesses" are not illnesses. I was tempted to elaborate at length on why Riel's behaviours and beliefs in late 1875 and early 1876 weren't symptoms of an illness, but it would all just be a rehash of what I wrote in my strip "My Mom Was a Schizophrenic" (which can be found in my book THE LITTLE MAN), so instead I'll just quote a brief passage by historian Thomas Flanagan and urge any of you who are puzzled by my statement that "'mental illnesses' are not illnesses" to read my schizophrenia strip, or (even better) to read MADNESS, HERESY, AND THE RUMOUR OF ANGELS by Seth Farber and/or TOXIC PSYCHIATRY by Peter Breggin.

> Much of what strikes modern readers as incomprehensible and therefore insane makes sense in the context of Riel's ultramontane worldview, which included a God who controls human affairs, punishes the evil and rewards the good, works miracles in daily life, and speaks directly to men through revelation and prophecy. A hasty resort to medical labels risks rendering this phase of Riel's life meaningless, when in fact it is the key to understanding his character, and thus the overall pattern of his career. [Flanagan, 1996, p. 80.]

(The ultramontanes were Roman Catholics who placed papal authority over state authority and who desired the reunion of church and state. Bishop Bourget was an ultramontane.)

For unknown reasons, Riel was transferred from L'Hospice de St Jean de Dieu to the St Michel-Archange asylum at Beauport (near Quebec City) in May 1876. Conditions at St Michel-Archange were about the same as those at St Jean de Dieu.
In January 1878, Riel was released and was

> whisked to the American border. The last thing the officials of the asylum wanted was the scandal that would surely result if it was ever discovered he had been living in Canada illegally for two years. [Siggins, p. 271.]

I suspect that the worry that the authorities might find out the true identity of "Mr David", impelled the asylum officials to release Riel sooner than they would have if he had been an ordinary Canadian citizen.

> [H]e was having visions and receiving revelations within a few weeks of his discharge from Beauport. If he ever did repudiate his prophetic beliefs, it was not very deeply and not for very long. Riel's cure meant that he had learned how to conduct himself externally, not that he had undergone a deep internal transformation. [Flanagan, 1996, p. 78.]

Riel went to Keesville and the home of Father Fabien Barnabé. With money borrowed from Barnabé, he rented a small farm and began working it. He also became engaged to the priest's 27 year-old sister Evelina. (Riel was then 33 and probably still a virgin.) The crop-yield at the end of the summer was disappointing, so Riel went to New York City to look for a job-- and also to try and raise support for an armed invasion of Manitoba. With no success achieved in either of these goals, he decided to go back to the west. He returned to Keesville only to pack his belongings and say good-bye to Evelina, assuring her that he'd send for her once he was "established". He settled in the St Joseph/Pembina area of the Dakota territory which was close to the Red River Settlement -- or Winnipeg, as the settlement was now being called. Many of his friends and family made the trip south to visit him. In the summer of 1879 he relocated to Montana and joined a nomadic, buffalo-hunting band of about 150 Métis families. Riel was planning a "confederacy of Indian and mixed-blood peoples who would fight for a country of their own" (Siggins, p. 293) and he spent a lot of time traveling around, trying to mobilize the Indian chiefs in the area. On April 27, 1881, he married 20 year-old Marguerite Monet Bellehumeur (having apparently forgotten his promise to Evelina Barnabé). He became involved in American politics in a minor way-- he campaigned for a Republican candidate in an 1882 congressional election. (Unlike Indians, the Métis could vote.) On May 9, 1882, Marguerite gave birth to a son, Jean. Riel became an American citizen in March 1883. The following month he was hired as a school-teacher at St Peter's Mission. And a month after that he was arrested and charged with election-fraud in relation to his role in the 1882 election. It was believed that he'd "induced Half-breeds who were not U.S. citizens to vote [.] [...T]he whole thing was patent nonsense". (Ibid, pp. 311, 312.) He was quickly released on bail, and in April 1884 the charges were dismissed. Marguerite gave birth to their second child, Marie-Angelique, in September 1883.

PAGE 117

"By 1886 all of the 1.4 million acres had been granted. Less than 20 per cent of the eligible Metis beneficiaries actually owned the land they were entitled to." (Purich, p. 70.)

PAGES 117, 118

The dispersal of the Métis and native English from Manitoba was gradual but perceptible between 1871 and 1876; it became remarkable from 1877 to 1880; and the migration increased to a rush of personnel between 1881 and 1884. Overall, more than 4,000 persons participated in the exodus, mainly to Saskatchewan. [Sprague, p. 139]

In CANADA AND THE MÉTIS, 1869-1885 (which the above quote is from), historian D.N. Sprague contends that the Canadian government consciously worked to deprive the Métis of the land it had promised them by legally rigging things against their interests. (See the Purich quote in the note for panel 77:5 for an example of this type of legal rigging.)

Occasionally historians disagree with one another:

[T]he government's administration of Manitoba lands was creditable. It was slower than people would have liked, but the situation was intrinsically complicated [...]. Several thousand Métis left Manitoba in the 1870s and 1880s, but not because the Canadian government deprived them of their river lots or any other lands. They left partly because the arrival of white immigrants changed the character of the Red River settlement, but mainly because the buffalo were withdrawing. [Flanagan, 2000, p. 33]

Flanagan argues his side of this particular matter (whether or not Canada lived up to its Manitoba Act promises) in his MÉTIS LANDS IN MANITOBA (1991). Anyone interested in getting into this subject in more depth should probably read both authors.

121:3

Father Alexis André (1833-1893) was an Oblate priest.

121:6

I really don't know, but I would guess that an ordinary citizen such as Dumont would have had to make an appointment with George Duck (the Dominion Lands agent in Prince Albert) to see survey maps of the area, and I doubt that Mr Duck would have allowed those maps to leave his presence-- nor would he have allowed those maps to be folded in the way that we fold mass-produced maps today.

122:5

Apparently the square lots lent themselves better to the kind of intensive commercial agriculture that the Canadian government was hoping to encourage. But the real reason that so much of the south branch of the Saskatchewan River was divided into "English lots" instead of "French lots" is that surveying long thin rectangles took longer than surveying squares and was therefore more expensive.

123:1

The Dominion Lands office didn't

officially open in Prince Albert until 1881, but George Duck moved to Prince Albert in 1878 and would have been available for consultations with settlers from that point on.

In 1888, the government finally did resurvey the Métis land along the south branch of the Saskatchewan River.

123:2 - 123:6

The Canadian government's homesteading system

involved the following stages:
- making "entry" on a quarter-section [160 acres] through registration at a Dominion Lands agency and paying the $10.00 fee;
- performing "settlement duties," usually uninterrupted residence of three years, construction of a home, and cultivation of thirty acres or raising a certain number of animals;
- obtaining "patent" or title after a Dominion Lands inspector ascertained that settlement duties had been performed;
- "pre-empting" neighbouring land. When a settler made homestead entry, he could also enter a pre-emption on an adjoining quarter-section [...]. Pre-emption was the right to buy those 160 acres at a specified price, once patent had been obtained on the homestead. The price was $2.50 per acre if the land was within a certain distance of a railway, $2.00 per acre otherwise. [Flanagan, 2000, pp. 26, 27.]

If one didn't want to wait three years for title -- if one wanted outright ownership immediately -- one could buy privately-owned land on the open-market (the CPR had lots of land to sell) but the market-price for land was a good deal more than the homesteading price of $10 for 160 acres.

125:2

The land-grants that Father André is referring to here are the lots that made up the 1,400,000 acres mentioned in panels 77:5 and 77:6 and on page 117.

125:2 - 125:4

After the 1885 rebellion, a land-grant was made to the Métis of the North-West in the form of scrip. Scrip was a certificate that could be traded for land or money. Most of the Métis chose to trade their scrip for money. Some argue that the scrip-system was designed to keep the Métis from acquiring more land and that the true beneficiaries were land-speculators who under-paid the Métis for the scrip. (See Purich, pp. 107-127.) On the other side are those who say that the Métis handled the scrip-system to their advantage. (See Flanagan, 2000, pp. 64-84.)

128:1

Charles Nolin had moved to the south branch of the Saskatchewan River and was one of the people who urged that a delegation be sent to Montana to meet with Riel. He was not, however, one of the four men who made the trip. The actual fourth man was named Michel Dumas.

129:3 - 130:4

Concerned that he might be detained at the border, Riel sent his papers up separately to minimize the chance that the police might seize them, so this scene is a fabrication. The book Riel was writing was titled MASSINAHICAN which was "the Cree word for book or Bible." (Flanagan, 1996, p. 125.) I don't know how much of this book Riel managed to write, but it seems that only a few pages still exist. (Riel, pp. 387-399.)

131:1 - 131:3

In late July 1884 Riel "met with twelve chiefs, including Big Bear and Poundmaker". (Siggins, p. 350.)

Treaty No. 6 [signed in 1876] contained the clause whose vague wording would soon make it the most controversial of all the treaty provisions: "That in the event hereafter of the Indians comprised within this treaty being overtaken by any pestilence, or by a general famine, the Queen, on being satisfied and certified thereof by her Indian Agent or Agents will grant to the Indians assistance of such character and to such extent as her Chief Superintendent of Indian Affairs shall deem necessary and sufficient to relieve the Indians from the calamity that shall have befallen them." [Beal & Macleod, p. 57.]

The Indians believed the treaty guaranteed them a sufficient supply of food until they were well-established enough as farmers to provide for themselves. [...] But the government took a radically different view of the famine clause. Government officials believed they were under no obligation to supply rations except in the case of a general famine. The Plains Indians had been consistently very hungry since the buffalo suddenly disappeared. Ottawa, however, refused to consider widespread hunger as the famine they interpreted the treaty to mean. [Ibid., p. 72.]

This wasn't the only grievance that the Indians had. "The chiefs complained their reserves were too swampy, [and] that the salty bacon they were usually provided was causing scurvy". (Ibid., p. 88.) They had been promised farming equipment and livestock, but "What equipment and animals the Indians received under the treaty provisions were of such obviously inferior quality that the Indians had understandably refused to take delivery of some of it". (Ibid., p. 63.) Also, the Indian agents and the men hired to teach the Indians how to farm were patronage appointees who had little understanding or sympathy for the Indians and the dramatic changes they faced. Their general unsuitability for the task at hand, often bordering on incompetence, led to a high turnover rate. [Stonechild & Waiser, p. 36.]

131:4

After the Pacific Scandal forced Sir John A. Macdonald from office in 1873, everyone -- including Macdonald -- assumed that he was washed-up politically. He tried to retire but could find no suitable replacement for the leadership of the Conservative party. Meanwhile, the Liberals under Alexander Mackenzie may have been in power, but that doesn't mean that things were going well for them.

The root of the problem was the great world trade depression that began in 1873 [...]. The Mackenzie government could hardly be blamed for the effects of depression on Canada -- but, human nature being what it is, it was blamed. [Careless, p. 268.]

As a result, when the next election came around in 1878, Macdonald found himself to be once again the prime-minister of Canada.

131:5

I mention Riel meeting with the English here. To his surprise, he received a favourable response from the North Saskatchewan's white-anglophone community in 1884. Like the other groups in the Canadian North-West, they were feeling tremendously frustrated with the government and they hoped that Riel's presence would convince Ottawa to address their concerns along with those of the Métis and the Indians.
Probably the prime concern of the white settlers was the railway.

The rapid construction of the main line ate up money at such a rate that there was none left over to build the branch lines, sidings, platforms, and grain elevators that would make the line usable. The CPR's insatiable appetite for capital and its monopoly position in the West meant that freight rates were set at very high levels, so high that farmers found they needed bumper crops just to get by. The poor crop of 1883 combined with falling prices threatened many with bankruptcy. [Beal & Macleod, p. 32.]

After Riel arrived in [the Batoche area] in early July, there ensued a lengthy period of peaceful political agitation. [...] Riel tried to frame a petition of grievances acceptable to all residents of the area, native as well as white, anglophone as well as francophone. This was no simple task [.] [Flanagan, 2000, p. 14.]

Support from the white community fell away when the Métis and Indians resorted to arms, with one

important exception. 23 year-old William Jackson met Riel in July 1884 and became his secretary. The young man was arrested in Batoche on May 12, 1885. He was thought to be crazy and was sent to an asylum.

The logic was simple : Jackson was the only white man among the Métis and Indians who participated directly in their rebellion, and therefore he must be insane." [Siggins, p. 420.]

133:3

In order to get British Columbia to become Canada's western-most province, Macdonald had promised to build a railway that linked it to eastern Canada. There was fear that British Columbia might leave confederation if the railway didn't get built.

132:6 - 137:2

The two disasters -- the revolt on the prairies and the collapse of the railway -- had come together in time. And together they might destroy [Macdonald] and his Canada. [...] They were separate problems. They could even be played off against each other. And in that possibility did not there lie a real hope ? He could use the railway to defend the West. He could use the West to justify the railway. [Creighton, p. 417.]

Don McLean, in his book 1885: MÉTIS REBELLION OR GOVERNMENT CONSPIRACY ?, prints the above quote from historian Donald Creighton -- he then comments:

Creighton saw the success of the CPR and the destruction of the Métis as two separate events that were somehow brought together in time. He recognized that these two "separate" events could be played off against each other by the prime minister in such a way as to save the CPR and the Conservative government. Creighton saw the Métis rebellion as a fortunate coincidence that simply provided Sir John A. Macdonald with the means to politically justify further financial support for the CPR syndicate. They were not, however, separate events. They were intricately interrelated events that came together not through coincidence but by design. [McLean, p. 86.]

D. N. Sprague hints at a similar conspiracy theory in his CANADA AND THE MÉTIS, 1869-1885. The notion that the 1885 rebellion happened by "design" makes a certain amount of sense. If the plan that I have Macdonald outline in panels 136:3 to 136:6 had occurred to him in real life, it's hard to see how he couldn't have been tempted by it. That said, it must be admitted that McLean and Sprague scratch up little in the way of hard evidence.

137:3

"The petition [...] had finally, on December 16, been sent off to the governor-general, with copies going to the government." (Siggins, p. 362.)

137:4 - 138:1

Creighton saw Riel's attempt to get money from the government (and apparent willingness to leave Canada if paid) as "cynically, almost brutally, selfish. " (Creighton, p. 413.) McLean, on the other hand, reasons that

> By this time he knew that he had done all that he could towards establishing a peaceful and just settlement in the West. Since his presence was now working against further progress, why should he not tend to his own financial affairs and return to his life as a teacher in Montana ? [McLean, p. 94.]

138:2 - 139:5

Sprague thinks that this telegram was a deliberate provocation.

> Telegraphed to Dewdney, the news was that Canada would "investigate claims of Half Breeds and with that view [Cabinet] had decided [to make an] enumeration of those who did not participate in Grant under Manitoba Act." The provocation was that only a small minority of the residents of [the area around Batoche] could benefit from awards to non-Manitobans. Moreover, the government already had the figures: 200 of 1,300 potential claiments. Dewdney was so stunned by the news he refused to pass on the information without alteration. Imagining the purpose of the Order in Council was conciliation rather than provocation, he changed the announcement before transmitting the telegram to [the Métis]: "Government has decided to investigate claims of Half Breeds and with that view has already taken preliminary steps." Then Dewdney reminded Macdonald that "the bulk of the French Half Breeds" had "nothing to expect" from the unrevised text. The original news would "start a fresh agitation." No prime ministerial congratulation came back over the wire thanking Dewdney for his editorial intervention[.] [Sprague, p. 170.]

The more conventional view is that Macdonald was not aware that the telegram would be seen as provocative -- that perhaps he was distracted by matters like the CPR crisis and so didn't give the concerns of the Métis the attention that they deserved and/or that perhaps the conflicting reports from the North-West made it difficult to accurately judge how the Métis would react to the telegram. The choice seems to be between believing that Macdonald abused his power or that the government operated inefficiently. People in positions of prominence frequently abuse their power, and governments always operate inefficiently, so both choices seem possible

to me. I've made the McLean/Sprague-theory part of my strip, not because I'm convinced that it's true (I honestly don't have a strong opinion on the matter one way or the other), but because it makes Macdonald seem more villainous -- villains are fun in a story, and I'm trying to tell this tale in an engaging manner.

Incidentally, even though I think that Macdonald was capable of abusing his power, I don't think that he actually was a villain. I disagree with much of what he did and stood for, but I recognize that he tried to do what he thought was best for the country. And, quite frankly, I'd rather have lived in a state run by John A. Macdonald than one run by Louis Riel.

140:1 - 140:5

> There is some doubt how far Louis Riel was sincere when he offered to return to the United States. Charles Nolin, a hostile witness, later declared that Riel never really intended to leave the Saskatchewan and that he engineered this demonstration on his own behalf. Schmidt [*] was disposed to take much the same view, writing to Archbishop Taché that it was Riel's personal claque that carried the métis in the demand that Riel stay in the North-West. On the other hand, there is some evidence to suggest that Riel did have notions of leaving the country. Father Vegreville, likewise no warm partisan of Riel, wrote to Taché on February 19, telling him Riel had made arrangements with Louis Marion to drive him to Winnipeg in mid-March -- probably, suggested Vegreville, to see the Archbishop. "The fact is that he is extremely poor and lives by charity," wrote the priest. [Stanley, p. 299.]

140:6 - 141:2

There is no evidence that a conversation like this took place between Clarke and Macdonald or that Clarke saw the prime-minister at all when he was in Ottawa. Whether or not the two men conspired together, it does seem that "Lawrence Clarke was playing a double game." (Sprague, p. 163.) In 1884 Clarke encouraged the Métis to invite Riel back to Canada. When they did, he informed the authorities that the Métis leader was returning and advised them to arrest Riel as he crossed the border. Clarke's advice was ignored -- no effort was made to detain the Montana schoolteacher as he re-entered Canada. Clarke then visited Riel, gave him money for his upkeep, and told him to "Bring on your rebellion as soon as you can. It will be the making of this country." (McLean, p. 90.) Then there's the incident described in the next note and also the way that Clarke encouraged the Mounties to fight the Métis. (see panel 153:1.) The Métis believed that they could trust

---

* Louis Schmidt was a childhood friend of Riel's who opposed taking up arms against the government.

Clarke, but he was reporting their actions to the government. In February 1885, the Métis sent Clarke to Ottawa to "make representations to the government on their behalf." (McLean, p. 96.)

141:4, 141:5

Clarke did not go to Riel to tell him all this.

> On March 18 [...] the French settlements were electrified by a rumour: Clarke had told some freighters whom he met on the trail that five hundred more. police were enroute to Saskatchewan and Riel and other leaders soon would be under arrest. [Howard, p. 322.]

"Clarke later denied saying any such thing but the story was quickly and widely circulated." (Beal & MacLeod, p. 139.) According to Beal & MacLeod and Siggins, Clarke met the freighters on the trail on the 17th, not the 18th. (Siggins, p. 371.)

> The truth behind the rumour was that the commander of the police, alarmed by reports of sedition, had ordered a column of 100 men north to reinforce Fort Carlton. [Flanagan, 1996, p. 151.]

141:6 - 142:4

"On March 4, the full details of the government's telegram to Dewdney announcing the Halfbreed Claims Commision were, at last, released." (Siggins, p. 367.) None of the books that I've read mention who released the original telegram to the Métis, or how it was done, but it's rather unlikely that Clarke was responsible, since he went to Ottawa in February and didn't get back to the Saskatchewan area until March 17th. Whoever did it, Dewdney seems to have been right that it would make the Métis angry: on March 5th, Riel, Dumont, and nine other Métis held a secret meeting at which they pledged to "save our country from a wicked government by taking up arms if necessary." (Beal & MacLeod, p. 135.)

142:5, 142:6

Early in the evening of March 18th, Riel, Dumont, and 70 Métis took 3 prisoners -- an Indian agent, his interpreter, and a Batoche magistrate who had been reporting the activities of the Métis to the police. Riel's group then went to the Kerr brothers' store near Batoche and took all the guns and ammunition. From there they headed to the Batoche church (St Antoine de Padoue) where a large crowd was waiting. This is where panel 142:5 takes up the story. The priest who refused to let the crowd into the church was Father Julien Moulin, not Father André. There were several priests in the area, they all disliked Riel, and I'm combining them all into one character.

143:1, 143:2

Refusing the sacrament to any who participated in armed rebellion was threatened on Sunday, March 15th, by Father Vital Fourmond in a sermon delivered at the St Laurent de Grandin church. Riel was in the congregation. He

> rose in his place and denounced the priest. "You have turned the pulpit of truth into one of politics, falsehood and discord. How dare you refuse the sacrament to those who would take up arms in defence of their most sacred rights!" [Siggins, p. 370.]

143:3

It would seem that Riel had others move the priest out of the way. "When Moulin, an elderly, small-boned man, still refused to let them in his church, Louis ordered, 'Take him away! Take him away!'" (Siggins, p. 373.)

146:1

As I mentioned above, three men had already been taken prisoner by the time the Métis got to the Walters & Baker store. By the end of the night they had eight hostages. (Beal & Macleod, pp. 140, 141.) There were more to follow, though (if I've counted correctly), the number of prisoners held at any one time never went over fourteen.

147:5

In December 1884, during a religious ceremony, Nolin's wife had been cured of "a disabling illness" (Siggins, p. 369) that had afflicted her for ten years.

> For the people [in the Batoche area], the recovery of Rosalie Nolin was indeed a miracle. Father André took every advantage of it; he wrested a promise from Charles Nolin that, in thankfulness to the Virgin, he would not engage in any civil disobedience. [Ibid.]

147:1 - 148:1

> Nolin was arrested and brought up for trial along with Louis Marion and William Boyer, two other métis who had refused to take up arms at Riel's request. [...] The trial itself was brief and Nolin, as the ringleader of the opposition, was sentenced to death. According to Philippe Garnot, Riel "made a long speech accusing Ch. Nolin of treason and said that an example was necessary and that it was essential that Nolin should be condemned to death." Riel, however, did not press for an immediate execution of sentence; he knew his man, and he wanted to leave a way open to force the hands of the clergy by granting Nolin his life in return for clerical approval, or at least clerical neutrality during the days to follow. Nolin, badly frightened and encouraged by Lépine, made his submission and agreed to support Riel. So, too, did Louis Marion. Boyer was discharged. [Stanley, p. 308.]

Nolin was arrested on the 19th, not the 25th.

148:2, 148:3

The world-famous Canadian Mounties are finally mentioned in this strip.

> Sir John A. Macdonald envisaged a mounted police force in 1869 to secure Rupert's Land [...] but, true to his nickname "Old Tomorrow," he procrastinated. Consequently, late in 1869 when the first Red River uprising flared, there was no force stationed in the West to deal with it. [Cruise & Griffiths, 1996, p.31.]

> During the early months of 1873, with pressure mounting on Macdonald to produce his police force, the prime minister became mired in a boozy rearguard defence of his office over the [Pacific] scandal. With British Columbia threatening to leave Confederation unless Macdonald kicked some life into the still moribund railway project, the prime minister pulled himself together sufficiently to draw up the legislation needed to make the police force a reality. [Ibid., p.34.]

The force was originally called the North West Mounted Police, but the name was later changed to the Royal Canadian Mounted Police. The Mounties first entered the North-West in 1874.

148:5

Dumont seems to imply here that the Métis were keeping the rebellion a secret, or at least had made no official declaration of hostility.

> On March 19, Riel sent an ultimatum to Major Crozier demanding the surrender of Fort Carlton and threatening a war of extermination if his demand was not obeyed. Major Crozier summarily rejected Riel's demand. [McLean, p.103.]

148:4 - 149:6

These panels simplify the events leading up to the Battle of Duck Lake. Dumont and ten men went over to the Mitchell store on the afternoon of March 25th. Riel and many more armed men joined them and they all went over to a nearby Cree reserve to spend the night. Two police spies were spotted and captured. The next morning, three police scouts were sighted, and Dumont and several of his men chased them to a group of fifteen Mounties and seven militia (local armed citizens -- probably all anglophones).

150:1 - 151:2

Several of the Mounties were actually in sleighs. The fellow who had the stand-off with Dumont was standing in his sleigh the whole time.

151:2

Dumont's rifle accidentally went off as he struck the Mountie.

151:3

The fellow who's shouting in this panel was also swatted by Dumont's gun. Another one of the Mounties "pushed Edouard Dumont into the snow." (Siggins, p.384.) There was also a good deal more yelling back and forth than I show.

153:2

I imply in the strip that the Fort Carlton fighting-force was made up only of North West Mounted Police officers. 56 of the men were Mounties, but fighting alongside them at Duck Lake were 43 men from Prince Albert's volunteer-militia.

154:3

Riel's reinforcements actually arrived at around the point when the shooting began.

155:5 - 156:4

The weaponless Assiyiwin is reported to have said to McKay, "If you haven't come to fight, what are you doing with so many guns, grandson?" (Siggins, p.384.) McKay was holding a rifle and Assiyiwin either grabbed it or reached out to push it in another direction. McKay later claimed that the rifle discharged without killing the Indian and that he (McKay) then drew his pistol and shot Assiyiwin and Isidore Dumont. (Charlebois, p.148.)

Assiyiwin, who lived at a nearby Cree reserve, had not considered himself to be affiliated with either side in the conflict. Siggins says that he was at Duck Lake to mediate. But, according to Stonechild & Waiser, he was not there to mediate or to have anything to do with either the Métis or the Mounties -- he had simply been walking his pony home, the path he took happened to lead between the two opposing forces, and he happened to get into an argument with McKay as Isidore Dumont rode up with a white flag. (Stonechild & Waiser, p.66.)

162:5

Only three of the dead were Mounties -- the other nine were militiamen.

162:6, 163:1

If you were to trust my drawings, you'd think that the Mounties fled from Fort Carlton in broad day-light, but that's not what happened. Fearing an attack of the kind that I have Dumont suggesting in panel 163:2, the Mounties decided to leave the fort under cover of darkness in the pre-dawn hours of March 27th. During the rush to leave, a fire started accidentally, and soon the fort was in flames. This drew the attention of the Métis, and the end-result was that the Mounties may as well have left in broad day-light.

The fire caused a great deal of damage to the fort, but there were still supplies and important papers to be found, as I show in panels 164:3 to 164:6.

167:5 - 168:2

> The decision to use the CPR imposed serious hardships on the troops and was almost certainly unnecessary. There would have been no difficulty shipping the men through the United States; most of the ammunition and supplies went that way anyway. [Beal & Macleod, p. 172.]

168:4

Saying that Battleford was "attacked" is perhaps overstating what happened, although the inhabitants of Battleford felt like they were being attacked. A large number of Cree ("hundreds" according to Beal & Macleod, p. 181 -- "about 120" according to Stonechild & Waiser, p. 92) advanced on the town and the Battlefordites fled to their fort. Stonechild & Waiser insist that the intentions of the Cree weren't hostile -- nevertheless, finding the town deserted, they decided to loot and destroy much of its property before they returned to Poundmaker's reserve.

168:5

Because he was the chief of the Cree at Frog Lake, Big Bear's name is associated with the Frog Lake massacre, but he himself did not participate in the murders and, in fact, tried to stop them.

> To the outside world, it was "Big Bear's band" that had committed unspeakable crimes that early spring day at Frog Lake, and as their leader, he was held personally responsible. [Stonechild & Waiser, p. 118.]

169:5 - 170:2

> Amazingly, in just over two weeks since the first shots at Duck Lake, more than three thousand men with all their equipment had been shipped to the West and were ready to be deployed. [Beal & Macleod, p. 177.]

Major-General Thomas Bland Strange (I love that name) lived near Calgary, Alberta, and he wouldn't have been in Qu'Appelle -- his orders were sent to him.

In Mid-April, Middleton wasn't in Qu'Appelle either. He started to march toward Batoche on April 6th.

The strip leaves unanswered what happened to Poundmaker and Big Bear, so I'll very briefly deal with that subject here.

Lieutenant-Colonel Otter did find Poundmaker, and on May 2, 1885, the Canadians attacked the Cree camp, but within hours the Indians had the whites on the run. Otter and his men would have all been killed if Poundmaker hadn't intervened and ordered his warriors to let the fleeing soldiers escape. On May 17th, Poundmaker and his followers were on their way to Batoche to aid Riel when they heard of the defeat of the Métis. The Cree chief led his people into Battleford and surrendered on May 26, 1885.

Major-General Strange managed to track down Big Bear's group, and on May 28th a battle ensued. The two sides fought for a few hours and then both retreated. On June 2nd, Sam Steele of the North West Mounted Police, and 60 mounties and soldiers, attacked the Indians, who managed to get away. The group traveling with Big Bear got smaller and smaller as various factions and individuals went off on their own, until the only person left with the chief was his youngest son. On July 4, 1885, the two of them surrendered at Fort Carlton.

Poundmaker and Big Bear were both sentenced to three years, even though Big Bear was clearly innocent of any treasonous or hostile intentions. * He had lost control of his band -- a guy named Wandering Spirit had initiated the Frog Lake massacre. Big Bear had tried to stop the bloodshed. Wandering Spirit and seven other Indians were hanged for the massacre and other murders committed during the Rebellion. If I'm counting right, around 40 Indians who were associated with either Poundmaker or Big Bear were sentenced to various prison terms. (Beal & Macleod, pp. 325-332.)

Poundmaker

> sickened rapidly in jail. After less than a year in Stony Mountain Penitentiary he was clearly dying and the authorities released him. Four months later [...] Poundmaker died on July 4, 1886. Big Bear lasted a little longer but he too was seriously ill by early 1887 and was released in March. [...] He spent the last few months of his life on Poundmaker's reserve, where he died on January 17, 1888. [Ibid., p. 339.]

170:6

On the afternoon of April 23, Riel and Dumont headed out with

---

* In their book, LOYAL TILL DEATH, Stonechild & Waiser argue that the same was true of Poundmaker.

200 men (Beal & Macleod, p. 229) or 230 men. (Siggins, p. 397.) They left 20 to 30 men in Batoche to guard it. That evening "a messenger rode in from Batoche with a report, which later proved false, that the Mounted Police were advancing from Prince Albert." (Beal & Macleod, p. 229.) In case the report was true, Riel took 50 of the men and returned to Batoche.

171:1

A coulee is a ravine.

171:3 - 174:1

[Dumont] tells how one of the [Canadian] scouts came riding towards him. Dumont's combative instinct rose up, and he forgot the need for concealment. "I had no wish to waste my cartridges on such a little matter. He saw us and made off; I chased him and was about to overtake him, when somebody fired at me. My people shouted to me that I was riding into a troop of forty men whom I had not seen, so intent was I on catching my prey. When I saw I had no time to club down the fugitive, I shot him, and at once I plunged into the coulée[.] [Woodcock, p. 199.]

The way I've drawn the scene implies that, had this incident not occurred, the Métis would have been able to take the Canadians by surprise -- this was not the case. Middleton's scouts had already seen signs of Métis presence in the area, and the soldiers were alert to the possibility of an ambush.

178:5 - 181:3

All day [Dumont] had hoped for help to come from Batoche, but Riel, who prayed for hours on end with his arms held up in the shape of a cross, and exhorted the women and children to do likewise, did not want to send any men, though the attack by Irvine and the Mounted Police did not materialize and the thunder of Middleton's guns could be heard quite distinctly in the village. Finally, Edouard Dumont's patience came to an end. "When my own people are in peril, I cannot remain here," he said, "My brothers are there and I cannot let them be killed without going to their aid." He was supported by an Indian named Yellow Blanket who added: "There is no need to wait until tomorrow to help one's friends." [... T]hey gathered eighty horsemen, and riding hard to Fish Creek, Edouard led his cavalry in a charge into the coulée that forced the Canadians back and made Middleton decide to withdraw[.] [Woodcock, p. 203.]

According to Morton and Beal & Macleod, Middleton's decision to withdraw had been made before the Métis

reinforcements showed up. (Morton, 1972, p.68 -- Beal & Macleod, p. 232.)

In panels 179:1 to 180:3, I have a Métis horseman riding from Tourond's Coulee to Batoche and convincing Riel to send reinforcements to the battle. As the above quote by Woodcock makes clear, it was Gabriel's brother, Edouard Dumont, who convinced Riel, and Edouard hadn't yet been at the battle-site. I didn't invent the horseman who rode from the coulee to Batoche -- he's mentioned by Howard. (P. 361.) Perhaps this man was simply deserting the battle with the excuse that he was going for help. A lot of Dumont's men did run away from the fight.

179:4 - 180:3

As mentioned in the above George Woodcock quote, Riel held his arms up in the shape of a cross. "[W]hen his strength had given out, the Métisses had taken turns holding [Riel's arms] up." (Siggins, p. 399.)

181:5

Of the forty-nine, four were mortally wounded.

181:6

One of the two was mortally wounded.

178:3 - 181:6

Snow and rain fell during the day (Siggins, p. 397), but the precipitation must have been light -- at one point in the battle, the Métis successfully lit the grass on fire, so it couldn't have been very wet or snow-covered.

182:1

While the precipitation was probably light on April 24th, there was a heavy snowfall on the next day, so my depiction of snow on the ground in this panel is accurate.

182:5 - 183:6

The gun-boat (the Northcote) approached from the south. If one was in Batoche, looking toward the South Saskatchewan River, a boat traveling from south to north would float by you from left to right, not from right to left.

Two men on the Northcote were wounded in the exchange of gunfire -- both of them were part of the boat's civilian crew.

183:5, 183:6

The fire that developed on the Northcote would probably not have been as large as I've drawn it in these panels.

"[I]t was quickly smothered."(Siggins, p. 402.)

185:4 - 186:5

I show Father André holding a white flag and walking from the church, past Métis rifle-pits, and toward the Canadian soldiers. Father André was not in Batoche during the battle. Also, the Canadians advanced from the south, and there were no Métis rifle-pits south of the Batoche church. (I'm not sure why -- perhaps because Dumont had expected the attack to come from the east rather than the south. (Siggins, p. 403.) Another reason could have been that the church and the parish-house were located at a bit of a distance from the rest of the village. In addition, the antagonism that had developed between the priests and much of the Batoche community may have influenced Dumont's thinking when planning the rifle-pits.) As they approached the church, the soldiers noticed that a "white handkerchief fluttered from the door of the parish house". (Howard, p. 392.) They walked up to the building and found several priests, nuns, "and the few Métis who had sought refuge with them". (Ibid, p. 393.)

> The missionaries in their later accounts of the Battle of Batoche insisted that they remained neutral and that they gave no information to the troops, in obedience to a written pledge the Métis had required of them. But against their words stands not only the testimony of the Métis veterans, including Gabriel Dumont, but also the accounts written on the battlefield by Canadian officers, volunteers and newspopermen. [Ibid, p.392.]

The Canadians held the church for the rest of the day (May 9th) but abandoned it when they retreated for their camp in the evening. The next day, the Métis positioned themselves in front of the church (to the south of it) and it remained behind their line of defence until the Canadians' final charge on May 12th.

190:1 - 191:3

Riel had Baptiste Boucher hear his confession on May 8th (the day before the Batoche battle began), not May 10th.

191:5

At some point on May 11th, 150 Mounted Police joined the Canadian force, bringing Middleton's army up to 950 men. (Siggins, p. 405.)

193:3

The Métis believed that General Middleton was waiting for them to run out of bullets. Historian Desmond Morton doesn't think that was

the case.

> In later years, commenting on his campaign, Middleton sought to leave the world with the impression that he had deliberately conducted a wearing battle at Batoche, seeking to tire out Dumont's men and to train his own. In fact, he does not seem to have known really what to do.
> [Morton, 1972, p. 87.]

194:2 - 194:6

The decision to charge the Métis was a little less spontaneous than I show in these panels. Lieutenant-Colonel Arthur Williams had gotten fed up with being held back by Middleton. He quietly consulted with his men (the Midland Battalion of Port Hope, Ontario) and they agreed that, if they got an order to advance, they would charge and disregard any attempts to call them back.

> [F]rom man to man the word spread [.] [...] Quickly the whispers came back from [other battalions], promising their support. [...] Then the Midland got its orders: a "reconnaissance in force" on the left flank.
> The Port Hope Battalion leaped up cheering and started on a run [...] with Williams at their head. The command, "Charge!" rolled along the line [and other battalions] too jumped up and ran, firing as they went.
> General Middleton watched aghast as the troops poured over the crest of the hill. "Cease Firing!" he roared. "Why in the name of God don't you cease firing ?"
> The bugle sounded the command to retire, again and again, but the troops ignored it. Within ten minutes the whole line was in motion. Middleton, realizing at last that his army was out of control, called up the rear echelons to support the charge.
> [Howard, p. 403.]

195:5, 195:6, 198:1

Dumont described a conversation that he had with 93 year-old Joseph Ouellette:

> What kept me there [on the battle-field], I should say, was the courage of old Ouellette. Several times I said to him: "Come on, Father, we must pull back !" and the good old man always replied: "Just a minute ! I want to kill another Englishman!" Then I said to him, "Very well, let us die here." [Siggins, pp. 406 & 407.]

while this conversation was iterated "several times" during the battle, there is no reason to think that Dumont and Ouellette repeated it during the Canadians' final charge or that they were side-by-side at that point.

The Métis casualties were

> twelve dead and three wounded, but two of these were not soldiers; a young girl had been killed by a burst

of shrapnel -- ten-year-old Marcile Graton had been shot dead on the doorstep of Fisher's store, where she had gone looking for her mother -- and a nine-month-old baby had died from machine-gun fire. All the Métis fatalities were suffered on the last day of fighting. The official count for the Canadians was ten dead, thirty-six wounded. [Siggins, p. 407.]

199:1

The two rebels did come across each other in the woods while fleeing the battle, but Riel hadn't yet made up his mind to surrender, or he kept it to himself if he had. Dumont and his wife hid out for several days, and when he was ready to head for the border on May 15 he tried to find Riel in order to ask him to come with him. Dumont was told that Riel had surrendered that day.

203:1 - 232:4

The black backgrounds that I've used here might give the impression of a spacious room. The court-room was actually very tiny and very crowded.

Most of the dialogue in these panels is based on the transcript of Riel's trial, published in book-form as THE QUEEN V LOUIS RIEL (which is listed under Morton, 1974, in the bibliography).

Below are the panel numbers, followed by the relevant page from THE QUEEN V LOUIS RIEL.

203:6

The Crown was represented by five prosecutors : Christopher Robinson, Britton Bath Osler, George Burbridge, David Lynch Scott, and Thomas Casgrain. To simplify things, I've eliminated Osler, Burbridge, Scott, and Casgrain from the story.

204:2

Riel was represented by four lawyers : François-Xavier Lemieux, Charles Fitzpatrick, James Green-shields, and T.C. Johnstone. Only Lemieux makes it into the strip, as if he was Riel's only lawyer.

209:1, 209:4 - 209:6

There is no evidence that such a book ever existed. In order to give Nolin the benefit of the doubt, I invented the scene in panels 129:3 - 130:5 to suggest that he might have gotten the buffalo-blood treaties and Riel's MASSINAHICAN mentally mixed-up in some manner. Still, Nolin was almost certainly lying when he claimed that Riel intended to "give the Province of Quebec to the Prussians [and] Ontario to the Irish" (Morton, 1974, p. 203). Even if Riel had wanted to do so (and there is no indication in his private writings that he did) he could not have gotten away with openly saying so -- the Métis were willing to fight for their homes along the Saskatchewan River, but they would have had no interest in militarily invading Ontario and Quebec.

221:4 - 222:1

Dr Clark testified at the trial, but he did not tell this story there -- it comes from one of his later lectures about Riel. (Flanagan, 1996, pp. 14-15.) Siggins believes that Clark's papers and lectures about Riel "were full of vicious lies". (Siggins, p. 427.) Flanagan admits that "most of Clark's material can be dismissed", but he makes an exception for the doctor's contention that Riel believed he was a Jew named David Morde-chai, because it "is supported by fragmentary evidence." (Flanagan, 1996, p. 16.)

It took the jury an hour and a half to come to a decision.

232:6

The three doctors "were appointed in secrecy [...]; each doctor was an employee or beneficiary of the federal government; and none was an expert in the field of inquiry." (Flanagan, 2000, p. 162.) Two of the doctors thought that Riel was sane, but the third one, Dr François-Xavier Valade, disagreed and said so in a telegram to Macdonald. When presenting the conclusions of the three doctors in the House of Commons, Macdonald rewrote Valade's telegram to make it look as if Valade had concurred with the other two.

233:2

Macdonald spoke these words to Roderique Masson, the Lieutenant-Governor of Quebec, who "discreetly approached Sir John and pleaded with him to change his mind." (Siggins, p. 442.)

233:3

Riel didn't sleep on the night before his execution. "With the assistance of André and Father McWilliams [...], Louis Riel spent the night in prayer and spiritual exercises." (Stanley, p. 369.) Father Charles McWilliams had been one of Riel's schoolmates in the Collège de Montréal. Flanagan writes that McWilliams didn't join Riel and André until the "early morning hours", by which he seems to mean sometime after 5:00 AM and sometime before Riel was led from his cell. (Flanagan, 1996, p. 194.) On the other hand, Howard thinks that McWilliams joined Riel only on the walk to the scaffold. (Howard, p. 467.)

233:4 - 234:2

Riel signed a recantation of his heresies on 5 August. Several motives impelled him, including a desire to have the help of the sacraments while facing death, as well as the lingering hope that he might yet bring the Church to support his mission. The abjuration seems to have been only external. Riel subscribed to certain formalities, but in such a way as to leave intact his underlying belief in himself. [Flanagan, 1996, p.178.]

On the morning of November 16th, Riel

wrote his last retraction and gave it to McWilliams. It was a short declaration of loyalty to the Church. Riel repudiated anything "too presumptuous" in his writings, subordinating himself "to the infallible decisions of the supreme

Pontiff. I die Catholic and in the only true faith." [Ibid. p. 194.]

233:5, 233:6

Riel described this vision to Dr Augustus Jukes on the evening of November 15th (Flanagan, 1996, p.191), not to Father André on the morning of the 16th. Dr Jukes was a surgeon for the Mounties and had testified at the trial (giving his opinion that Riel was sane). Jukes and Riel became friendly while Riel was imprisoned in Regina.

234:4

"[Riel] embraced me saying: 'How happy and content I am! I feel my heart will overflow with joy.'" (Father André quoted by Flanagan, 1996, p. 194.)

234:5, 234:6

Deputy-Sheriff Gibson arrived at Riel's cell-door at 8:15. Reluctant to fulfill his task, he stood at the door without knocking or speaking until Riel noticed him.

235:2

I'm pretty sure that I didn't make this up -- that Riel said or wrote something like this about his executioners (i.e. his executioners in general, not the Deputy-Sheriff specifically) but I can't find the reference right now. Anyway, he probably didn't say it to Gibson on the morning of November 16th.

235:4 - 236:5

Slowly they climbed the staircase towards the exit leading to the scaffold. The two priests recited the office of the dying. At the top, Riel knelt again with McWilliams, while André bestowed upon him a final absolution [.][...] Riel rose. The hangman approached and bound his hands behind his back. André kissed Riel, and together they walked towards the scaffold. [Stanley, pp. 370, 371.]

It seems that Stanley thought that Riel's arms were tied before he stepped onto the scaffold. This is confirmed by Howard who describes Riel's hands being "pinioned" before he "stooped and passed through the window onto a small ledge above the gallows platform." (Howard, p. 468.) From Siggins' book: "Louis mounted a ladder that led to a window, and climbed outside onto the scaffold without help". (Siggins, p. 445.) Howard writes that, on the scaffold, "The priests and Dr. Jukes shook hands with [Riel]." (Howard, p. 468.) Flanagan states that Riel "helped put the rope around his own neck." (Flanagan, 1996, p. 194.)

Manoeuvring up a ladder and through a window with one's hands tied behind one's back ("without help"!) would be awkward but probably possible, but I have a hard time seeing how Riel could have shaken anyone's hand or adjusted the noose around his neck. Perhaps Stanley and Howard were wrong about when Riel's hands were tied, or perhaps Howard and Flanagan were wrong about the hand-shaking and noose-assistance.

On a related matter: Of the books before me, only Howard's mentions that Dr Jukes was present on the scaffold. Given his connection to the Mounties, it's possible that he could have been there but, according to Charlebois and Stanley, the doctor's last visit with Riel was on the evening of November 15th. (Charlebois, p. 233 & Stanley, p. 368.)

236:1, 236:2

He asked God to bless his mother, his wife and children. "My Father bless me according to the views of Thy Providence which are beautiful and without measure." [Siggins, p. 445]

236:3 - 236:5

The gallows had been erected in a fenced enclosure adjoining the guard-room in which Riel was confined [.] [...] The platform [of the gallows], concealed by the fence, had been placed so that the only access to it was through an upstairs window [...]. At dawn [a crowd] began to assemble in the field before the barracks square. A strong cordon of Mounties had been drawn up around the enclosure and no one with-out a pass could approach. [Howard, pp. 466, 467.]

236:6 - 237:2

On the evening before the execution, Riel

asked the sheriff if he would have the opportunity to speak from the scaffold.
Father André forbade Riel to speak, arguing that he might say something that would disturb his union with God. His mission now was not to prove to the spectators that he was a prophet, but to demonstrate how a Christian should die. Riel submitted, impressed by André's additional argument that he should imitate the silence of Jesus [.] [Flanagan, 1996, p. 193.]

On the scaffold, after the noose had been placed around Riel's neck, Father André

turned away to conceal his face; he was crying.
Deputy Gibson spoke. "Louis Riel, have you anything to say before sentence of death is carried out?"
Riel glanced toward Father André, whose back was now turned to him. "Shall I say something?" he pleaded.
"No," the priest said. [Howard, p. 468.]

237:4

Riel "asked me not to forget Mr. and Mrs. Forget for their kindness to him". (Father André quoted by Charlebois, p. 234.)

Amédée-Emmanuel Forget was a clerk of the North-West Council who agitated to have Riel's life spared. (Flanagan, 2000, p. 162, & Howard, p. 466.) Mrs Forget gave Riel a crucifix that he carried to the gallows. (Stanley, p. 370.)

237:6, 238:1

Two versions of the hangman's words:

"Louis Riel," he said in a hoarse, angry whisper, "do you know me? You cannot escape from me today!" [Howard, p.468.]

"Louis Riel," he whispered, "you had me once and I got away from you. I have you now and you'll not get away from me." Jack Henderson had been a prisoner in Fort Garry in 1870 and had sworn then to take revenge not only for his humiliation, but for the death of his friend Thomas Scott. [Siggins, p.445.]

Strangely, Father André claimed that Henderson began weeping after Riel fell through the trap-door. (Charlebois, p. 234.)

238:2 - 238:5

"Courage, bon courage, mon père," [Riel] called to Father André, who was dissolved in tears. After a few more prayers and farewells, the time had come. Riel and Father McWilliams said the "Our Father" together in English; and on the phrase "deliver us from evil," the trap was dropped. [Flanagan, 1996, pp. 194, 195.]

241:1

My count of 24 men comes from Beal & Macleod (pp. 309-313, 326, 327). (This wasn't the total number of men who were punished for participating in the North-West Rebellion. See the note for panels 169:5 to 170:2 regarding the punishment of the Indians who were associated with Poundmaker and Big Bear.)

241:5

George Stephen, Donald Smith, and James J. Hill

comprised the triumvirate that formed and controlled the original syndicate of investors in the CPR. [...] At their peak these three associates individ-ually and collectively wielded unmatched financial and political power in North America. A few short years after the last spike [November 7, 1885], they would be among the richest men not just in North America, but in the entire world. [Cruise & Griffiths, 1988, pp. 5,6.]

The above-mentioned Donald Smith is the same Donald Smith who appears in panels 34:3 to 35:3.

BIBLIOGRAPHY

Beal, Bob, and Rod Macleod. PRAIRIE FIRE: THE 1885 NORTH-WEST REBELLION. 1984. Toronto: McClelland & Stewart, 1994.

Bumsted, J.M. THE RED RIVER REBELLION. Watson & Dwyer, 1996.

Careless, J.M.S. CANADA: A STORY OF CHALLENGE. 3rd ed. 1970. Toronto: Stoddart, 1991.

Charlebois, Peter. THE LIFE OF LOUIS RIEL. Toronto: NC Press, 1978.

Creighton, Donald. JOHN A. MACDONALD: THE OLD CHIEFTAIN. 1955. Toronto: Macmillan, 1968.

Cruise, David, and Alison Griffiths. THE GREAT ADVENTURE: HOW THE MOUNTIES CONQUERED THE WEST. 1996. Toronto: Penguin, 1997.

----------. LORDS OF THE LINE: THE MEN WHO BUILT THE CPR. 1988. Toronto: Penguin, 1996.

Ferguson, Will. BASTARDS AND BONEHEADS. Vancouver: Douglas & McIntyre, 1999.

Flanagan, Thomas. LOUIS 'DAVID' RIEL: 'PROPHET OF THE NEW WORLD'. Rev. ed. Toronto: University of Toronto, 1996.

----------. RIEL AND THE REBELLION: 1885 RECONSIDERED. Rev. ed. Toronto: University of Toronto, 2000.

Gentilcore, R. Louis, ed. HISTORICAL ATLAS OF CANADA, VOLUME 2: THE LAND TRANSFORMED, 1800-1891. Toronto: University of Toronto, 1993.

Howard, Joseph Kinsey. STRANGE EMPIRE: THE STORY OF LOUIS RIEL. 1952. Toronto: Swan, 1965.

McLean, Don. 1885: MÉTIS REBELLION OR GOVERNMENT CONSPIRACY? 2nd printing. Winnipeg: Pemmican, 1985.

Morton, Desmond. THE LAST WAR DRUM: THE NORTH WEST CAMPAIGN OF 1885. Toronto: Hakkert, 1972.

----------, intro. THE QUEEN V LOUIS RIEL. Toronto: University of Toronto, 1974.

Oppen, William A. THE RIEL REBELLIONS: A CARTOGRAPHIC HISTORY. 1979. Toronto: University of Toronto, 1980.

Purich, Donald. THE METIS. Toronto: Lorimer, 1988.

Racette, Calvin. FLAGS OF THE MÉTIS. Regina: Gabriel Dumont Inst. 1987

Riel, Louis. THE COLLECTED WRITINGS OF LOUIS RIEL / LES ECRITS COMPLETS DE LOUIS RIEL. 5 vols. Ed. George F. G. Stanley. Edmonton: University of Alberta Press, 1985. Vol. 2.

Ryerson, Stanley B. THE FOUNDING OF CANADA: BEGINNINGS TO 1815. Toronto: Progress, 1960.

----------. UNEQUAL UNION: CONFEDERATION AND THE ROOTS OF CONFLICT IN THE CANADAS, 1815-1873. Toronto: Progress, 1968

Senior, Hereward. "Orange Order." THE CANADIAN ENCYCLOPEDIA. 1999.

Siggins, Maggie. RIEL: A LIFE OF REVOLUTION. 1994. Toronto: HarperCollins, 1995.

Sprague, Douglas Neil. CANADA AND THE MÉTIS, 1869-1885. Waterloo: Wilfred Laurier UP, 1988.

Spry, Irene M. "The 'Memories' of George William Sanderson, 1846-1936". CANADIAN ETHNIC STUDIES, vol. 17, no. 2, 1985.

Stanley, George F.G. LOUIS RIEL. Toronto: Ryerson, 1963.

Stonechild, Blair, and Bill Waiser. LOYAL TILL DEATH: INDIANS AND THE NORTH-WEST REBELLION. Calgary: Fifth House, 1997.

Woodcock, George. GABRIEL DUMONT: THE MÉTIS CHIEF AND HIS LOST WORLD. 1975. Edmonton: Hurtig, 1976.

INDEX

Chester William David Brown was born in
1960 and grew up in Chateauguay, Quebec.
He currently lives in Toronto.